SOCIAL ACTION

A MANDATE FOR COUNSELORS

edited by
Courtland C. Lee
Garry R. Walz

Developed Collaboratively
by the American Counseling Association and
ERIC Counseling & Student Services Clearinghouse

SOCIAL ACTION: A MANDATE FOR COUNSELORS

10 9 8 7 6 5 4 3 2 1

American Counseling Association
5999 Stevenson Avenue
Alexandria, VA 22304

ERIC Counseling and Student Services Clearinghouse
201 Ferguson
Greensboro, NC 27402

Director of Acquisitions
Carolyn Baker

Director of Publishing Systems
Michael Comlish

Copyeditor
Lucy Blanton

Cover design by Brian Gallagher and Kim DiBona

This publication was funded in part by the U.S. Department of Education, Office of Educational Research and Improvement, Contract No. RR93002004. Opinions expressed in this publication do not necessarily reflect the positions of the U.S. Department of Education, OERI, ERIC/CASS, or ACA.

Library of Congress Cataloging-in-Publication Data

Lee, Courtland C.
    Social action : a mandate for counselors / Courtland C. Lee, Garry R. Walz.
        p.   cm.
    Includes bibliographical references and index.
    ISBN 1-55620-213-X (alk. paper)
    1. Counseling.   2. Social action.   I. Walz, Garry Richard.   II. American Counseling Association.   III. Title.
HM132.L4   1998
361′.06—DC21   97-43987
                                                    CIP

To Jackie Robinson,
whose social action on the baseball field changed a nation

Table of Contents

PART TWO
Social Action: A Focus on Assessment, Research, and Technology

PART THREE
Social Action: A Focus on Professional Issues

CONCLUSION

Foreword

On behalf of the American Counseling Association I am pleased to introduce this book, *Social Action: A Mandate for Counselors*, to you. It represents an important collaboration between ACA and the ERIC/Counseling and Student Services (ERIC/CASS) Clearinghouse. The editors, Courtland C. Lee, PhD, and Garry R. Walz, PhD, are both outstanding scholars and leaders in the profession of counseling. Each has served as president of ACA, Dr. Lee during 1997-98 and Dr. Walz during 1971-72. Together, they have been able to enlist some of the best scholars, practitioners, and leaders in the field of counseling as contributors.

This book comes at an important time in the history of the world and in the profession of counseling. As we prepare to enter the 21st century and a new millennium of human history, we are witnessing a dizzying panorama of change throughout all societies. This change suggests there is a major shift in worldwide social, cultural, and economic perspectives. It is evident that with the start of the new millennium comes a greater global view of human need and potential. Professional counselors therefore need to rethink their views on human development and refine their methods of promoting it.

The authors who contributed to this book will help counselors engage in such rethinking. The book focuses on social action and its place in the counseling profession. It is designed to provide counselors with direction for becoming agents of social change who intervene not only in the lives of their clients but also in the world around them as well.

The book provides a critical analysis of social action and counseling. Its major theme is that counselors should be social change agents and that this should be reflected in practice, training, and research. Lee, Walz, and their contributors deftly explore the counselor's role in addressing a number of pressing contemporary social issues that affect academic, career, and personal development.

I urge you to consider how the ideas and strategies that follow can impact your role as a counselor, regardless of your professional identity or work setting. As the text makes clear, you can make a difference not only at the individual level but also at the societal level. In so doing, you can truly promote public confidence and trust in the counseling profession, which is the stated mission of ACA in our strategic plan.

It is indeed an honor to welcome this important new work to the ACA publication list. Drs. Lee and Walz provide us with a manifesto for social change. It will help guide ACA and the profession as we work to help the clients we serve build a better life in the new millennium.

John L. Jaco
Executive Director
American Counseling Association

Preface

This book is about social action and its role in the counseling profession. Social action refers to two important interrelated concepts. The first is that social action involves a counselor's ability to intervene not only into client's lives to help with problem resolution or decision making but also into the social context that affects those lives. Social action is based on the premise that the environment is the key factor in determining behavior. Problematic behavior can often be traced to the negative effects of the environment on cognitive and affective functioning. Client issues, therefore, are often merely reactions or symptoms to deep-seated problems in the social environments in which people must interact.

The second concept, from a preventive perspective, is that social action encompasses the professional and moral responsibility that counselors have to address the significant social, cultural, and economic challenges that have the potential to impact negatively upon psychosocial development. This second concept relates to a counselor's sense of social responsibility and involves counselors taking stands on social issues as well as working to eradicate systems and ideologies that perpetuate discrimination and disregard human rights.

Social Action: A Mandate for Counselors is designed to provide counselors with new direction for becoming agents of social change who intervene not only in the lives of their clients but also in the world around them. It emphasizes the need to direct counseling skills toward the significant social, cultural, and economic issues that often impact negatively upon the lives of clients in the contemporary world.

The profession of counseling has a limited tradition of confronting social issues that is reflected in a relatively small body of literature on the role of the counselor as social change agent. This book provides a critical analysis of social action in contemporary counseling practice.

OVERVIEW OF CONTENTS

This book is divided into five sections: Introduction (chapter 1); Part One—Social Action: A Focus on Promoting Diversity and Challenging Oppression (chapters 2–9); Part Two—Social Action: A Focus on Assessment, Research, and Technology (chapters 10–14); Part Three—Social Action: A Focus on Professional Issues (chapters 15–17); and Conclusion (chapter 18). Courtland C. Lee provides the Introduction to the book. In chapter 1 he offers a definition of social action within the context of counseling and explores the tradition of social action in the profession. Ways in which counselors have engaged in social action, and some of the challenges they face as social change agents, are also discussed in this introductory chapter.

Part One—Social Action: A Focus on Promoting Diversity and Challenging Oppression offers direction for promoting diversity and overcoming oppression with specific client populations. Ingrid Grieger and Joseph G. Ponterotto specify ways that counselors can challenge intolerance in chapter 2. They discuss how counselors can combat intolerance by challenging their own intolerance, facilitating multicultural organizational development, and engaging in outreach, consultation, teaching, training, curriculum development, advocacy, and activism. The authors focus on how counselors can facilitate more empathic intergroup communication and create strategies for increasing access to opportunities and resources by nonprivileged groups and individuals. Two appendixes are included with this chapter to help counselors assess intolerance at both the individual and institutional levels.

In chapter 3, Judith A. Lewis and Mary Smith Arnold use the lens of multiculturalism to examine the impact of systemic oppression on client groups. They discuss four important ways that counselors can engage in social action to challenge systemic oppression: addressing the inadvertent tendency of the counseling profession to collude with oppression, supporting community empowerment efforts, engaging in political advocacy, and emphasizing the social action agenda of the American Counseling Association.

Courtland C. Lee and Jennifer L. Brydges explore the etiology of interpersonal violence in U.S. culture, including demographic patterns and psychological forces that contribute to the phenomenon, in chapter 4. They provide a comprehensive social action plan that counselors can employ to dispel violence and that includes public awareness initiatives, professional collaboration, legislative action, and program development.

Among the many opportunities for counselors to become activists for social change, perhaps the most daunting challenge lies in assisting the gay and lesbian community as it attempts to gain social justice. In chapter 5, Bob Barret provides background for working with gay and lesbian clients and offers suggestions for counselors working for social change with respect to the discrimination and homo-prejudice that exist within every community as well as the mental health profession.

David Capuzzi addresses the impact of at-risk behaviors and choices engaged in by vulnerable youth in chapter 6. He also focuses on the need for early prevention with and systemic intervention for this client group. Through the use of numerous examples, the qualities of prevention programming and aspects of systemic intervention with at-risk youth are discussed and described. The chapter concludes with additional suggestions for strategies to address the needs of at-risk youth more successfully.

In chapter 7 Edwin L. Herr and Spencer G. Niles explain that counselors involved in career intervention are engaged in social action in much of what they do. This chapter examines the counselor's various roles in social action and explores how career guidance, the client's context, unemployment, and other factors influence counselors who strive for nonbiased access to opportunities, individual purpose, and achievement.

Jane E. Myers in chapter 8 discusses demographic changes in the United States with a focus on the aging of our population. Counselors' responses to the graying of American society are considered, and the consequences of counselors' responses to the needs of older persons are explored. The phenomenon of ageism, an unreasonable prejudice against persons based on chronological age, is discussed, as is the personal impact of ageism on older individuals. Recommended strategies and actions for counselors are considered from the macro and micro perspectives, and suggestions for advocacy for and empowerment of older clients are provided.

In chapter 9 Judith G. Miranti and Mary Thomas Burke discuss social change through the incorporation and integration of the spiritual dimension into counseling practice. The authors contend that a willingness by counselors to be creative architects, to bear witness to their transcendent beliefs, will result in resisting and changing the persistent structures of injustice, dehumanizing poverty, and humiliating domination of certain segments of society.

The chapters in Part Two—Social Action: A Focus on Assessment, Research, and Technology focus on how to redirect counseling research and assessment initiatives to foster social change. Similarly, they examine how emerging technologies can foster social action in counseling. Nicholas A. Vacc in chapter 10 discusses the events shaping the assessment process in counseling and counselors' use of assessment instruments. He presents assessment as a multidimensional, continuous process for establishing a base of information about clients. The focus of the chapter is on using information in a way that is helpful to clients rather than as a way to find a truth for placement selection.

In chapter 11, John A. Casey explores the gap that has developed between the technologically advantaged and disadvantaged. As companies downsize, restructure, and reengineer, those workers without technology skills are let go, whereas the remaining front-line workers are using their technology skills to work harder for less money. In U.S. schools a growing gap has similarly developed between wealthy districts using state-of-the-art technology and poor districts struggling to meet basic needs. The author examines how professional counselors can be social change agents in combating these disturbing trends by using their expertise to secure technological resources that will benefit all citizens.

James P. Sampson examines the use of the Internet as a tool for social change in chapter 12. After briefly describing the nature of the Internet, he presents a model for Internet use and discusses the potential benefits and problems associated with Internet use. The chapter concludes with recommendations for using the Internet for social action.

What are the factors that shape social change research? In chapter 13 William E. Sedlacek explores the importance of understanding one's audience, the need to focus research questions, the importance of ethics, and other essential components of a social action research agenda. He provides a case study that illuminates the power and potential of social action research.

The accumulated knowledge of over 60 years of counseling outcome research can help direct and give credibility to our efforts to advocate for social change, according to Thomas L. Sexton and Susan C. Whiston in chapter 14. They outline an activist agenda consistent with current research findings, identify additional areas that outcome research can investigate, and comment on the synergistic relationship between research and social action.

Part Three—Social Action: A Focus on Professional Issues examines several important areas that the profession of counseling must consider in order to operationalize a social action agenda for the 21st century. In chapter 15, Brooke B. Collison, Judith L. Osborne, Lizbeth A. Gray, Reese M. House, James Firth, and Mary Lou consider important issues in preparing counselors for social action. They contend that counselors will best be prepared to answer the call for social action when counselor education programs begin to emphasize social activism within all aspects of counselor preparation. This chapter outlines a frame of reference for social action, explores the personal side of social activism, and stresses the importance of counselor educators modeling a social conscience for their students.

Fred Bemak in chapter 16 discusses the idea that the 21st century will require a reconceptualiztion of the role of counselors that incorporates interdisciplinary collaboration and social change. He offers a critique of dominant paradigms and some of the social, cultural, and political trends in the counseling profession. He also provides counselors with recommendations and strategies for interdisciplinary collaboration.

In chapter 17, Courtland C. Lee discusses professional counseling and social action in a global context. Worldwide social and economic challenges should compel counselors to action. This chapter describes ways that counselors can engage in such action through international collaboration, a global social action agenda, and support for families. Some of the challenges counselors will encounter as they strive for social change at the international level are also discussed.

Courtland C. Lee and Garry R. Walz provide the Conclusion of the book. In chapter 18 they summarize the key concepts related to social action set forth in the preceding chapters and present a call to action for counselors that is inherent throughout the book.

ACKNOWLEDGMENTS

We are indebted to a number of individuals for their assistance with the development of *Social Action: A Mandate for Counselors*. First and foremost are the contributors to this book. Thank you for the time and thought you put into preparing your chapters. Your scholarly efforts are greatly appreciated.

A special note of appreciation goes to Carolyn Baker, ACA Director of Acquisitions, for her support and guidance. Your professional insight into the publishing process aided significantly in the completion of this project. Likewise, we extend thanks to John L. Jaco, Executive Director of ACA, and Richard Yep, Senior Associate Executive Director of ACA, for their support of this project.

Special appreciation is due to Kaye Davis, Assistant Director for Creative Services, and Jay Malone, Editorial Consultant from ERIC/CASS, for their continued contributions throughout the development of this book. We also want to thank the editorial assistant who contributed significantly to this project, Jennifer L. Brydges at the University of Virginia.

About the Editors

Courtland C. Lee received his PhD from Michigan State University. He is professor of counselor education at the University of Virginia. Dr. Lee is the editor of three books on multicultural counseling and has also published numerous articles and book chapters on counseling across cultures. He is also the author of two books on counseling African American males. Dr. Lee is the former editor of the *Journal of Multicultural Counseling and Development*. In addition, he has served as president of the American Counseling Association (1997–98) and is a past president of the Association for Multicultural Counseling and Development and Chi Sigma Iota, the international counseling honor society. He has also served on the Executive Council of the International Round Table for the Advancement of Counselling. Dr. Lee is a consultant on multicultural issues both in the United States and abroad.

Garry R. Walz received his PhD from the University of Minnesota in counseling psychology. He currently is director of the ERIC Counseling and Student Services Clearinghouse and senior research scientist at the University of North Carolina at Greensboro and professor emeritus from the University of Michigan. He has authored or coauthored 10 books relating to counseling and has served as editor-in-chief of the ERIC/CASS publication program since its inception in 1966. His special areas of interest are counselor efficacy, career development, research in counseling, knowledge utilization, and educational technology. He is a past president of the American Counseling Association and the Association for Counselor

Education and Supervision, and chair of the Counseling and Human Development Foundation. His awards include the National Career Development Association (NCDA) Eminent Professional Career Award, Gilbert and Kathleen Wrenn Humanitarian Award, and the Association for Counselor Education and Supervision (ACES) Innovation in Counselor Education Award.

About the Authors

Mary Smith Arnold is a professor in the Division of Psychology and Counseling at Governors State University in University Park, Illinois. She has been recognized for many years as a leader in multicultural and diversity counseling. She designed the "unlearning oppression" workshop, which has been presented to hundreds of groups over the last 15 years. She received her PhD from the University of Iowa.

Bob Barret, PhD, is professor of counseling at the University of North Carolina at Charlotte, a psychologist in private practice, and president of the Association for Gay, Lesbian, and Bisexual Issues in Counseling. He has been a counselor interested in social activism throughout his career and is perhaps best known for his work on behalf of people with HIV disease.

Fred Bemak, EdD, is an associate professor of counselor education in the College of Education at the Ohio State University. His professional focus has been on at-risk populations from cultural, social, and political perspectives. He has consulted, lectured, researched, published, and directed federal and state grants aimed at personal, social, political, and systemic change.

Jennifer L. Brydges received her MEd in counselor education from the University of Virginia. She is a National Certified Counselor and has experience in counseling and coordinating programs for single parents, displaced homemakers, and low-income adults. Currently, she is a career counselor at the University of California, Los Angeles, Career Center.

Mary Thomas Burke, PhD, is a professor and coordinator of counselor education in the Department of Counseling, Special Education, and Child Development at the University of North Carolina, Charlotte. She has served as president of the Association for Spiritual, Ethical, and Religious and Value Issues in Counseling (ASERVIC). She is currently chairperson of the CACREP Board, president of Chi Sigma Iota, and president of the North Carolina ACES.

David Capuzzi, PhD, is a Licensed Professional Counselor and National Certified Counselor. He is professor of counselor education at Portland State University in Portland, Oregon, and a past president of the American Counseling Association. He is an author, coauthor, or coeditor of textbooks and monographs including *Youth At Risk* and *Suicide Prevention in the Schools*. Dr. Capuzzi is a frequent keynote and conference presenter and has worked with school districts and communities all over the country interested in addressing the needs of youth at risk. He is the first recipient of ACA's Kitty Cole Human Rights Award.

John A. Casey, EdD, NCC, is associate professor in the Department of Counseling and Educational Psychology at the University of Nevada, Reno. He has served on the governing councils for both ACA and ACES. He is a frequent contributor to journals and conferences on the topic of technology and counseling.

Brooke B. Collison is professor and coordinator of counselor education at Oregon State University. He received a PhD in counseling psychology from the University of Missouri-Columbia. He served as president of the American Association for Counseling and Development in 1988–89 and was formerly a faculty member in counselor education at the Wichita State University, Kansas.

James Firth received his PhD in counseling psychology from Arizona State University. He is an associate professor of counselor education at Oregon State University and specializes in group counseling procedures. He is a senior associate in the Yarbrough Group emphasizing group process training for middle- and upper-level managers in business and industrial settings.

Lizbeth A. Gray is an associate professor of counselor education at Oregon State University. She received a PhD in counseling psychology from Washington State University and an MSW from the University of Chicago. Dr. Gray's area of specialty is in human sexuality and HIV/AIDS education programs. She has taught and consulted internationally in her specialty area.

Ingrid Grieger recieved her BA in English from Brooklyn College of the City of New York, her MA in counseling from Virginia Commonwealth University, and her EdD in counselor education from the University of Virginia. Currently, she is director of counseling services at Iona College in New Rochelle, New York. Among her recent publications are those that focus on cross-cultural counseling assessment and multicultural issues in college student development.

Edwin L. Herr received his BS from Shippensburg State College, Pennsylvania, and his MA, Professional Diploma, and EdD from Teachers College, Columbia University. He is currently distinguished professor of education (counselor education and counseling psychology) and associate dean for graduate programs, research, and technology, College of Education at the Pennsylvania State University. Herr has served as the president of the American Counseling Association, the National Career Development Association, and the Association for Counselor Education and Supervision. The author of some 300 articles and 31 books and monographs and the immediate past editor of the *Journal of Counseling and Development*, Herr has received a number of professional awards including the Eminent Career Award of the National Career Development Association, the Professional Development Award of the American Counseling Association, and the 50th Anniversary Professional Leadership Award of the Association for Counselor Education and Supervision. Internationally, he has lectured in some 15 nations and been elected to the board of directors of the International Round Table for the

Advancement of Counselling and the International Association for Education and Vocational Guidance.

Reese M. House received his BS and MA from Ball State University, Indiana, and his EdD from Oregon State University. He currently works for the Education Trust in Washington, D.C., on a project to transform how school counselors are prepared. He is on leave from Oregon State University where he focused on preparing school counselors to be proactive change agents and advocates for social, economic, and political justice. He has written extensively about gay, lesbian, and bisexual issues in counseling and HIV/AIDS prevention. His background includes experience as a school counselor, community activist, and HIV/AIDS educator.

Judith A. Lewis is a professor in the College of Health Professions at Governors State University in University Park, Illinois. She is the author of numerous publications addressing issues related to social action. She is president of the International Association of Marriage and Family Counselors and has been the recipient of several awards, including the American Counseling Association's Professional Development Award and the Ohana Award. Her PhD is from the University of Michigan.

Mary Lou is an assistant professor in counselor education at Oregon State University (OSU). She earned an MAT from Lewis and Clark College, and an MS and PhD in counseling from Oregon State University. Her primary focus for several years has been field supervision of school counseling interns. Prior to joining the faculty at OSU, she worked as a school counselor with high-risk students and as a counselor in a middle school.

Judith G. Miranti, EdD, is professor of counselor education and dean of graduate studies at Our Lady of Holy Cross College in New Orleans, Louisiana. She has held leadership positions on the national and local levels by serving on the American Counseling Association Governing Council and as president of the Association for Spiritual, Ethical, and Religious Values in Counseling, the Louisiana Counseling Association, and Chi Sigma Iota International.

She is the recipient of the Gilbert and Kathleen Wrenn Humanitarian and Caring Person Award.

Jane E. Myers, PhD, LPC, is a professor and coordinator of the Gerontological Counseling Program Track and Post-Master's Certificate in Gerontological Counseling in the Department of Counseling and Educational Development at the University of North Carolina at Greensboro. She is a past president of the American Counseling Association, the Association for Adult Development and Aging, and Chi Sigma Iota.

Spencer G. Niles, DEd, LPC, NCC, is an associate professor of counselor education at the University of Virgina. He is the incoming editor of the *Career Development Quarterly* and serves on editorial boards for the *Journal of Career Development, Journal of Counseling and Development,* and *Journal of College Student Development.* Niles also serves on the board of directors for the National Career Development Association. He has written 40 refereed journal articles and delivered over 50 presentations at international and national conferences.

Judith L. Osborne received her EdD from Oklahoma State University. She is an assistant professor in counselor education at Oregon State University where she is centrally involved in preparation of school counselors. Her recent publications have emphasized program evaluation as well as advocacy issues.

Joseph G. Ponterotto received his BA from Iona College, New York, and his MA and PhD degrees in counseling psychology from the University of California, Santa Barbara. He is currently professor of education in the counseling programs at Fordham University-Lincoln Center (New York), where he also coordinates the master's degree program in bilingual school counseling. He is a frequent contributor to the multicultural counseling literature.

James P. Sampson, Jr., PhD, is professor and codirector of the Center for the Study of Technology in Counseling and Career Development at Florida State University in Tallahassee.

William E. Sedlacek, PhD, is a professor of education and assistant director of the Counseling Center at the University of Maryland, College Park. He is also an adjunct professor of pharmacy at the University of Maryland at Baltimore. He earned bachelor's and master's degrees from Iowa State University and a doctorate from Kansas State University.

Thomas L. Sexton is an associate professor in the Department of Counseling at the University of Nevada, Las Vegas. He teaches courses in counseling research and marriage and family therapy, and directs the Counselor Training Clinic. He is the coauthor of three books, *Integrating Outcome Research Into Counseling Practice and Training* (with Susan C. Whiston, Jeanne Bleuer, and Garry R. Walz), *Constructivist Thinking in Counseling Research and Practice* (with Barbara Griffin), and *The Heart of Healing* (with Jeffrey Kottler and Susan Whiston). He has also written numerous articles applying outcome research to counseling practice. He received his PhD from Florida State University in counseling psychology.

Nicholas A. Vacc is currently the Rosenthal Excellence Professor in the Department of Counseling and Educational Development at the University of North Carolina at Greensboro. He has served as president of the Association for Assessment in Counseling, editor of the *Measurement and Evaluation in Counseling and Development* journal, and president of Chi Sigma Iota International, the international counseling honor society.

Susan C. Whiston is an associate professor in the Department of Educational Psychology at the University of Nevada, Las Vegas, and teaches courses in school and career counseling. She is an associate editor for research for the *Journal of Counseling and Development*. She is coauthor of two books, *Integrating Outcome Research Into Counseling Practice and Training* (with Thomas L. Sexton, Jeanne Bleuer, and Garry R. Walz), *The Heart of Healing* (with Jeffrey Kottler and Thomas L. Sexton). She is also author of numerous articles in the area of outcome research. She received her PhD in counselor education from the University of Wyoming.

INTRODUCTION

1

Counselors as Agents of Social Change

COURTLAND C. LEE

Gang violence. The burning and desecration of places of worship. Acts of intolerance against individuals from culturally diverse groups. Homelessness. Domestic and international terrorism. Environmental pollution. The rampant spread of HIV/AIDS. Abuse and neglect of children and older persons.

These are just some of the issues that reflect profound social, cultural, and economic dilemmas confronting society at the end of the 20th century. Such phenomena negatively affect the quality of life for millions of people and impact psychological and social development across the life span.

For the profession of counseling, these pressing social issues suggest an examination of the current philosophy and practice of mental health intervention. They provide the opportunity to reexamine and redefine a commitment to the art of helping on the part of counselors. Traditionally, counselor energy and skill have been focused on helping individuals resolve problems and make decisions. Yet the origin of problems and impediments to effective decision making often lie not in individuals but in an intolerant, restrictive, or unsafe environment.

The focus of this chapter is on social action and its role in the practice of counseling. It provides a conceptual basis for the role of counselor as social change agent. Improving society through helping people empower themselves has always been a major objective of the counseling profession. Through promoting decision making, problem resolution, and values clarification, counselors have contributed to the betterment of their clients, thereby promoting an improved society. This chapter, however, provides counselors with a context for becoming agents of social change who intervene not only in the lives of their clients but also in the world around them.

This chapter first defines social action in counseling and explores the tradition of social action in counseling. It then provides a conceptual overview by looking at empowerment and advocacy as the basis for the role of counselor as social change agent and describes some of the ways that counselors have engaged in social action. The chapter next considers the professional and personal challenges and risks of social action and concludes with a look at its possible limits in counseling.

SOCIAL ACTION IN COUNSELING DEFINED

Social action as a concept must be considered within the context of a counselor's personal awareness of himself or herself as both a person and a professional. In order to be effective as a helper, it is important that a counselor possess three levels of awareness:

- *Level 1—Awareness of Self.* A counselor must understand the important dynamics of his or her personality and how they contribute to the counseling process (Gladding, 1992; Meier, 1989; Nugent, 1990).
- *Level 2—Interpersonal Awareness.* A counselor must be able to enter a client's reality in a nonjudgmental manner (Rogers, 1951). He or she must possess both an appreciation of another person's perception of the world and the psychosocial context for that worldview. The essence of counseling lies at this level; it is the art of helping another person to resolve problems or make decisions.
- *Level 3—Systemic Awareness.* A counselor must be able to perceive accurately environmental influences on client development and possess skills to intercede at an environmental level to challenge systemic barriers that block optimal mental health (Cook, 1972; Gunnings & Simpkins, 1972; Katz, 1985; Lee, Armstrong, & Brydges, 1996)

It is the third level of counselor awareness that forms the basis of social action. Within the context of counseling, social action refers to two important interrelated concepts. The first is that social action involves the ability to intervene not only into client's lives to help with problem resolution or decision making but also in the social context that affects those lives. Social action is based on the premise that the environment is the key factor in determining behavior. Problematic behavior can often be traced to the negative effects of environment on cognitive and affective functioning. Client issues, therefore, are often merely reactions to or symptoms of deep-seated problems in the social environments in which people must interact.

The second concept, from a preventive perspective, is that social action encompasses the professional and moral responsibility that counselors have to address the significant social, cultural, and economic challenges that have the potential to impact negatively upon psychosocial development. This second concept relates to counselors' sense of social responsibility and involves counselors taking stands on social issues as well as working to eradicate systems and ideologies that perpetuate discrimination and disregard individual rights. A sense of social responsibility implies that professional counselors have an important role to play in fostering and supporting a society that is more enlightened, just, and humane (Lee & Sirch, 1994; McWhirter, 1997).

SOCIAL ACTION: A COUNSELING TRADITION

Although often viewed as a relatively conservative and somewhat passive profession, counseling has established a tradition of social action. McWhirter (1997) suggested that social action is implicit in the work of Frank Parsons and Carl Rogers. Both of these giants in the profession advocated that counselors respond to the injustice of the status quo, work to change social policy, and intervene at both the individual and societal level.

"Counseling and the Social Revolution," a special issue of the *Personnel and Guidance Journal,* was published in May 1971. This seminal issue, edited by Michael D. Lewis, Judith A. Lewis, and Edward P. Dworkin, was published near the end of the great social revolution begun the 1960s that saw massive protest against a war considered to be unjust and various forms of social discrimination. The goal of the special issue was to put the realities of the social revolution before the counseling profession and to suggest that counselors need not only to understand but also to participate in the social change process. The articles in this issue dealt with the counselor facing social issues such as racism and sexism, ecological issues, and antiwar issues. There were also articles about counselor self-evaluation and training with respect to social action.

This special issue was followed by a number of articles in professional counseling journals exhorting counselors to social action. Some of these articles accused the profession of being reactionary and serving oppressive social systems that negatively impacted on client groups (Banks & Martens, 1973). Others called on counselors to become social change agents (Cook, 1972; Gunnings & Simpkins, 1972; Herbert, 1971; Kincaid & Kincaid, 1971; Schlossberg, 1977; Smith, 1971; Tucker, 1973; Warnath, 1973).

In the 1980s a wave of conservatism swept the United States and severely challenged the relevance of social action and social responsibility on the part of professionals. Nevertheless, the counseling profession continued to build on a tradition of confronting social issues. This tradition is reflected in the literature on counselor training, research, and client service delivery of that era (Burhke, 1988; Cook, 1983; Corvin & Wiggins, 1989; Crabbs, 1989; Downing, 1982; Eldridge, 1983; Lee, 1989; Ponzo, 1981; Sander, 1982; Wilcoxon, 1989).

Significantly, in 1987 the American Association for Counseling and Development published a position paper on human rights (AACD, 1987). The paper was a clarion call to professional counselors to advocate for social change through personal, professional, and political activity.

The 1980s also witnessed the rise of multicultural counseling as a major discipline, and multicultural concepts in counseling fostered a new sense of social responsibility and activism within the profession (Lee, 1997). Counselors who worked with culturally diverse clients were often forced to consider the negative effects of racism, sexism, classism, homophobia, and other forms of oppression on psychosocial development (Cook, 1993; Priest, 1991; Schreier, 1995; Solomon, 1992). This contributed to increased professional awareness that the etiology of problems often lies not in clients but, rather, in intolerant or restrictive environments. Counselors who worked with culturally diverse client groups, therefore, were called on to become agents of systemic change, to channel energy and skill into helping clients from marginalized or powerless groups break down institutional and social barriers to optimal development (De La Cancela & Sotomayor, 1993; Evans & Wall, 1991; Lee, 1991; Ponterotto & Pedersen, 1993).

As the profession prepares for the 21st century, the concept of social action has taken on new dimensions. In the 1990s, counselors have witnessed a dizzying panorama of change throughout the world, including the collapse of communism and the end of apartheid in South Africa as well as the introduction of major new technologies for improving the quality of life.

Counselors have also observed that these same technologies impact negatively upon both the environment and human interaction. Likewise, counselors have seen historical racial/religious/ethnic hostility and violence fractionalize many areas of the world from Los Angeles to Sarajevo, the rampant spread of HIV/AIDS, a rise in the number of hungry and homeless people throughout the world, and a declining quality of life due to worldwide economic recession.

The nature of these changes suggests a major shift in global social and cultural perspectives and a new set of human challenges. As the 20th century wanes, counselors often have to rethink their views on human development and refine their methods for promoting it (Lee & Sirch, 1994). It is evident that the start of the 21st century will bring a wider global view of both human need and potential. This has led to a renewed focus on counselors and their social responsibility (Arredondo & D'Andrea, 1995; Lee & Sirch, 1994; McWhirter, 1994, 1997; Morrow & Deidan, 1992; Parette & Hourcade, 1995; Ponterotto, 1991; Robinson, 1994; Yep, 1992).

COUNSELING AND SOCIAL ACTION:
A CONCEPTUAL OVERVIEW

In order to fully understand the role of social action in counseling, several concepts must be considered. Social responsibility on the part of counselors is predicated on a comprehensive understanding of the interrelation of empowerment and advocacy as the basis of counselor social change agency.

EMPOWERMENT

The 1990s have seen an increased awareness of the importance of the concept of empowerment to counseling theory and practice. This concept, which has its origins in social work, community psychology, feminist therapy, multicultural counseling, and education, forms a framework for social action in counseling (McWhirter, 1994, 1997). McWhirter (1994) offered the following definition of empowerment:

> . . . the process by which people, organizations, or groups who are powerless or marginalized (a) become aware of the power dynamics at work in their life context, (b) develop the skills and capacity for gaining reasonable control over their lives, (c) which they exercise, (d) without infringing on the rights of others, and (e) which coincides with actively supporting the empowerment of others in their community. (p. 12)

This definition suggest that empowerment is a complex process that encompasses self-reflection and action, awareness of environmental power dynamics that may impact upon psychosocial development, and the development of skills to promote community enhancement (McWhirter, 1997).

With its focus on environmental awareness and community action as well as individual insight, the concept of empowerment provides an important foundation for social action. The process of empowerment puts the onus on both client and counselor to look beyond mere intervention at an individual level.

ADVOCACY

Advocacy refers to the process or act of arguing or pleading for a cause or proposal. An advocate, therefore, is an individual who pleads for a cause. In addition, an advocate can be a person who argues another individual's cause or proposal.

The concept of advocacy also helps to frame the social action context of counseling. As advocates, counselors are called upon to channel energy and skill into helping clients challenge institutional and social barriers that impede academic, career, or personal-social development. When necessary, counselors need to be willing to act on behalf of marginalized or disenfranchised clients and actively challenge long-standing traditions, preconceived notions, or regressive policies and procedures that may stifle human development. Acting as advocates, through efforts both with and/or for clients, counselors can help people become empowered so that they can challenge systemic barriers and seize new educational, career, or personal-social opportunities (Lee, 1989).

There are three important aspects of the advocate role for professional counselors. First, advocates are counselors who view helping from a systemic perspective. Second, advocates attempt systemic change in partnership with clients who often lack the knowledge or skill base to effect such change alone. Third, advocates must have an understanding of important systems change principles along with the skill to translate them into action.

Counselor as an Agent of Social Change

The concepts of empowerment and advocacy provide the basis for the role of counselor as social change agent. Any counselor with a belief in the possibility of a better world should develop a sense of social responsibility. Part of such a counselor's philosophy should be a commitment to the idea of social change and his or her role as catalyst for such change.

A counselor who is an agent of social change possesses the awareness, knowledge, and skill to intervene not only at an individual level but also at a system-wide level. Either in partnership with and/or for clients, a social change agent challenges cultural, social, historical, or economic barriers that stifle optimal mental health and human development. Such a professional should have two important goals in the counseling process: (1) to help clients understand problem causation by recognizing the influence of the social context on human development and (2) to help empower clients by assisting them in developing and implementing strategies to eliminate or reduce systemic discrimination or oppression in all forms.

A counselor who is a social change agent works with and for clients in a variety of ways. Examples of social action initiatives for professional counselors include

- participating with clients in an AIDS Walk to make a statement to the government and the public about his or her commitment to fighting the AIDS epidemic;
- helping to educate economically disadvantaged women about changes in welfare laws that may impact them and their children; organizing them to make their voices heard in the corridors of power about how potential changes in such laws could negatively effect their ability to care for their children;
- facilitating educational programs in prisons that insure offenders gain knowledge and skills for success on the outside as way to reduce recidivism rates;
- working to insure that affirmative action and other equity issues remain central to policy and procedures in both education and the work world;
- speaking out at legislative forums and hearings about how cutbacks in school counseling programs have the potential to impact negatively the academic, career, and personal-social development of young people;
- volunteering at soup kitchens, homeless shelters, or other social welfare agencies; and
- participating in community-building efforts such as Habit for Humanity; insuring that clients and others have decent places to live.

The chapters that follow offer multifaceted analyses of such actions.

SOCIAL ACTION: THE PROFESSIONAL AND PERSONAL RISKS

Inherent personal and professional risks are involved when social action is incorporated into a counseling philosophy and skills repertoire. However, the crucial tasks of helping to empower clients to challenge social problems and/or socially responsible acts on the part of counselors themselves are worth the risks.

Still, counselors need to be aware that speaking or acting out against social problems may engender professional or personal consequences. For example, counselors may become vulnerable to different forms of harassment in the workplace when taking a stand on a controversial issue. Likewise, they may develop reputations as "troublemakers" in their efforts to challenge social problems. Such a reputation could lead to professional backlash in the form of disciplinary action or limited opportunities for advancement. In addition, choosing to promote social causes may result in being ostracized by professional colleagues.

A counselor who chooses to advocate for social change also runs the risk of stretching ethical limits. An important example of this is losing sight of relationship boundaries with clients. This is a particularly acute risk when and if a counselor assumes the role of client advocate. For example, while acting on behalf of marginalized or disenfranchised clients in challenging institutional or social barriers, a counselor may find himself or herself fostering dependent relationships. It is important, therefore, that client advocacy be part of an integrated individual or group counseling intervention that is jointly planned by counselor and client. Advocacy on the part of a counselor should be part of an intervention that ultimately aims to help clients become empowered so that they can develop the skills to challenge systemic barriers and seize new educational, career, or personal-social opportunities for themselves.

Counselors choosing to confront social challenges in their work must understand that such a choice transcends the boundary between personal life and professional role. Professional actions taken to promote social action may resonate in personal life. Counselors need to consider that various forms of harassment may impact upon their home and family life. Moreover, they may run the risk of becoming so associated with this concept that it can jeopardize relationships with people who do not share such views.

Counselors striving to become agents of social change must consider such risks as part of the process of promoting an enlightened and humane society. They must reach a point in their own personal and professional lives where they believe that the benefit to individuals and society from their social action is well worth the risks.

POSSIBLE LIMITS OF SOCIAL ACTION IN COUNSELING

It can be argued that the definition of counselor as social change agent emphasizes the remedial and negates the preventive dimension of counseling. However, helping empower clients to challenge intolerant, restrictive, or oppressive environments effectively should be considered a way to prevent them from returning to such environments. The ultimate goal of social action, like that of individual or group counseling, is both remedial and preventive in nature. Social action aims to prevent individuals from returning to disempowering environments by establishing social structures that empower people.

It may also be argued that the definition of social change agent does not differentiate counseling from other professions. For example, social work is predicated on assisting persons to establish emotional and social subsistence for themselves (Crouch, 1979). As a profession, social work has a proud tradition of social advocacy. However, what seems to distinguish counseling from other professions is its unique emphasis on wellness, personal growth, and career development. A unique goal of counseling is to facilitate human development and adjustment throughout the life span. Systemic intervention strategies, which lie at the heart of social action in counseling, should be conducted within this important developmental context.

CONCLUSION

Professional counselors can and should be agents of both individual and social change. This chapter has provided a conceptual basis for the role of counselor as social change agent and outlined how counselors can become engaged in helping to address serious social problems and build stronger communities. We can employ our diverse expertise not only to help people but also to resolve the profound social, cultural, and economic dilemmas challenging the world. Through our own social action, we can help to empower people and to foster a healthy society as well.

REFERENCES

American Association for Counseling and Development. (1987). *Human rights position paper*. Alexandria, VA: Author.

Arredondo, P., & D'Andrea, M. (1995). The challenge of multiculturalism and organizational development: Outlining the "call of conscience." *Counseling Today*, 37 (12).

Banks, W., & Martens, K. (1973). Counseling: The reactionary profession. *Personnel and Guidance Journal*, 51, 457-462.

Buhrke, R. A. (1988). Lesbian-related issues in counseling supervision. *Women and Therapy*, 8, 195-206.

Cook, D. R. (1972). The change agent counselor: A conceptual context. *The School Counselor*, 20, 9-15.

Cook, E. P. (Ed.). (1993). *Women, relationships, and power: Implications for power*. Alexandria, VA: American Counseling Association.

Cook, J. A. (1983). The hydra-headed nature of prejudice: Research perspectives concerning cross-cultural counseling with elementary age children. *Elementary School Guidance and Counseling*, 17, 294-300.

Corvin, S. A., & Wiggins, F. (1989). An antiracism training model for White professionals. *Journal of Multicultural Counseling and Development*, 17, 105-114.

Crabbs, M. A. (1989). Future perfect: Planning for the next century. *Elementary School Guidance and Counseling*, 24, 160-166.

Crouch, R. C. (1979). Social work defined. *Social Work*, 46-48.

De La Cancela, V., & Sotomayor, G. M. (1993). Rainbow warriors: Reducing institutional racism in mental health. *Journal of Mental Health Counseling*, 15, 55-71.

Downing, C. J. (1982). Counseling the culturally different. *Counseling and Values*, 26, 259-263.

Eldridge, W. D. (1983). Affirmative social action and the use of power in clinical counseling. *Counseling and Values*, 27, 66-75.

Evans, N. J., & Wall, V. A. (Eds.). (1991). *Beyond tolerance: Gays, lesbians and bisexuals on campus*. Alexandria, VA: American College Personnel Association.

Gladding, S. T. (1992). *Counseling: A comprehensive profession (2nd ed.)*. New York: Merrill.

Gunnings, T. S., & Simpkins, G. A. (1972). A systemic approach to counseling disadvantaged youth. *Journal of Non-White Concerns in Personnel and Guidance*, 1, 4-8.

Herbert, R. (1971). Ecology: A shared journey. *Personnel and Guidance Journal*, 49, 737-739.

Katz, J. H. (1985). The sociopolitical nature of counseling. *The Counseling Psychologist*, 13, 615-624.

Kincaid, M., & Kincaid, J. (1971). Counseling for peace. *Personnel and Guidance Journal*, 49, 727-735

Lee, C. C. (1989). Needed: A career development advocate. *Career Development Quarterly*, 37, 218-220.

Lee, C. C. (1991). Empowerment in counseling: A multicultural perspective. *Journal of Counseling and Development*, 69, 229-230.

Lee, C. C. (1997). The promise and pitfalls of multicultural counseling. In C.C. Lee (Ed.), *Multicultural issues in counseling: New approaches to diversity* (2nd ed., pp. 3-13). Alexandria, VA: American Counseling Association.

Lee, C. C., Armstrong, K. L., & Brydges, J. L. (1996). The challenges of a diverse society: Counseling for mutual respect and understanding. *Counseling and Human Development, 28,* 1-8.

Lee, C. C., & Sirch, M. L. (1994). Counseling in an enlightened society: Values for a new millennium. *Counseling and Values, 38,* 90-97.

Lewis, M. D., Lewis, J. A., & Dworkin, E. P. (Eds.). (1971). Counseling and the social revolution [Special issue]. *Personnel and Guidance Journal, 49*(9).

McWhirter, E. H. (1994). *Counseling for empowerment.* Alexandria, VA: American Counseling Association.

McWhirter, E. H. (1997). Empowerment, social activism, and counseling. *Counseling and Human Development, 29,* 1-14.

Meier, S. T. (1989). *The elements of counseling.* Pacific Grove, CA: Brooks/Cole.

Morrow, K. A., & Deidan, C. T. (1992). Bias in the counseling process: How to recognize and avoid it. *Journal of Counseling and Development, 70,* 571-577.

Nugent, F. A. (1990). *An introduction to the profession of counseling (2nd ed.).* New York: Merrill.

Parette, H. P., Hourcade, J. J. (1995). Disability etiquette and school counselors: A commonsense approach toward compliance with the Disabilities Act. *The School Counselor, 42,* 224-232.

Ponterotto, J. G. (1991). The nature of prejudice revisited: Implications for counseling intervention. *Journal of Counseling and Development, 70,* 216-224.

Ponterotto, J. G., & Pedersen, P. B. (1993). *Preventing prejudice: A guide for counselors and educators.* Newbury Park, CA: Sage.

Ponzo, Z. (1981). Counseling the elderly: A lifetime process. *Counseling and Values, 26,* 68-80.

Priest, R. C. (1991). Racism and prejudice as negative impacts on African American clients in therapy. *Journal of Counseling and Development, 70,* 213-215.

Robinson, K. E. (1994). Addressing the needs of gay and lesbian students: The school counselor's role. *The School Counselor, 41,* 326-332.

Rogers, C. (1951). *Client-centered therapy.* Boston: Houghton Mifflin.

Sander, D. (1982). Age discrimination in employment: Counselor responsibilities. *Counselor Education and Supervision, 21,* 213-217.

Schlossberg, N. K. (1977). Hide and seek with bias. *Personnel and Guidance Journal, 55,* 481-484.

Schreier, B. A. (1995). Moving beyond tolerance: A new paradigm for programming about homophobia/biphobia and heterosexism. *Journal of College Student Development, 36,* 19-26.

Smith, P. M. (1971). Black activists for liberation, not guidance. *Personnel and Guidance Journal, 49,* 721-726.

Solomon, A. C. (1992). Clinical diagnosis among diverse populations: A multicultural perspective. *Families in Society, 73,* 371-77.

Tucker, S. J. (1973). Action counseling: An accountability procedure for counseling the oppressed. *Journal of Non-White Concerns in Personnel and Guidance, 2,* 35-41.

Warnath, C. F. (1973). The school counselor as institutional agent. *The School Counselor, 20,* 202-208.

Wilcoxon, S. A. (1989). He/she/they/it?: Implied sexism in speech and print. *Journal of Counseling and Development, 68,* 114-116.

Yep, R. K. (1992). Advocating in the public policy arena. In C. Solomon & P. Jackson-Jobe (Eds.), *Helping homeless people: Unique challenges and solutions* (pp. 29-40). Alexandria, VA: American Counseling Association.

PART ONE

Social Action: A Focus on Promoting
Diversity and Challenging Oppression

2

Challenging Intolerance

INGRID GRIEGER AND JOSEPH G. PONTEROTTO

As we approach the 21st century, intolerance is one of the major social problems facing the United States and the world. Consider the following two quotations, which span the second half of the 20th century:

> Civilized men [and women] have gained notable mastery over energy, matter, and inanimate nature generally, and are rapidly learning to control physical suffering and premature death. But, by contrast, we appear to be living in the Stone Age so far as our handling of human relationships is concerned. (Allport, 1954, p. xiii)

> Within the last several years, we have witnessed a disturbing backlash to gains in civil rights and progress in intergroup communication. This is symptomatic of a growing climate of intolerance that seems to pervade the 1990s. An atmosphere has developed throughout the country in which differences are not accepted, but rather feared. Such fear is perpetrated by ignorance about ethnic, gender, class, religious, sexual orientation, and other cultural differences. (Lee, 1997, xxi)

The first quotation is taken from one of the most important books written in this century: Allport's (1954) *The Nature of Prejudice*. The second excerpt, written over four decades later, comprises part of ACA President Courtland Lee's foreword to Sandhu and Aspy's (1997) *Counseling for Prejudice Prevention and Reduction*, a book that will be influential well into the 21st century.

If the Allport and Lee quotations are taken at face value, and we believe that they can be, we are left with the impression that U.S. society has made little progress either in fighting intolerance or in building a healthy climate of intergroup harmony and respect. Given the target audience of this book, it is instructive to look at the development of the counseling profession over the time span covered by the two quotations. During the four decades in question, the counseling profession has grown rapidly, with ACA reaching a membership total of roughly 57,000. The vibrancy of the counseling profession can also be seen in the fact that 42 of 50 states (as of this writing) have enacted some form of legislation certifying or licensing the work and/or titles of professional counselors.

Given the growth and development of the counseling profession over the last four decades, the following questions can be raised: What role has the counseling profession played in fighting intolerance? What role should our profession play? What can professional counselors offer by way of their unique skills in this area? How can the profession be more involved in broadly based systemic efforts designed to challenge intolerance and facilitate intergroup understanding?

This chapter answers, at least in part, all of these questions, within the primary goal of empowering our readers to fight intolerance both in their personal and professional lives. The chapter begins with a brief overview of the nature and prevalence of intolerance in U.S. society. The discussion then moves to counselor skills effective for challenging intolerance, such as facilitating empathic intergroup communication and creating strategies for increasing group and individual access to opportunities and resources. The chapter next specifies actions that counselors can take to challenge intolerance, including individual assessment; multicultural organizational development (MOD); outreach and consultation; teaching, training, and curriculum development; and advocacy and activism. Two appendixes are provided to help counselors in their assessment of intolerance at both individual and institutional levels.

THE NATURE AND PREVALENCE OF INTOLERANCE

The American Heritage Dictionary (1992) has defined tolerance as "the capacity for or the practice of recognizing and respecting the beliefs or practices of others" (p. 1884). Lack of tolerance, or intolerance, forms the root of ethnocentrism, which is at the heart of prejudice (Ponterotto & Pedersen, 1993). Intolerance and prejudice take many forms and can be directed at any number of groups based, for example, on race, ethnicity, gender, sexual orientation, income level, religion, and disability.

There is little question that intolerance is alive and well at the dawn of the 21st century. Recent major treatments of prejudice and intolerance (e.g., Jones, 1997; Sandhu & Aspy, 1997), which extend previous work in the area (e.g., Jones 1972; Ponterotto & Pedersen, 1993), document all too well the continuing pervasive nature and destructive consequences of intolerance in U.S. society.

Why is intolerance so prevalent in society? The answer is deceptively simple: intolerance and prejudice develop naturally and easily. Humans have a propensity for intolerance, and prejudice develops easily from an interaction of three factors: our natural tendency toward ethnocentrism, our lack of meaningful contact with other groups, and our need to categorize and classify people (and things) to help manage "information overload" (see extensive discussion in Allport, 1954, and Ponterotto & Pedersen, 1993).

Ethnocentrism develops because people tend to cling to their own (or family's or community's) values and personal beliefs. Individuals naturally tend to be more comfortable with their own "in group"— whether that be family, ethnic group, or work group—than with some "out" or different group. Furthermore, many individuals in U.S. society lack meaningful intergroup contact because the history and continuing legacy of our nation is stratified along racial, religious, and income lines. Despite increasing racial/ethnic diversity in this country, society is still segregated on many levels. Finally, to help manage information overload that results from a highly technological society, people tend to categorize information (and people) into manageable segments. Often these perceptive clusters are established on the basis of faulty or incomplete information, which results in negative stereotyping.

Though developing rather naturally, intolerance and prejudice are still learned. Infants are not born racist or homophobic; rather, through subtle and sometimes overt messages from parents, older siblings, the media, the school system, the world of work, and some political legislation, individuals are taught to love themselves first and to distrust others not like themselves.

This book is one that calls for action while at the same time inspiring hope that professional counselors can contribute significantly to building a more tolerant and accepting society. The profession has not been totally silent on the issue, and in fact, we believe that many front-line counselors are committed to challenging intolerance and that, in many cases, they have devoted their professional careers to realizing more constructive, respectful, and humane intergroup interaction. We want to acknowledge the thousands of front-line counselors who work everyday in schools, colleges, clinics, hospitals, and corporations as well as in their communities to stem the tide of intolerance.

Nevertheless, we also believe that the counseling profession, as a whole, can play a more significant social action role in challenging intolerance. Counselors, in particular, have a cluster of skills that are unique among professionals.

COUNSELOR SKILLS IN CHALLENGING INTOLERANCE

Through their training and their general orientation to helping, counselors are the ideal professionals to address intolerance on both a preventive and remediative level. Counselors have the requisite listening and communication skills; they are adept at problem solving; they can effectively mediate conflict and intervene in a crisis; and they can work toward cognitive restructuring and attitude change.

In their extensive discussion of this topic, Ponterotto and Pedersen (1993) outlined five necessary steps in prejudice prevention programs with students and clients: (a) facilitate healthy racial and ethnic identity development, (b) promote critical thinking skills, (c) support and enact multicultural and nonsexist education, (d) facilitate meaningful interracial contact among groups, and (e) work to transform underlying negative racial attitudes. Though these authors were focusing primarily on racial and ethnic prejudice, we believe their strategies are appropriate to fighting intolerance in all its many expressions.

We also believe that counseling and psychotherapy, in and of themselves, should be viewed as powerful skills for using social action to challenge intolerance. For clients who have been the victims of intolerance in any of its virulent forms, speaking the truth of their experience in the presence of an empathic and compassionate listener is an important part of their healing process. The counselor's shared sense of outrage with the client is empowering; the counselor's framing of the client's pain as emanating from sociopolitical injustice rather than from intrapsychic conflict is transformational. The ability of the counselor to deliver culturally sensitive, non-victim-blaming, voice- and dignity-restoring counseling is surely among the most significant in the counselor's arsenal of skills relevant to healing the insidious effects of intolerance.

COUNSELOR ACTIONS IN CHALLENGING INTOLERANCE

We assert that the moral and ethical imperative to take action in challenging intolerance is clear, and that the possibilities are virtually limitless. For the purpose of this relatively brief discussion, however, we designate five areas of counselor action and provide specific suggestions for change-oriented activities in each area. They are as follows:

- Self-assessment
- Multicultural organizational development (MOD)
- Outreach and consultation
- Teaching, training, and curriculum development
- Advocacy and activism.

SELF-ASSESSMENT

Professional counselors are not exempt from socialization pressures that promote ethnocentrism and prejudice; we are all prejudiced to some degree. It makes intuitive sense that to challenge intolerance in others effectively, we must first process it within ourselves. To that end, counselors can ask themselves the following four questions:

1. How do I feel about my own racial/religious/sexual identity?
2. How comfortable am I with friends/colleagues/students/clients who differ from me based on gender, race, religion, ethnic group, or sexual orientation?

3. What have I done recently to enhance my knowledge and awareness of self as a cultural being as well as of others of different groups?
4. What steps am I willing to take, both personally and professionally, to feel more comfortable and to be more competent with
   persons who have a worldview and life history that differs markedly from my own?

Appendix A presents the Quick Discrimination Index (QDI)
(Ponterotto et al., 1995), a 30-item self-report assessment of racial
and gender attitudes. The QDI yields three factors: (a) general
(cognitive) attitudes about racial diversity and multiculturalism, (b)
affective attitudes regarding racial diversity related to personal life,
and (c) general attitudes regarding women's equity issues. The QDI
serves as an individual assessment instrument that can be used
with high school juniors and seniors and with adults. Readers may
want to complete the instrument themselves to see their stance on
the three measured attitude clusters. (Development, reliability, and
validity information on the QDI is presented in Ponterotto et al.,
1995.)

Multicultural Organizational Development

Historically, efforts to challenge intolerance within organizations
and institutions, although well-intentioned, have been at best reactive, fragmented, and crisis oriented; at worst, they have been nonexistent, ineffectual, or counterproductive (Grieger, 1996; Stage &
Hamrick, 1994). We believe that coherent and systemic organizational transformation is necessary in order to challenge intolerance
effectively, promote diversity, and incorporate social justice issues
into the very fabric of our societal institutions.

Organizational development (OD) provides a well-established
methodology for creating long-term systemic change within an organization, usually in the direction of higher functioning (Gibson,
Ivancevich, & Donnelly, 1994). Using principles and methods of
applied behavioral science, OD involves a planned, systemic, complex educational strategy that aims to change beliefs, attitudes,
values, and structures of organizations in order to help them adapt to
change (Conyne, 1991). The changes that traditional OD addresses

typically involve emerging technologies, expanding markets, and handling new competitors and challenges.

Building upon traditional OD, multicultural organization development specifically addresses and integrates diversity and social justice issues into its change process (Jackson & Holvino, 1988; Pope, 1993; Sue, 1995). It is a methodology for transforming monocultural, Eurocentric, intolerant, and discriminatory organizations into multicultural ones, organizations that not only value diversity but also challenge intolerance at all levels and in all aspects of organizational functioning. Informed by issues of social justice, the multicultural organization addresses issues of racism, sexism, homophobia, ableism, ageism, and other forms of intolerance; allows equal access to resources and opportunities; and remains fluid and adaptive with regard to "continuing attempts to accommodate ongoing cultural change" (Sue, 1995, p. 485). The multicultural organization also increases its "awareness and knowledge about human diversity in ways that are translated into more respectful human interactions and effective interconnection" (D'Andrea & Daniels, 1995, p. 18).

To summarize, Grieger (1996) has described the multicultural organization as one which

(a) is inclusive in composition of staff and constituencies served; (b) is diversity-positive in its commitment, vision, mission, values, processes, structure, policies, service delivery, and allocation of resources; (c) is permeated by a philosophy of social justice with decisions informed by considerations of ensuring fairness, ending oppression, and guaranteeing equal access to resources and opportunities for all groups; (d) regards diversity as an asset and values the contributions of all members; (e) values and rewards multicultural competencies, knowledge about salient aspects of diverse groups, and skills in interacting with and serving diverse groups effectively, sensitively, and respectfully; and (f) is fluid and responsive in adapting to ongoing diversity-related change. (pp. 563-564)

Sue (1995) and D'Andrea and Daniels (1995) have argued persuasively for the relevance of MOD for the counseling profession specifically, and for transforming organizations in general. Pope (1993) has noted the applicability of MOD to transforming divisions of student affairs on our campuses, and Grieger (1996) has created a Multicultural Organizational Development Checklist (MODC) for departments of student affairs that wish to transform themselves into multicultural organizations (see Appendix B). We believe that MOD is the "gold standard" for challenging institutional intolerance, that it represents the highest evolution of "counselor as an agent of change," and that counselors, in particular, are the professionals within an organization who have the constellation of skills needed to initiate and to implement this complex multidimensional system for change.

Specific actions that counselors can take in order to create multi-cultural organizations include

- helping their organizations view diversity as a challenge and as an opportunity rather than as a problem;
- helping the institution develop a coherent plan of action with regard to MOD;
- assisting upper-echelon administrators/executives in articulating a multicultural vision and mission;
- helping their institutions to reevaluate policies, practices, and structures that perpetuate exclusion, cultural privilege, and dis-crimination;
- developing coherent educational programs that challenge intoler-ance by addressing issues of racism, prejudice, and oppression and that include affective, as well as cognitive and attitudinal, components;
- advocating for and assisting with the recruitment, retention, and promotion of a diverse and inclusive employee and/or student population;
- helping make multicultural competency a criterion for hiring, retention, and promotion of employees;
- assisting the institution in providing incentives for the implemen-tation of MOD;
- assisting the institution in conducting periodic audits with regard to its climate for enhancing diversity and challenging intolerance;
- helping the organization resist the current backlash against and trivialization of multiculturalism and stay the course of developing a multicultural organization; and

- ensuring that the counselor's own area or unit is a model for valuing diversity and challenging intolerance, that is, that the staff is diverse in composition, space is physically accessible, the mission embraces diversity, art work and written material reflect diversity, and programming addresses issues of racism, sexism, bias, and intolerance.

Sue (1995) has argued that "MOD represents the next major frontier on which issues of diversity will be fought" (p. 490). We agree, and we add that it is the best approach for challenging intolerance holistically, systemically, and effectively in our educational institutions and in the workplace. (For a more complete discussion of MOD in the workplace see Sue, 1995; for MOD on the campus, see Grieger, 1996.)

OUTREACH AND CONSULTATION

Presenting psychoeducational outreach programs in schools, in colleges, and in the community, and offering consultation to student groups, to other professionals, and to members of the community create virtually unlimited opportunities to educate and to intervene with regard to challenging intolerance. As counselors, we have the power to keep this topic on the front burner of our constituencies' awareness. Framing conversations, dialogue, exchanges, and experiential programs around the issue of challenging intolerance is dependent only upon our own energy, creativity, and commitment.

College Campus

Specific suggestions and recommendations for actions to challenge intolerance on the college campus, the setting with which we are the most familiar, include the following:

- Piggyback workshops dealing with intolerance on established campus programs such as New Student Orientation, Black History Month, Women's History Month, and Rape Awareness/Gay Awareness/HIV Awareness events. In general, well-established campus events tend to draw large numbers of students and are well publicized.
- Volunteer to do training with resident advisers, coaches, teaching assistants, security personnel, faculty, and administrators on challenging intolerance and appreciating diversity.

- Make sure that your training program includes affective/experiential as well as attitudinal/cognitive components. Handle potential resistance right at the beginning. Create cross-cultural case vignettes relevant to the specific population you are training.
- Use specific workshop titles to challenge intolerance, such as Understanding Racial Identity Development; Combating Stereotypes; Gender Violence: Not Just A Woman's Problem; Racism and White Privilege; and Student Leaders' Round Table on Diversity.
- Consider creating sequential workshops on challenging intolerance that increase in depth and that keep the topic alive on the campus throughout an academic year (cf. Grieger & D'Onofrio, 1996).
- Ask the campus newspaper to cover each workshop you present on challenging intolerance so that the topic reaches and sensitizes other members of the campus community.
- Invest in a few good commercially produced videos, particularly those that include manuals for discussion and experiential exercises, which you can then modify for use on your campus. Videos that we particularly like include
  —*Skin Deep* and *Talking About Race* (Iris Films, 2600 10th Street, Suite 413, Berkeley, CA 94710; phone: 510-845-5414). These videos can be used to create workshops and presentations on such topics as racism, institutional racism, White privilege, racial identity development, and experiencing and challenging stereotypes.
  —*Healing the Harm* (The Bacchus and Gamma Peer Educational Network, P.O. Box 100430, Denver, CO 80250-0430; phone: 303-871-0901; E-mail: BACGAM@AOL.com). This video can be used to present workshops on gender violence, changing attitudes about gender stereotypes and rape myths, sexual assault prevention, and creating environmental change with regard to gender violence.
  —*Tom* (UCSB Student Health Service, University of California, Santa Barbara, CA 93106). This video presents a monologue by an HIV-positive college student struggling with maintaining a sense of meaning in his life. It can be used for workshops on attitudes towards HIV-positive individuals.

—*Dream World II* (Media Education Foundation, 26 Center Street, Northampton, MA 01060; phone: 413-586-4170/800-659-6882). This video presents a frank and graphic look at the portrayal of women in music videos as inviting sexual objectification and sexual assault. It can be used to present workshops on challenging damaging societal attitudes toward women, exploring rape-supportive cultures, and examining male/female relations.

—*Athletes for Sexual Responsibility* (NCAA, Champs Life Skills Program, 6201 College Boulevard, Overland Park, KS 66211-2422; phone: 913-339-1906). This video presents a model program in which athletes serve as peer educators on gender violence. It can be used both in workshops for awareness building with coaches and in training for peer educators regarding taking action against gender violence on campus. (The Champs Life Skills Program offers videos on other aspects of student life as well as material on diversity for student athletes.)

- Use full-length motion pictures, or portions thereof, that focus on diversity/intolerance issues, such as *Do the Right Thing, Schindler's List, Long Time Companion*, and *Malcolm X*, and television news magazine segments that deal with intolerance/diversity issues in creative ways as stimuli for workshops.
- Create opportunities for students to process any high-profile incident of intolerance in a timely fashion, using open forums, town meetings, interdisciplinary panel discussions, conversation hours, and student roundtables.
- Use campus newspaper reports of bias incidents as the basis for experiential exercises that involve role-playing each of the constituencies in the story: victims, perpetrators, and bystanders. These stories can also be used in a talk-show format with protagonists appearing on the panel and the other workshop participants comprising the audience. The purpose of this exercise is to explore attitudes and feelings that lead to intolerance and to promote understanding and empathy for the victim's experience. Using real-life incidents eliminates the denial factor, as in "things like that don't happen here."
- Provide on-line information on diversity and challenging intolerance from your counseling center or division of student affairs'

home page. Students enjoy surfing the net, which makes this an accessible way for them to receive diversity-related information.

Other Settings

Specific suggestions and recommendations for actions to challenge intolerance in settings other than the college campus include the following:

- Volunteer to do parent training for prejudice prevention, particularly for parents of nursery school and K-8 students. Obviously, parental attitudes with regard to appreciating or deprecating diversity are critical in shaping the attitudes of the next generation. Targeting parents constitutes primary prevention for lessening intolerance in the society.
- Volunteer to consult with police departments with regard to their handling of bias incidents, and with regard to providing awareness training on diversity and on fostering tolerance.
- Participate in youth conferences or other community initiatives that target young people for diversity awareness/increasing tolerance programs.
- Become a member of your school's, college's, or company's speakers' bureau as an avenue for presenting programs on challenging intolerance.

TEACHING, TRAINING, AND CURRICULUM DEVELOPMENT

Because teaching, training, and curriculum development allow access, directly and indirectly, to the formation of students' attitudes at critical junctures in their education, these functions offer counselors important opportunities for challenging intolerance. Of course, as trainers and educators of future counselors, we must recognize our responsibility for creating and nurturing professionals who are themselves tolerant, accepting, aware of their own biases and areas of intolerance, and willing to challenge these biases. Therefore, issues related to multiculturalism, diversity, bias, and prejudice must be addressed on an affective and cognitive level, not only in the designated multicultural course but also across the counselor education curriculum. Courses dealing with ethics, counselor role and function, understanding the individual, psychopathology, individual and group interventions, assessment, and counseling theories must include components that challenge the intolerance and narrowness of the Eurocentric perspective and of conventional assessment and intervention. The very nature of bigotry, oppression, and intolerance must in and of themselves be a part of the counseling curriculum. We must specifically teach counselors to understand, to prevent, and to remediate prejudice, racism, bigotry, and other forms of intolerance as a part of their formal professional training.

Furthermore, in many educational settings, counselors may also be involved in teaching noncounselor preparatory courses on a number of levels and across the disciplines. For example, counselors are often involved in teaching introductory undergraduate courses in psychology and extended "freshmen experience" courses and seminars. In addition, counselors are often called upon (and should, in fact, make themselves available to be called upon) to assist other faculty in transforming the classroom and the curriculum to embrace diversity and to challenge intolerance. With regard to structuring classroom teaching and/or in assisting others in teaching tolerance and challenging intolerance, we offer the following guidelines:

- Be aware of your own areas of bias and intolerance and how you may be communicating them in the classroom, for example, engaging in gender- or race-based differential treatment of students.
- Use nonsexist and inclusive language. Correct students when they use sexist language and explain why this is important. Require nonsexist and inclusive language on all written assignments.
- Examine the textbook(s) used in your classroom critically. Does it use inclusive language? Does it speak to the contributions of women and persons of color to your discipline or to the subject matter at hand? If not, find an alternative text; at the very least, supplement it with more inclusive material. If you must use a noninclusive text, point out its limitations to your students.
- Educate yourself about the contributions of women and persons of color to your discipline, if you are not knowledgeable.
- Incorporate information about and contributions of women and persons of color into your lectures and presentations. Do not handle them as separate and special topics.

- Invite speakers who bring diverse perspectives into your class-room.
- Address directly the topics of racism, sexism, homophobia, and other forms of intolerance in your classroom wherever appropriate.
- Promote critical thinking, open-mindedness, flexibility, and respect for diverse opinions in your classroom.
- Create an atmosphere of safety and trust in your classroom so that students are willing to examine and to discuss their own biases, prejudices, and areas of intolerance.
- Create experiential exercises and activities in which students are asked to challenge their intolerance on an affective level through, for example, role-plays of bias incidents, cultural simulation games, and solving ethical dilemmas related to intolerance.
- Invite students to create projects about racism, sexism, homopho-bia, ageism, ableism, and other forms of intolerance.
- Create opportunities for students to share their own cultural heritage and perspective with each other.
- Create opportunities for cooperative learning activities in order to facilitate intergroup contact among students.
- Have students research the contributions of women and persons of color to your discipline and ask them to share their findings with each other.
- Challenge intolerant behavior as it occurs in your classroom and use it as a teachable moment.

ADVOCACY AND ACTIVISM

Although both advocacy and activism are infused explicitly and implicitly across the other categories we have discussed, we have chosen to highlight and to delineate them separately. We believe that of all of the possible types of actions that counselors can undertake in order to challenge intolerance, advocacy and activism are potentially the most aggressive, the most controversial, and the most public. These functions run the gamut from relatively safe to openly high risk with regard to the counselor's sense of personal and professional safety in the workplace and in the community.

Advocacy and activism in relation to fighting intolerance challenge us, as counselors, to take a moral and ethical stand with regard to the touchiest issues within our organizations, to publicly articulate our stand, and to risk the displeasure, if not the wrath, of those who hold power and authority. It may mean being unpopular, becoming a lightning rod for the anger and resistance of colleagues, and at times, it may mean being willing to put our jobs on the line in order to do the right thing.

In our roles as advocates and activists, counselors are asked to do the following:

- Champion the causes of equality, justice, inclusion, diversity, and tolerance in our schools, in our communities, and in the workplace.
- Empower the weakest and the most disenfranchised in our organizations and communities so that they demand inclusion and justice.
- Insist upon the establishment of policies and procedures that address and redress intolerance in the workplace and in educational institutions.
- Confront and challenge the racial/ethnic/sexist/homophobic and otherwise intolerant comment at the moment that it is uttered, tactfully but firmly, no matter who has uttered it.
- Support individuals who are victims of intolerance, such as sexual harassment, gender violence, gay bashing, racism, and other forms of discrimination, and shepherd them through organizational and/ or legal grievance processes.
- Be willing to confront directly colleagues who you firmly believe to be engaging in behaviors that are sexually harassing, racist, biased, demeaning, and otherwise intolerant of and damaging to less powerful individuals, such as students or lower echelon employees.
- Help students or lower echelon employees create mechanisms and forums for making their concerns known and for being taken seriously.
- Work actively toward the adoption of a zero-tolerance policy toward incidents of bias, prejudice, and discrimination in the workplace and in educational institutions, and toward the imposition of clear sanctions and consequences for engaging in these behaviors.

- Assist in the creation of multicultural and diversity-positive groups, spaces, events, and resource centers in our schools, communities, and workplaces.
- Support multicultural events and causes actively through sponsorship, attendance, and participation.
- Volunteer time to organizations that promote peace and justice and that challenge intolerance.
- Boycott organizations, events, and individuals that promote intolerance and reduce appreciation for diversity.
- Serve on committees, task forces, and ad hoc groups that oversee the recruitment, retention, and promotion of a diverse population of constituencies, that frame policy vis á vis diversity-related issues such as sexual harassment, bias incidents, and discrimination, and that monitor the allocation of resources to underrepresented constituencies.
- Become a public spokesperson for issues related to challenging intolerance and embracing diversity.
- Become an institutional advocate or ombudsperson for underrepresented constituencies.
- Challenge policies that promote intolerance or limit access of underrepresented constituencies to resources and opportunities actively and vocally.
- Intervene directly when witnessing incidents of bias, prejudice, violence, and/or intolerance.
- Be willing "to take it to the streets" in protest of policies that promote intolerance and/or support policies and individuals who promote tolerance, equality, and appreciation for diversity.

Our role as advocate and activist is a radical departure from the very private, often gentle, one-on-one counseling relationship. It catapults the counselor into a public arena fraught with controversy, confrontation, and risk. Yet we believe that however uncomfortable it may be at first, we cannot challenge intolerance effectively without stepping out of the relative safety of our offices and our roles as therapists into the larger world that is filled with issues, individuals, and tasks that demand our attention, commitment, and, especially, our active participation.

CONCLUSION

We conclude this chapter as we opened it, with an urgent call to action in challenging intolerance. We believe that counselors, perhaps more than any other highly trained professional cohort, are best equipped to intervene in the area of tolerance enhancement and prejudice reduction. We also believe that we, as counselors, need "to rock the boat" in order to create change, and that includes rocking our own professional ship. Quite simply stated: If we do not take action to stem the tide of intolerance and to nurture intergroup acceptance, empathy, and respect, who will?

REFERENCES

The American Heritage Dictionary of the English Language (3rd ed.). (1992). Boston: Houghton Miflin

Allport, G. W. (1954). *The nature of prejudice.* Reading, MA: Addison-Wesley.

Conyne, R. K. (1991). Organization development: A broad net intervention for student affairs. In T. K. Miller, R. B.Winston, & Associates (Eds.), *Administration and leadership in student affairs: Actualizing student development in higher education* (2nd ed., pp. 72-109). Muncie, IN: Accelerated Development.

D'Andrea, M., & Daniels, J. (1995). Promoting multiculturalism and organizational change in the counseling profession. In J. G. Ponterotto, J. M. Casas, L. A. Suzuki, & C.M. Alexander (Eds.), *Handbook of multicultural counseling* (pp. 17-33). Thousand Oaks, CA: Sage.

Gibson, J. L. , Ivancevich, J. M., & Donnelly, J. H., Jr. (1994). *Organizations: Behavior, structure, processes* (8th ed). Burr Ridge, IL: Irwin.

Grieger, I. (1996). A multicultural organizational checklist for student affairs. *Journal of College Student Development, 37,* 561-573.

Grieger, I., & D'Onofrio, A. (1996). Free your mind: A three-part sequential series of multicultural programs. *Journal of College Student Development, 37,* 591-594.

Jackson, B. W., & Holvino, E. (1988). Developing multicultural organizations. *Journal of Religion and Applied Behavioral Sciences, 9,* 14-19.

Jones, J. M. (1972). *Prejudice and racism.* Reading, MA: Addison-Wesley.

Jones, J. M. (1997). *Prejudice and racism* (2nd ed.). Englewood, NJ: Prentice Hall.

Lee, C. C. (1997). Foreword. In D. S. Sandhu & C. B. Aspy, *Counseling for prejudice prevention and reduction* (pp. xxi-xxii). Alexandria, VA: American Counseling Association.

Ponterotto, J. G., Burkard, A., Rieger, B. P., Grieger, I., D'Onofrio, A., Dubuissson, A., Heenehan, M., Millstein, B., Parisi, M., Rath, J.-F., & Sax, G. (1995). Development and initial validation of the Quick Discrimination Index (QDI). *Educational and Psychological Measurement, 55,* 1016-1031.

Ponterotto, J. G., & Pedersen, P. B. (1993). *Preventing prejudice: A guide for counselors and educators.* Thousand Oaks, CA: Sage.

Pope, R. L. (1993). Multicultural organization development in student affairs: An introduction. *Journal of College Student Development, 34,* 201-205.

Sandhu, D. S., & Aspy, C. B. (1997). *Counseling for prejudice prevention and reduction.* Alexandria, VA: American Counseling Association.

Stage, F. K., & Hamrick, F. A. (1994). Diversity issues: Fostering campus-wide development of multiculturalism. *Journal of College Student Development, 35,* 331-336.

Sue, D. W. (1995). Multicultural organizational development: Implications for the counseling profession. In J. G. Ponterotto, J. M. Casas, L. A. Suzuki, & C. M. Alexander (Eds.), *Handbook of multicultural counseling* (pp. 474-492). Thousand Oaks, CA: Sage.

Appendix A

Quick Discrimination Index (QDI)
AKA Social Attitude Survey

Please respond to all items in the survey. Remember there are no right or wrong answers. The survey is completely anonymous; do not put your name on the survey. Please circle the appropriate number to the right.

	Strongly Disagree	Disagree	Not Sure	Agree	Strongly Agree
1. I do think it is more appropriate for the mother of a newborn baby, rather than the father, to stay home with the baby (not work) during the first year.	1	2	3	4	5
2. It is as easy for women to succeed in business as it is for men.	1	2	3	4	5
3. I really think affirmative action programs on college campuses constitute reverse discrimination.	1	2	3	4	5
4. I feel I could develop an intimate relationship with someone from a different race.	1	2	3	4	5
5. All Americans should learn to speak two languages.	1	2	3	4	5
6. It upsets (or angers) me that a woman has never been President of the United States.	1	2	3	4	5

5   7. Generally speaking, men work harder than women.   ① 2 3 4 5

3   8. My friendship network is very racially mixed.   1 2 ③ 4 5

4   9. I am against affirmative action programs in business.   1 ② 3 4 5

3   10. Generally, men seem less concerned with building relationships than women.   1 2 ③ 4 5

4   11. I would feel OK about my son or daughter dating someone from a different race.   1 2 3 ④ 5

2   12. It upsets (or angers) me that a racial minority person has never been President of the United States.   1 ② 3 4 5

4   13. In the past few years there has been too much attention directed toward multicultural or minority issues in education.   1 ② 3 4 5

2   14. I think feminist perspectives should be an integral part of the higher education curriculum.   1 ② 3 4 5

2   15. Most of my close friends are from my own racial group.   1 2 3 ④ 5

3   16. I feel somewhat more secure that a man rather than a woman is currently President of the United States.   1 2 ③ 4 5

4   17. I think that it is (or would be) important for my children to attend schools that are racially mixed.   1 2 3 ④ 5

36

4   (18.) In the past few years there   1   (2)   3   4   5
         has been too much
         attention directed toward
         multicultural or minority
         issues in business.

4   (19.) Overall, I think racial   1   (2)   3   4   5
         minorities in America
         complain too much about
         racial discrimination.

4   20. I feel (or would feel) very   1   2   3   (4)   5
         comfortable having a
         woman as my primary
         physician.

4   21. I think the President of the   1   2   3   (4)   5
         United States should make
         a concerted effort to appoint
         more women and racial
         minorities to the country's
         Supreme Court.

5   22. I think White people's   1   2   3   4   (5)
         racism toward racial
         minority groups still
         constitutes a major problem
         in America.

4   (23.) I think the school system,   1   (2)   3   4   5
         from elementary school
         through college, should
         encourage minority and
         immigrant children to learn
         and adopt fully traditional
         American values.

4   24. If I were to adopt a child, I   1   2   3   (4)   5
         would be happy to adopt a
         child of any race.

3   (25) I think there is as much   1   2   (3)   4   5
/   female physical violence
27   toward men as there is male
         physical violence toward
         women.

5   26. I think the school system,   1   2   3   4   ⑤
        from elementary school
        through college, should
        promote values
        representative of diverse
        cultures.

4   27. I believe that reading the   1   2   3   ④   5
        autobiography of Malcolm X
        would be of value.

5   28. I would enjoy living in a   1   2   3   4   ⑤
        neighborhood consisting of a
        racially diverse population
        (i.e., Asians, Blacks,
        Hispanics, Whites).

4   ㉙ I think it is better if people 1   ②   3   4   5
        marry within their own race.

4   ㉚ Women make too big a deal   1   ②   3   4   5
        out of sexual harassment
   22   issues in the workplace.

SCORING DIRECTIONS FOR THE QUICK
DISCRIMINATION INDEX (QDI)

Users of the QDI must have completed the "Utilization Request Form" before incorporating the QDI in their professional work.

The QDI is a 30-item Likert-type self-report measure of racial and gender attitudes. The instrument itself is titled "Social Attitude Survey" to control for some forms of response bias. Users on the QDI should read the development and validity studies on the QDI before use.

There are two methods of scoring the QDI. The first procedure is that you can simply use the total score, which measures overall sensitivity, awareness, and receptivity to cultural diversity and gender equality.

The second scoring procedure involves scoring three separate subscales (factors) of the QDI. This is the preferred method at this time (1998), given that both exploratory and confirmatory factor analysis support the construct validity of the three-factor model.

METHOD ONE: QDI TOTAL SCORE

Of the 30 items on the QDI, 15 are worded and scored in a positive direction (high scores indicate high sensitivity to multicultural/gender issues), and 15 are worded and scored in a negative direction (low scores indicate high sensitivity). Naturally, when tallying the total score response, the latter 15 items need to be *reverse scored*. This simply means that if respondents circle a 1 they get five points, a 2 four points, a 3 three points, a 4 two points, and a 5 one point.

The following QDI items need to be reversed scored:

1, 2, 3, 7, 9, 10, 13, 15, 16, 18, 19, 23, 25, 29, 30.

Score range is 30 to 150, with high scores indicating more awareness, sensitivity, and receptivity to racial diversity and gender equality.

METHOD TWO: THREE-FACTOR MODEL

If scoring separate subscales (factors), the researcher should not also use the total score. As expected, the total score is highly correlated with subscale scores and to use both would be somewhat redundant.

When scoring separate subscales, only 23 of the total 30 items are scored.

Factor 1: General (Cognitive) Attitudes Toward Racial Diversity/ Multiculturalism (Items in parentheses are reverse scored)

9 items: (3), (9), (13), (18), (19), 22, (23), 26, 27
(Score range = 9 to 45)   37/45
3 44 4 4 5 4 5 4

Factor 2: Affective Attitudes Toward More Personal Contact (Closeness) With Racial Diversity (Items in parentheses are reverse scored)

7 items: 4, 8, 11, (15), 17, 24, (29)
(Score range = 7 to 35)
5 3 4 2 4 4 4   27/35

Factor 3: Attitudes Toward Women's Equity (Items in parentheses are reverse scored)

7 items: (1), 6, (7), 14, (16), 20, (30)
(Score range = 7 to 35)

2352344   23/30

Appendix B

Multicultural Organizational Development (MOD) Checklist for Student Affairs

	Goals			
Mission	Met	Unmet	In Progress	Timetable for Completion
1. The mission, philosophy, and goals of the division of student affairs clearly address issues of diversity and multiculturalism.	____	____	____	____
2. The mission, philosophy, and goals of each office within the division clearly address issues of diversity and multiculturalism.	____	____	____	____
Leadership and Advocacy				
3. Women, persons of color, and members of other underrepresented populations are in positions of leadership within the division.	____	____	____	____
4. The chief student affairs officer is a vocal advocate for diversity and multiculturalism within the division and on an institutional level.	____	____	____	____
5. Student affairs professionals view advocacy for diversity and multiculturalism on campus as a part of their role and function.	____	____	____	____

6. Student affairs professionals collaborate with faculty and others to advocate for a positive campus climate with regard to diversity.   _____ _____ _____ _____

7. A clearly defined advocacy/ombudsperson/ special services position exists within the division to address the needs of a diverse student population (e.g., students with disabilities, older students, religious and racial/ethnic minority students, female students), albeit with a clear understanding that advocacy is the responsibility of all student affairs professionals.   _____ _____ _____ _____

Policies

8. The division has promulgated and distributed to all students clearly articulated policies and procedures relevant to a diverse student population (e.g., HIV, AIDS, sexual assault, sexual harassment, bias incidents, nondiscrimination on the basis of race, ethnicity, religion, age, sexual orientation, nationality).   _____ _____ _____ _____

9. The student code of conduct clearly prohibits engaging in racist, sexist, biased, sexually harassing, or sexually or physically assaultive behavior.   _____ _____ _____ _____

10. Infringements of the student code of conduct in the areas delineated in item 9 are taken seriously and disciplinary sanctions are imposed. _____ _____ _____ _____

11. Infringements of the student code of conduct in the areas delineated in item 9 are viewed as signals for ongoing assessment, dialogue, and intervention with regard to valuing diversity. _____ _____ _____ _____

12. Staffing patterns within the division reflect campus demographics and diversity. _____ _____ _____ _____

13. Women, persons of color, and members of other underrepresented populations are actively recruited for positions within the division. _____ _____ _____ _____

14. Student affairs professionals actively assist the institution in efforts to recruit and retain a diverse student population. _____ _____ _____ _____

15. Multicultural competencies (i.e., attitudes, knowledge, and skills) are a hiring criterion for student affairs professionals. _____ _____ _____ _____

16. Performance appraisals of student affairs professionals include a review of their contributions to creating a multicultural organization. _____ _____ _____ _____

Expectations for
Multicultural Competency

17. Student affairs
    professionals possess
    multicultural
    competencies appropriate
    for their role and function. _____   _____   _____   _____

18. Student affairs
    professionals are
    knowledgeable about the
    specific multicultural
    competencies that have
    been delineated for their
    particular discipline. _____   _____   _____   _____

19. Student affairs
    professionals are
    knowledgeable about the
    standards of ethical
    practice with regard to
    multiculturalism within
    their particular discipline. _____   _____   _____   _____

20. Student affairs
    professionals take
    responsibility for
    continuously developing
    and enhancing their multi-
    cultural competencies by
    remaining current on the
    professional literature and
    by availing themselves of
    training opportunities. _____   _____   _____   _____

Multicultural Competency
Training

21. The division provides
    systematic ongoing
    training regarding the
    development of
    multicultural
    competencies (i.e.,
    attitudes, knowledge, and
    skills). _____   _____   _____   _____

22. Support staff, including office managers, clerical staff, graduate assistants, and student workers, are systematically trained in multicultural awareness.   _____ _____ _____ _____

23. Residence hall staff, including residence hall directors, resident advisers, security personnel, and others who have contact with students in residence halls are systematically trained in multicultural awareness.   _____ _____ _____ _____

24. Review of multicultural competency training and education literature regarding effective training models informs multicultural competency training within the division.   _____ _____ _____ _____

25. Professionals designated to provide multicultural competency training within the division are fully competent to do so.   _____ _____ _____ _____

26. Funds are available for professional development opportunities with regard to multiculturalism (e.g., inviting trainers to campus, attendance at conferences, off-campus training).   _____ _____ _____ _____

Scholarly Activities

27. Student affairs professionals engage in research, writing, and professional presentations on multicultural issues.   _____ _____ _____ _____

28. Financial and administrative support are available for student affairs professionals to engage in scholarly activities pertaining to multicultural issues.

    _____   _____   _____   _____

Student Activities and Services

29. Student groups and organizations reflect campus demographics (e.g., Black Students Association, Gay/Lesbian Students Association, Italian Heritage Society, Women Students Concerns Group).

    _____   _____   _____   _____

30. Student activities are planned and designed to meet the cocurricular needs of a diverse student population.

    _____   _____   _____   _____

31. Student activities include the systematic development of leadership skills in people who are female, members of an ethnic/racial minority, physically disabled, and members of other underrepresented student groups.

    _____   _____   _____   _____

32. Mechanisms are in place for ongoing cross-cultural communication and dialogue among student groups and organizations.

    _____   _____   _____   _____

33. Annual programming for students reflects an appreciation for diversity and addresses multicultural issues (e.g., New Student Orientation, Black History Month, Women's History Month, Minority Career Day, Disabilities Awareness Day, Gay Awareness Day).   _____   _____   _____   _____

34. Psychoeducational workshops, lectures, and presentations offered on campus by student affairs professionals regularly address issues of diversity and multiculturalism.   _____   _____   _____   _____

35. Programs offered in residence halls regularly address issues of diversity and multiculturalism.   _____   _____   _____   _____

36. Student affairs professionals actively support and attend campus events that celebrate diversity.   _____   _____   _____   _____

37. Programs offered by student affairs professionals are physically accessible and provide interpreters for hearing-impaired persons and bilingual translators when appropriate.   _____   _____   _____   _____

38. All student services are fully responsive to the needs of a diverse student population.   _____   _____   _____   _____

39. All student affairs publications, including the student handbook, office brochures, flyers, resource guides, and announcements, are multiculturally sensitive in use of language, photographs, and illustrations. _____ _____ _____ _____

40. Student groups and organizations are expected to be multiculturally sensitive in their distribution of printed materials, such as advertisements and flyers. _____ _____ _____ _____

Internships and Field Placements

41. Interns and practicum students are exposed to a diverse client population. _____ _____ _____ _____

42. Internships and practicums offered within the division specifically include training in multicultural competencies. _____ _____ _____ _____

43. Student affairs professionals supervising interns and practicum students are knowledgeable about multicultural aspects of supervision. _____ _____ _____ _____

44. Interns and practicum students are specifically trained in multicultural aspects of ethical professional practice. _____ _____ _____ _____

45. Internship or practicum evaluations include an appraisal of students' multicultural competency. _____ _____ _____ _____

Physical Environment

46. All offices and spaces used by student affairs professionals are physically accessible. _____ _____ _____ _____

47. Artwork, posters, and other visual displays reflect an appreciation for diversity. _____ _____ _____ _____

48. Multicultural student groups have appropriate spaces on campus (e.g., Multicultural Resource Center, Women's Resource Center). _____ _____ _____ _____

Assessment

Diagnosis

49. This checklist or a similar instrument is used for diagnostic purposes. _____ _____ _____ _____

50. Individual and systemic barriers to creating a multicultural organization within the division of student affairs are assessed. _____ _____ _____ _____

51. Individual and institutional barriers to creating a multicultural campus environment are assessed. _____ _____ _____ _____

52. Student needs with regard to multicultural issues are assessed regularly. _____ _____ _____ _____

53. Student attitudes about campus climate with regard to diversity are assessed regularly (e.g., focus groups, surveys). _____ _____ _____ _____

54. When using standardized diagnostic instruments, student affairs professionals are aware of possible cultural bias. _____ _____ _____ _____

Evaluation

55. Goals within the division are examined and evaluated annually with regard to multiculturalism. _____ _____ _____ _____

56. The effectiveness of multicultural programs, strategies, and interventions is systematically evaluated. _____ _____ _____ _____

57. Systematic evaluations of student services include a multicultural component. _____ _____ _____ _____

58. This checklist or a similar instrument is reviewed, discussed, and updated annually within the division. _____ _____ _____ _____

The Multicultural Organizational Development (MOD) Checklist for Student affairs was developed by Ingrid Grieger and first published in Grieger (1996). Reprinted with permission of the American College Personnel Association.

3

From Multiculturalism to Social Action

JUDITH A. LEWIS AND MARY SMITH ARNOLD

M ost counselors today are very much aware that multiculturalism must play an integral part in any work that we do with
our clients. In the few short years since awareness of the concept
of multiculturalism as the "fourth force" in counseling has become
widespread (Pedersen, 1991), we have learned that multiculturalism
involves more than an acquaintance with the customs of distant
populations, more than tolerance of differences, and even more
than expertise in cross-cultural communication. Multicultural counseling is built on an understanding that all of us—counselors and
clients alike—are cultural beings who are exposed to "a complex
melange of cultural influences" (Szapocznik, Scopetta, Ceballos, &
Santisteban, 1994, p. 23), all of which affect our life situations and
worldviews. It is a short step from becoming aware of the impact
of the cultural milieu to noticing the role of oppression in our clients'
lives. Once we begin to notice systemic oppression, it is just one
more short step to accepting our responsibility for social action.

This chapter first explores how through multiculturalism we as
counselors can begin to notice our clients' oppression and to see
both internalized oppression and systemic oppression in an environmental context. The chapter then examines how counselors can take
social action on behalf of their multicultural clients by addressing the
inadvertent tendency of counselors to collude with oppression as
well as by supporting community empowerment efforts, engaging
in political advocacy, and emphasizing the social action agenda of
our professional associations. The chapter includes a table illustrating the complementarity of multiculturalism and social action.

NOTICING OPPRESSION

When we view our counseling relationships through the lens of multiculturalism, we see ourselves and our clients in an environmental context. This awareness of context enables us to make an important transition in our own thinking from assuming that our clients' problems are caused solely by intrapsychic or intrafamilial factors to recognizing that political, social, and economic explanations are often more accurate (Aubrey & Lewis, 1983; Lewis, Lewis, Daniels, & D'Andrea, 1998). We notice oppression.

OUR CLIENTS' OPPRESSION

Consider the application of multiculturalism to family counseling. Many counselors used to assume that they could define what was meant by the concept of family. Now we know that what some people previously believed to be universal values were in fact culture-bound. We know that concepts of family life differ among and within cultures with regard to such factors as individuation, family unity, and variations in family structure. Multiculturalism has taught us that the family-oriented norms of the dominant culture should not be imposed on clients whose definitions of family may differ from those accepted by the counselor.

As we work to avoid imposing our own biased views of family life onto our clients, we learn to be truly open to their experiences—including their experiences of oppression. Boyd-Franklin (1993) has pointed out that African American clients whose experiences of racism are foremost in their minds sometimes avoid raising these issues on their own. "They know that many therapists will try to talk them out of what they are feeling because they do not understand the need for African American individuals and families to vent their rage about situations in which there is an undercurrent of racism" (p. 56). As Franklin (1993) also pointed out,

> Once the pervasive impact of racism is acknowledged as a force in a Black family's experience, the family can move on to confront other issues. But if the impact of racism is ignored, it's unlikely that therapy will go anywhere. (p. 36)

The same kinds of processes occur with regard to other forms of oppression. Clearly, effective family counseling requires attention to the differential power and privilege our society accords to men and women, to straight and gay people, to rich and poor.

Environmental factors are just as apparent when we carry out multicultural counseling in our work with individuals.

> [These] factors clearly contribute to the development of almost any kind of problem a client may face. Sometimes the connection is overt and definable: the adult denied vocational options because of racism or sexism, the child victimized by a destructive family environment, the ex-offender or chronically ill client denied free entry into the mainstream community. Just as often, however, problems that have their source in environmental factors have become so much a part of the person that their cause cannot be clearly attributed. In such cases, the individual may feel powerless or lack a sense of purpose, be unable to recognize alternatives and make decisions, feel trapped in highly restrictive roles and unrewarding interpersonal relationships, be unclear about his or her personal values, or feel that the community is hostile to his or her development. (Lewis & Lewis, 1989, p. 3)

Today's environment is, in fact, hostile and disempowering for many people. Paying real attention to our clients' experiences opens our eyes to their oppression. In contrast, ignoring the reality of a cruel environment prevents us from becoming the caring helpers we hope to be. If we want to help our clients, "we should alleviate feelings of powerlessness not by altering perceptions but by altering reality" (Joffe & Albee, 1981, p. 323).

INTERNALIZED OPPRESSION

The most insidious effect of oppression is the internalization of the distortions and lies of the oppressor by the victims of oppression (Fanon, 1967; Freire, 1983). Internalized oppression is the acceptance, most often unconscious, of the myths, misinformation, and stereotypes the dominant culture constructs about a person's own group. Victims take on the values and norms of the dominant group and cast aspersions on the experiences and traditional values of their own group.

In order to take on the values of the dominant culture, a person must repudiate his or her self and live with contradictions in how he or she experiences self-in-the-world. DuBois (1953) described a duality, a double consciousness that entails incorporating the oppressor's worldview into the psychological life of the oppressed. The process is often conflictual because it involves what seems to be mutually exclusive emotional responses of acceptance and rejection of the oppressor.

Consider, for instance, the legions of African American women who chemically process their hair to conform to European standards. Many women of color reject other aspects of the dominant culture while embracing the notion that straight hair is better than kinky hair. This phenomenon resonates in the lives of women of color from early childhood through adulthood (Sanders, 1996). For people of color in the United States, issues of skin color, facial features, and hair length and color can be seen as indicators of self-acceptance or self-rejection. These attitudes are not pathological, but they are indicators of assent to the oppressor's view that people of color are unattractive. A women of color may view her own hair as unacceptable and, at the same time, view the hair of White women as beautiful and desirable. Hence, a woman of color could spend all of her life trying to obtain a look that is physically unattainable, expending large amounts of money, time, and energy and never quite meeting the standard.

Such a seemingly minor acquiescence to the values of the dominant culture can have major implications for counseling. When women of color present in counseling as having difficulty identifying their personal worth and accepting their inherent beauty, an approach that incorporates an understanding of internalized oppression is needed. It is certainly imperative for the counselor to understand the manifestations of oppression, but it is just as important that the counseling process help the client to understand its meaning in her own life. "Clients who recognize the role of oppression in their lives are most likely to be able to move from the morass of self-blame to the solid ground of self-management" (Carlson, Sperry, & Lewis, 1997, p. 132) and most likely to find their way past the theme of never feeling "good enough."

The example of internalized oppression that we have used here indicates the dual impact of two dimensions of oppression: racism and sexism. Oppression is so pervasive in our society, however, that almost all of our clients are likely to be grappling with its effects in some form.

SYSTEMIC OPPRESSION

It is not just our clients who live in the context of oppression but ourselves as well. If we define oppression as the systemic disadvantaging of one group by another group that holds the collective power of the state or society, we recognize that it is integral to all of our lives. It is so much a part of our everyday existence that people seldom question their roles either as perpetrators or as victims of oppression (Arnold, 1997).

Although oppression is pervasive, it is not based in human nature. We can understand systemic oppression and choose to alter our responses to it. Each person who makes this conscious choice plays a role in dismantling systems of oppression. The reason for making this choice is that all of us are hurt by oppression, even in those situations when we are in positions of power and privilege.

> We often act as if oppression hurts only the victim of oppression. Therefore, we think that sexism hurts women and not men, that racism wounds people of color and not White people, and that gay oppression has no impact on heterosexuals. It is important to note that victims and oppressors are hurt differently but that each is still hurt. People who identify with their oppressor status often feel that they have a stake in maintaining what they believe is their power. However, many persons are totally unaware that the cost of holding on to such "power" is disconnectedness and alienation from one's self and others. Another cost is having their own lives constrained and limited by the prescriptions that oppression imposes. (Arnold, 1997, p. 42)

Oppression is not our fault. If we had the power to design a new society, none of us would purposely choose to create oppressive systems. Despite the fact that oppression is not our fault, however, its elimination is our responsibility. We have the obligation to challenge oppression when we see it and, ultimately, to end it.

All of us are both victims and perpetrators of oppression. We are socialized to recognize our own victim status and to overlook our collusion in the oppression of others.

> White women who are victims of sexism are socialized to accept
> and participate in racism. By the same token, men of color who
> are victims of racism are socialized to accept and participate in
> sexism, which degrades women of color as well as White women.
> The inability to see the parallels and intersections of racism keeps
> both in place. (Arnold, 1997, p. 42)

The same kinds of parallels occur with regard to all forms of oppression, with most people being able to claim both victim and perpetrator statuses. Guilt and shame may make us uncomfortable with
facing our participation in oppression, but recognizing that we have
been enrolled in this process is a prerequisite for freeing ourselves
and our clients from its grip. It is our recognition of the pervasiveness
of oppression that can guide our efforts in the realm of social action.

SOCIAL ACTION

Although all people share a responsibility to recognize and counter
oppression, counselors are in an especially good position to carry
out this mission because we see the undeniable results of oppression
every day.

> Their work brings . . . counselors face to face with the victims of
> poverty, racism, sexism, and stigmatization; of political, economic,
> and social systems that leave individuals feeling powerless; of
> governing bodies that deny their responsibility to respond; of
> social norms that encourage isolation. In the face of these realities,
> counselors have no choice but to promote positive changes in
> those systems that directly impact the psychological well-being
> of their clients or to blame the victims. (Lewis et al., 1998, pp.
> 23-24)

Social action on behalf of our multicultural population of clients
should include (a) addressing the inadvertent tendency of the counseling profession to collude with oppression, (b) supporting community empowerment efforts, (c) engaging in political advocacy,
and (d) emphasizing the social action agenda of our professional
association.

ADDRESSING THE TENDENCY TO COLLUDE WITH OPPRESSION

People are frequently victimized by the very systems and institutions that have supposedly been set up to serve them. Impersonal bureaucracies such as welfare and child protective services may intrude in and constrict the lives of individuals through the imposition of dominant cultural values. Health care, educational, and legal systems often play abusive roles in the lives of people who should be able to receive help from them. Many people are shocked when they learn about egregious examples of exploitation, such as the Tuskegee experiment, which withheld readily attainable medicine from African American men in order to study the natural progression of untreated syphilis. People want to believe that this kind of abuse is a relic of the distant past. In reality, however, people suffer every day from oppression by health, education, and human service systems that should be ameliorating their pain instead of adding to it. How else but as an example of oppression can we interpret the punitive attitude that suggests imprisonment rather than treatment for pregnant, addicted women? How else can we account for the number of children of color who are inappropriately funneled into special education classes within public educational systems or for the number of men of color who are victimized by the criminal justice system? How else can we explain welfare systems that go to the extremes first of creating dependency by penalizing people who seek a degree of self-sufficiency or a family life and then trying to solve systemic problems by blaming the victims and cutting off aid altogether?

Because of these negative experiences with the human service network, people who are members of oppressed groups may distrust counseling and the counseling process.

> This is due, to a large extent, to the fact that the only counseling many of these people have received has been a forced, rather than a voluntary, experience with a culturally insensitive agent of some social welfare agency. In addition, counseling has often followed the commission of an offense against the social order. Generally, in both situations the goal of counseling is not development, but either remediation or punishment. Many people from diverse cultural backgrounds, therefore, perceive counseling as

a process that the dominant society employs to forcibly control their lives and well-being. (Lee, 1997, p. 9)

Certainly, part of this problem has to do with perception. As counselors, we do not think of ourselves as part of an oppressive army of social control agents. We hope that potential clients will learn to place us in a different category. At the same time, however, we need to recognize again the potency of the Joffe and Albee comment cited earlier in this chapter. If people feel powerless in their relationships with the helping professions, we need to change not just their perception but also their reality.

The reality is that we can find instances of inadvertently oppressive practices within our own profession. Ina (1994) described the disastrous consequences set in motion by a counselor who, unaware of the cultural values underlying family life, encouraged a Japanese American college student to carry out a public confrontation with his traditional father. Inclan and Hernandez (1992) recounted numerous cases of Hispanic families being pathologized by helpers who interpreted their family closeness and loyalty as codependence or enmeshment. Examples abound of counselors who think that they are being "objective" when they fail to address issues of gender-role socialization and thereby support the status quo.

How can we, as counselors, find our way out of an unknowing collusion with oppressive practices? Certainly, we need to recognize our responsibility to increase the responsiveness of the human service systems that affect our clients. We play an important role in interrupting oppressive processes within those systems when we speak up on behalf of our clients and when we work to enhance the cultural understanding and accountability of people in authority. We need first to notice and then to confront the examples of oppression that we see every day.

Even more pressing is our responsibility to interrupt oppressive and culturally biased practices within our own profession. It takes great courage to confront racism and other forms of oppression as they occur within our professional lives. Probably the most difficult—and most necessary—challenge is to become continuously involved in taking honest inventory of our own lives as community members and as counselors.

It is ludicrous to believe we therapists can live our lives outside of our offices never challenging references to niggers, spics, and White trash and then treat African Americans, Puerto Ricans, and Whites respectfully in therapy. As professionals, the looking-within process means ending the denial that racism exists both within the profession and in the therapy room. (Hardy, 1993, pp. 50-57)

Supporting Community Empowerment Efforts

If "empowerment is the antidote of oppression" (Wilson, 1987, p. 20), then our action strategies should focus on mechanisms that give individuals and communities as much control as possible over their own lives and environments. Counselors have a special role to play in community empowerment efforts because of two distinct strengths. First, the counseling process helps to build our own awareness of the common problems faced by our clients. Second, we bring to the table a unique set of interpersonal skills useful to community organizations.

Counselors are privy to the common problems faced by community members because we tend to perceive recurring themes in our work with clients. When negative environmental factors impinge on our clients' lives, we know it. We can use this perspective to encourage action for change by taking the following steps (Lewis et al., 1998):

- making the community as a whole aware of specific problems affecting its members;
- alerting existing community organizations that might be interested in joining an alliance to work on a particular issue; and
- participating with other individuals and groups to act as allies for people who are fighting for change on their own behalf.

These actions allow counselors to make one of their most significant contributions: acting as allies and supporters of groups seeking their own solutions.

It is important that counselors use their interpersonal and organizational skills not to control social movements but rather to be participants in actions that enhance self-empowerment. Sometimes counselors can support the growth of new self-help organizations, allowing leadership to emerge from among group members and providing leadership training as it is needed. Often counselors find opportunities to share their interpersonal and communication skills with people who can use these competencies in their efforts to organize for change. Counselors who know their communities well can identify groups and organizations that are doing antioppression work, possibly playing a role in linking factions that have common goals.

This kind of work takes place in schools as well as in community agencies. School counselors know that many parents and children perceive schools as hostile and punitive environments designed more to impose the will of the state than to encourage growth and learning. Poor children, children of color, and children for whom English is a second language are often neglected, labeled, and left to wither in the lowest tracks in our schools. Just as counselors in agency settings alert the community to the oppression of its members, so can school counselors voice opposition to oppressive and punitive practices affecting children and youth. Just as agency counselors participate in alliances with community organizations seeking change, so can school counselors affiliate with groups working toward the creation of schools that are distinguished by warm and welcoming climates for learning.

Counselors have many opportunities to be in contact with people whose lives are characterized by oppression and lack of privilege. Those counselors who have developed an affinity for social action are able to move past the customary emphasis on helping clients adjust to society's demands. They focus instead on the reverse: helping society adjust to the demands of its least powerful members.

Engaging in Political Advocacy

In recent years, counselors have become increasingly active in efforts to affect public policy and legislation. Although these endeavors represent important progress for our profession, they have remained somewhat limited because so much of their emphasis has been on advocacy in the interest of the profession itself. Clearly, counselors must address such issues as licensing and certification if we are to remain a viable profession. Just as clearly, our struggle to maintain our professional status has positive, if indirect, implications for the clients we serve. Still, the advocacy skills we have developed should be put to work more directly on behalf of our clients. Our vision of advocacy must expand so that we see as part of our domain the act of influencing policy on a broader stage. This change in vision will help us become more actively involved in advocating for the kinds of social, political, and economic changes that tend to counter oppression in all its forms.

By its very nature, political advocacy is always in flux. Both client needs and political pressures change over time. As this chapter is being written, we are in a historical period when virtually all of the basic benefits that protect families from poverty, violence, and despair are under attack at local, state, and federal levels. As child and family advocate Bernardine Dohrn pointed out in a recent interview,

> We have a quarter of our children being born into poverty in the wealthiest country in the world. . . . Some people seem to have the notion that part of the population can insulate itself or separate itself from the ravages of exclusion from education, exclusion from health care, exclusion from housing, and exclusion from the job market. The consequences of that underlying poverty are unfolding now and I think it's very ominous. (Arnold & Lewis, in press)

According to Dohrn, universal health care, child support payments, and paid parental leave are all examples of solutions that could create a range of options for families and help to provide them with a social floor. Yet legislative efforts in these areas are nowhere near the top of the agenda in the United States.

What Dohrn described is the lack of a serious national commitment to meeting the needs of people who have been excluded from the privileges this country has to offer. Just as devastating for many of the clients we serve is the trend toward punitive and damaging social policies. Among the issues that should be on the minds of counselors are attacks on affirmative action, destruction of the welfare system, the English-Only movement, and assaults on the rights of immigrant families (D'Andrea, 1997). Each of these social trends is related to oppression, and each is associated with a concrete legislative agenda that should be discredited. Attacks on affirmative action programs turn the clock back on efforts at diversity and place roadblocks in the paths of clients whose career development we, as counselors, have tried to enhance. The destruction of the welfare system in the name of reform places individuals and families in serious jeopardy because of the falsity of the underlying assumption that people could easily move from welfare to work if they chose to do so. The English-Only movement demeans and oppresses people who are not associated with the dominant culture (D'Andrea, 1997). Similarly, attempts to discourage immigration by withholding access to supportive benefits from immigrant families increases stress and fosters intergroup hostility.

Each of these destructive social policies undermines the work that we, as counselors, do with our clients. The specifics may change between one era and another, but the basic idea remains the same: we as counselors must confront the social policies that interfere with the healthy development of our clients.

Emphasizing the Social Action Agenda of Professional Counseling Associations

If we agree that counselors should be involved in social action on behalf of their clients, then we must look to the American Counseling Association and its divisions and branches to play a leading role in this effort. Recent years have seen a vastly increased interest among ACA's entities in raising the awareness of all members concerning multiculturalism and diversity. This effort, with its emphasis on multicultural competencies (Sue, Arredondo, & McDavis, 1992), is largely educational and is well under way. As we become more knowledgeable about the cultural context of people's lives, however, we increase our readiness to take the next step and move into the complementary realm of social action (see Table 3-1).

As the table indicates, the complementary focus on multiculturalism and social action can be part of the mission both of the association as a whole and of each of its entities. The association-wide activities and goals recognize the necessity for all counselors, regardless of setting or specialization, to be well trained in multiculturalism. The importance of a social action agenda that permeates all policies and processes of the association is also addressed. Entity-

Table 3-1
From Multiculturalism to Social Action:
An Organizational Framework

	Multicultural Education	Social Action
Association-Wide Activities	Multicultural/ diversity consciousness raising and training is association-wide. *Goal:* Every ACA member is trained in the awareness, knowledge, and skills underlying effective multicultural practice.	The antioppression/ social action mission is association-wide. *Goal:* An antioppression/social action agenda permeates all ACA policies and processes.
Entity-Focused Activities	Multicultural training/education is focused on concerns of specific ACA entities. *Goal:* All ACA entities provide multicultural/ diversity training appropriate to special emphasis of members.	Antioppression/social action missions are in all ACA entities, with attention focused on clients and communities served by members of the entity. *Goal:* Antioppression/ social action agendas permeate policies and processes of each ACA entity.
Collaborative Activities	ACA entities share expertise to provide diversity-related training across divisional and geographical lines. *Goal:* Each ACA entity has a collaborative training plan in effect.	ACA entities join in alliances for antioppression work. *Goal:* Each ACA entity has a social action alliance plan in effect.

focused activities recognize the issues and concerns that might be unique to specific divisions or geographical entities. The educational efforts of the family counseling division, for instance, focus on identifying and promulgating multicultural family counseling competencies, whereas the division's social action agenda emphasizes family-oriented legislation. In this ideal organization, all entities are involved in collaborative activities, and all entities demonstrate commitment to multiculturalism and social action.

CONCLUSION

Multiculturalism and social action are highly complementary efforts. The lens of multiculturalism helps us as counselors to view our clients within a complex environment, and we see ourselves and our clients in a new light. We learn that all of us exist in a social, economic, and political context. The reality of oppression is brought to the forefront of our perceptions, and our awakening to oppression leads us inexorably toward social action. We know that the most isolated and powerless among our clients need to be able to count on us to speak up on their behalf. We know that our social action should include not only addressing the inadvertent tendency of the counseling profession to collude with oppression but also supporting community empowerment efforts, engaging in political advocacy, and emphasizing the social action agenda of our professional association.

REFERENCES

Arnold, M. S. (1997, May). The connection between multiculturalism and oppression. *Counseling Today, 39,* 42.

Arnold, M. S., & Lewis, J. A. (in press). A conversation with Bernardine Dohrn. *The Family Journal.*

Aubrey, R. F., & Lewis, J. A. (1983). Social issues and the counseling profession in the 1980s and 1990s. *Counseling and Human Development, 15* (10), 1-15.

Boyd-Franklin, N. (1993, July/August). Pulling out the arrows. *Family Networker,* 54-56.

Carlson, J., Sperry, L., & Lewis, J. A. (1997). *Family therapy: Ensuring treatment efficacy.* Pacific Grove, CA: Brooks/Cole.

D'Andrea, M. (1997). Social action and family advocacy: Current issues and future challenges. *The Family Digest, 10* (1), 3, 10.

DuBois, W. E. B. (1953). *Souls of black folks.* New York: Blue Heron Press.

Fanon, F. (1967). *Black skin, White mask: The experiences of a Black man in a White world.* New York: Grove Press.

Franklin, A. J. (1993, July/August). The invisibility syndrome. *Family Networker*, 33-39.

Freire, P. (1983). *Pedagogy of the oppressed* (M. B. Ramos, Trans.). New York: Continuum. (Original work published 1970)

Hardy, K. (1993, July/August). War of the worlds. *Family Networker*, 50-57.

Ina, S. (1994, April). *Culturally sensitive family therapy*. Paper presented at the Forum on Racism and Sexism: Promoting Dignity and Development Through Diversity at the national conference of the American Counseling Association, Minneapolis, MN.

Inclan, J., & Hernandez, M. (1992). Cross-cultural perspectives and codependence: The case of poor Hispanics. *American Journal of Orthopsychiatry, 62* (2), 245-255.

Joffe, J. M., & Albee, G. W. (1981). Powerlessness and psychopathology. In J. M. Joffe & G. W. Albee (Eds.), *Prevention through political action and social change*. Hanover, NH: University Press of New England.

Lee, C. C. (1997). The promise and pitfalls of multicultural counseling. In C. C. Lee (Ed.), *Multicultural issues in counseling: New approaches to diversity* (2nd ed., pp. 1-13). Alexandria, VA: American Counseling Association.

Lewis, J. A., & Lewis, M. D. (1989). *Community counseling*. Pacific Grove, CA: Brooks/Cole.

Lewis, J. A., Lewis, M. D., Daniels, J. A., & D'Andrea, M. J. (1998). *Community counseling: Empowerment strategies for a diverse society*. Pacific Grove, CA: Brooks/Cole.

Pedersen, P. B. (1991). Multiculturalism as a generic approach to counseling. *Journal of Counseling and Development, 70*, 6-12.

Sanders, J. L. (1996). *My face holds the history of my people and the feelings in my heart: Racial socialization and evaluations of facial attractiveness of preadolescent African American girls*. Unpublished doctoral dissertation.

Sue, D. W., Arredondo, P., & McDavis, R. (1992). Multicultural counseling competencies and standards: A call to the profession. *Journal of Counseling and Development, 70*, 477-486.

Szapocznik, J., Scopetta, M.A., Ceballos, A., & Santisteban, D. (1994). Understanding, supporting, and empowering families: From microanalysis to macrointervention. *Family Psychologist, 10* (2), 23-27.

Wilson, M. (1987). Classnotes on the psychology of oppression and social change. *The Community Psychologist, 20* (2), 19-21.

4

Challenging Interpersonal Violence

COURTLAND C. LEE AND JENNIFER L. BRYDGES

• *Two men delivering a pizza to a house in a small New Jersey town are murdered by two teenagers who called in the order. The teenagers revealed to police that they shot the delivery men in cold blood merely for the "joy of killing."*

• *On the same day that the son of a famous entertainer is murdered in a robbery attempt on a Los Angeles freeway, a young high school senior is riding the bus home from school. Five months shy of her graduation, she is killed by a stray bullet, the innocent victim of gang warfare. Her mother buries her in her cap and gown.*

• *For the third time in a 3-month period a District of Columbia police officer is shot to death on the streets of the nation's capital. As with the previous two victims, this officer was young and had a wife and small children. In each of these incidents, the officers were gunned down without the opportunity to defend themselves. A month preceding his death, one of the slain officers remarked that youth today "have no regard for life."*

• *A teenage murder defendant in northern Virginia tells a judge that he shot and killed a man and wounded a youth in order to earn membership in a gang. The defendant smoked marijuana and got drunk in order to find the courage to shoot his victims.*

• *The estranged wife of a famous athlete is found brutally murdered in the yard of her expensive Los Angeles townhouse. Her husband is arrested and tried for the murder. Even though it is revealed that there is a history of abuse in the family, he is acquitted. The trial sparks new interest in domestic violence.*

News stories like these underscore a major challenge in contemporary American society. The United States is experiencing a plague of interpersonal violence. Individuals, regardless of social class, ethnic background, age, or gender have been adversely affected, either directly or indirectly, by indiscriminate acts of interpersonal violence. These include sexual assault, youth and gang-related violence, robberies, drug-related violence, hate crimes, and domestic violence.

Interpersonal violence affects the health and well-being of millions of people in the United States each year. According to the U.S. Department of Justice (1994), an individual has a greater chance of being a victim of a violent act than of being injured in an automobile accident. Data from a variety of sources (U.S. Department of Justice, Federal Bureau of Investigation, Bureau of Justice Statistics, American Medical Association, Family Prevention Fund, National Clearinghouse for the Defense of Battered Women, Childrens' Defense Fund) offer the following picture with respect to violence in the United States:

- In 1994, U.S. residents age 12 or over experienced approximately 42.4 million crimes.
- Homicide was the 10th leading cause of death for all Americans in 1991. For Whites ages 15 to 24, homicide was the third leading cause of death, exceeded only by accidents and suicide. For Blacks ages 15 to 24, homicide was the leading cause of death.
- In 1991 homicide was the fourth leading cause of death for 1- to 4-year-olds and the third leading cause of death for 5- to 14-year-olds.

- Criminologists expect juvenile crime to rise 114% over the next decade.
- Every 2 hours a child is killed with a gun in the United States.
- Approximately 1 in 10 high school students has experienced physical violence in dating relationships. Among college students, the figure rises to 22%.
- Battered women may account for 22% to 35% of women seeking care in hospital emergency rooms.
- More than 90 women were murdered every week in 1991.
- Family violence cost the nation from $5 to 10 billion annually in medical expenses, police and court costs, shelter and foster care, sick leave, and absenteeism.
- Every year domestic violence results in almost 100,000 days of hospitalization, almost 30,000 emergency room visits, and almost 40,000 visits to a physician.
- In 1994, for every 1,000 persons age 12 or over there occurred two rapes or attempted rapes, three assaults with serious injury, and four robberies.
- One hundred and five school-associated violent deaths occurred in the United States from 1992 to 1994.
- The lethality of violence among youth has significantly increased over the past decade, and this increase is associated with the use of firearms.
- Each year nearly 1 million individuals become victims of violence while working or on duty.
- Violent street gangs are active in 94% of all medium- and large-sized cities in the United States.
- Studies have shown that as many as 92% of gay men and lesbians have been the targets of verbal abuse and over one third have endured physical violence.

This chapter first looks at the underlying culture of such interpersonal violence and explores its etiology, including demographic patterns, psychosocial forces, and contextual factors. The chapter then challenges counselors to confront the culture of violence that pervades the country and work to establish a culture that fosters respect for human life through social action initiatives that include promoting public awareness, building coalitions, advocating public policy and legislation, and developing prevention programs.

A CULTURE OF VIOLENCE

Violence is pervasive in American society. It has been ominously suggested that violence has become the defining characteristic of American culture. Significantly, it has been reported that the United States is the most violent country in the Western world (Emde, 1993).

It is important to consider that violence permeates American history and cultural development. Through a violent revolutionary war, the country established its independence. A battle during the War of 1812 provided the inspiration for the country's national anthem. The true identity of the United States as one nation was forged in the 19th century only after a protracted and bloody civil war. This new-found identity prompted an expansionist movement across the North American continent that was often predicated on violence and manifested in physical domination and subjugation of Native Americans.

In the 20th century, as media have become more dominant and sophisticated, mainstream America has become more exposed to violence. This greater exposure, at increasingly younger ages, has lead to a glorification of and fascination with violence and its perpetrators. For example, the cultural icons of American society include the Western gunslinger, the rogue cop, the suave gangster, and the cut-throat business tycoon. The electronic and print media have immortalized these figures, largely because of their violent and relentless behavior. Such media praise for solving problems and gaining status through the use of violence has fostered (and perpetuated) a "shoot first and ask questions later" mentality that seems particularly attractive to American youth.

In recent years, the recording industry has contributed to the growing culture of violence by promoting the often violent, racist, and misogynistic lyrics of both heavy metal and so-called Gangsta rap artists. The recent fatal incidents involving several of these artists amplify the glorification of violence inherent in this music genre (Constable, 1996; Waxman & Iverem, 1997).

Moreover, advances in computer technology have provided yet another outlet for exposure to violence. From violent video games to exposure to the World Wide Web, young people today are inundated with images of aggression and domination.

America's historical progression coupled with a media fixation on aggressive behavior has produced an atmosphere in which violence has become accepted, and even more tragically expected, as the norm. Most Americans encounter daily at least a few data on violence through television and print media. However, although the data on violence (such as that cited earlier) are troubling when considered in total, this constant bombardment of disturbing facts and figures has served to desensitize many individuals to the magnitude of interpersonal violence in American society. This phenomenon is particularly disturbing with respect to young people. In response to environmental factors, American youth have often become both fascinated with and immune to the horror associated with violent acts. Significantly, empirical evidence has suggested that exposure to media violence is a risk factor for the development of aggressive behavior (Donnerstein, Slaby, & Eron, 1994).

THE ETIOLOGY OF VIOLENCE

Broadly defined, *violence* is any act, whether overt or covert, that coerces or causes physical hurt, material loss, or mental anguish, or that degrades human beings or that militates against human rights, dignity, and decency (Rajgopal, 1987). Despite its seemingly epidemic proportions in the United States, violence is not inevitable. The reasons that people engage in violent acts are complex. Researchers have suggested that violent behavior often results from the interaction of myriad variables, including demographic patterns, psychosocial forces, and contextual factors (Page, Kitchin-Becker, Solovan, Golec, & Hebert, 1992).

DEMOGRAPHIC PATTERNS

Research has suggested that the factors related to the development of violent behavior are often most evident among young males, primarily in their late teens to early 30s situated in the lowest socioeconomic levels. Demographic patterns suggest that this group is most likely to be the perpetrators and victims of violent behavior (Page et al., 1992).

With respect to vulnerable groups, data suggest that ethnic minorities are most often the target of violence. For example, with regard to African American and White victims of violence, the lifetime odds of dying by interpersonal violence in the United States have recently been estimated. Excluding violent deaths by suicide, by war, or by acts of law enforcement, it has been estimated that 1 in 27 African American males will die by violence as compared to 1 in 205 White males; 1 in 117 African American females will die by violence in comparison to 1 in 496 White females (Prothrow-Stith, 1991).

In considering demographic patterns regarding violent behavior, however, it must be stressed that the majority of research has been epidemiological in nature. There is little or no research to demonstrate unique psychobehavioral characteristics that predispose any group of people to violent behavior. The explanations for the etiology of violence must be considered within the context of other influential variables.

Psychosocial Forces

In a society that is generally characterized by high levels of prejudice and intolerance, significant disparities in economic and social opportunity, a strong emphasis on individualism and competition, and assertiveness that often degenerates into aggression, psychosocial development is often negatively impacted. As developmental tasks at each stage of life are adversely affected by such forces, the trajectory toward violence can be established. Feelings of mistrust, shame, doubt, guilt, anger, inferiority, role confusion, isolation, stagnation, and despair can result when individuals fail to master developmental tasks due to deleterious environmental influences. Such feelings often mutate into anger, frustration, and hatred that are the impetus for violent behavior.

Contextual Factors

In addition to demographic patterns and psychosocial forces, the etiology of violent behavior can be traced to a number of interrelated environmental influences. Contextual factors such as the widespread availability of weapons, rampant substance abuse, and dysfunctional family dynamics, to name a few, all combine to promote and sustain violence as a defining characteristic of American culture.

A first major contextual factor to consider in the etiology of violence is the availability of weapons, particularly guns in American society. Authorities contend that the availability of guns is a primary contributor to the growing number of homicides in the country. For example, in 1994 alone, nearly 40,00 people in the United States died from firearm injuries. In 1995, three times as many murders were committed with firearms as with all other methods combined. Significantly, the American Medical Association has labeled assault weapons *a public health hazard* and has called for restrictions on the sale and ownership of these most deadly weapons. In a 1993 national survey of junior and senior high school students, 59% reported that they could get a gun if they needed one, and two out of three of these students said they could get a gun in 24 hours (LH Research, 1993).

The Second Amendment to the U.S. Constitution protects the right of an individual to own a gun. This legal right has contributed in no small measure to an atmosphere where easy access to firearms has become a disturbing aspect of American life.

A second important contextual factor that must be considered is the pervasive problem of substance abuse in American society. To underscore this phenomenon, a number of studies have found that in 60% of homicides the perpetrator, the victim, or both, had consumed alcohol, and that violence frequently occurs in places where alcohol is used (National Committee for Injury Prevention and Control, 1989). The connection between alcohol consumption and interpersonal violence is well documented due to the common use of blood alcohol tests on homicide victims. Whereas the effects of other substances are less evident, it can be estimated that drugs have a similar impact (Goldstein, Hunt, Des Jarlais, & Deren, 1987).

In addition to the potential for controlled substances to contribute directly to violent behavior, drugs also play two salient and well-documented indirect roles in violent behavior. First, the expense related to drug addiction compels many users to engage in violent crime to support their habit. Second, because many drugs are illegal and highly valuable, many individuals involved in the drug trade resort to violence related to the buying and selling of controlled substances. A conservative estimate by the National Institute on Drug Abuse suggests that at least 10% of homicides occur during drug-related transactions (Harwood, Napolitano, Kristiansen, & Collins, 1984).

A third contextual factor contributing to the etiology of violence is ever-increasing family dysfunction. In recent years greater attention has been focused on the violent nature of many American families. According to the U.S. Department of Justice (1995), for example, in 29% of the violent crimes against women by lone offenders the perpetrators were intimates—husbands, former husbands, boyfriends, or former boyfriends. In 1995, over 3 million children were reported for child abuse or neglect to child protective service agencies in the United States (Lung & Daro, 1996). It is estimated that more than 800,000 older Americans were victims of various types of domestic abuse in 1994.

Such family dysfunction often manifests itself in aggressive or violent behavior, which in turn adversely impacts child development. This is particularly evident in families where there is a lack of parental supervision, a lack of parent-child involvement, or parental neglect and abuse. Such parenting styles are generally predictors of the development of conduct disorder and juvenile delinquency, problems that frequently involve violence.

Studies of families of aggressive children have suggested that caregivers fail to teach compliance to social norms and appropriate problem-solving strategies by reinforcing aggressive behavior rather than rewarding prosocial acts. Furthermore, the use of harsh physical punishment has been positively correlated with the development of aggressive behavior patterns in youth. Parents who engage in domestic violence thwart a child's ability to learn positive and effective conflict-resolution skills (Kazdin, 1985; Robbins, 1991; Rutter & Giller, 1983).

This analysis of the etiology of violence underscores the fact that this phenomenon impacts upon the quality of life and negatively influences psychosocial development. Although the course of violent behavior is disturbing, it is neither inevitable nor irreversible. Changing the course of violence in American society offers a unique challenge to professional counselors. Those counselors committed to preventing violence and promoting a safe environment for optimal psychosocial growth and development can play an important role as social advocates and systemic change agents.

CHALLENGING VIOLENCE: A COUNSELOR CALL TO SOCIAL ACTION

Counselors and other mental health professionals have begun to focus attention on the issue of violence (Anderson & Bauer, 1987; Andrews & Brewin, 1990; Aizenman & Kelly, 1988; Brown, 1996; Herek, 1989). Significantly, during her presidency of the American Counseling Association (1993–94), Beverly O'Bryant called for declaring a state of emergency in American communities where violence pervades everyday life. She also called on counselors to commit themselves to reducing violence on the streets, in homes, in schools, and in the workplace. One result was the development of an initiative, "Healing a Violent Society: The Counselor as a Resource for Life," to provide a framework for social action on the part of counselors to alleviate societal violence.

Given the continuing and insidious nature of violence in American society, professional counselors need to make further commitment to intervene not only on an interpersonal level but on a systemic level as well. As with any counseling issue, counselors should facilitate individual and group interventions for both the victims and perpetrators of violence. However, given the magnitude of the culture of violence found in American society such interventions are often not enough. This is because the etiology of violence is often not found within the individual but rather in a societal context. Therefore, working to help individuals deal effectively with their own violent behavior and its consequences or to assist victims of violence demands that the societal context for violence be addressed as well. Without such systemic intervention it is highly probable that the phenomenon of violent interpersonal behavior will continue. Counselors committed to the eradication of societal violence, therefore, are not only able to work with clients on an individual level but also have the skills to empower themselves and others to advocate for social change.

Social action initiatives that demonstrate such action and commitment to challenge violence on the part of professional counselors include promoting public awareness, building coalitions, supporting public policy and legislation, and developing prevention programs.

Promoting Public Awareness

It is important that counselors find ways to raise levels of awareness and sensitivity to the issue of violence in American society. Ways that counselors can promote public awareness include the following:

- Make a personal statement concerning zero tolerance for violence. For example, boycott movies and television programs with violent content or refuse to purchase violent toys and video games, or compact discs with violent or misogynistic lyrics.
- Work in communities to develop public service announcements for local radio, television, and newspapers that provide a strong message about how violence negatively impacts upon the quality of life. Such announcements might also include messages about how to prevent violent behavior and provide referral sources. A strategy to develop such public service announcements might be to find an advertising agency willing to provide creative expertise free of charge. Working with such an agency, counselors can develop powerful messages about violence and its negative effect on human growth and development.
- Prepare packets of information that address issues of violence and that can be mailed to key sectors of the public. These public awareness packets can be sent to community agencies for distribution to selected client populations. For example, develop packets that focus on the dangers of handguns.
- Facilitate community forums on the nature and prevention of violence. These forums might include roundtable discussions in community or religious centers, community focus groups, brown bag lunches, and presentations to PTAs or other civic groups.
- Prepare and disseminate specialized information for families, youth, educators, and community leaders on a variety of issues related to violence. For example, prepare information for parents on how to improve parenting skills in order to prevent family violence, provide youth with information on conflict resolution, consult with educators on how to organize peer mentoring programs, and work with community leaders on strategies for redirecting gang violence into more constructive activity.

BUILDING COALITIONS

Because the problem of violence is multidimensional, its solution requires an interdisciplinary approach. It is important that counselors find ways to collaborate with colleagues in other professions in their attempts to challenge the climate of violence. Professional alliances are needed to promote an atmosphere of respect for human life.

- Develop alliances with law enforcement officials to work with first-time and repeat offenders in developing the attitudes and skills necessary to solve problems in an effective and nonviolent manner.
- Collaborate with members of the medical profession in helping them find ways to recognize the signs of domestic abuse and other violent behavior.
- Collaborate with educators, psychologists, criminologists, anthropologists, sociologists, and the medical community to improve the scope and quality of research on the etiology and prevention of violence.
- Work closely with teachers, administrators, and other educational professionals to establish and implement primary prevention programs. With the passage of the Safe Schools Act (Improving America's Schools Act of 1994), such collaboration seems to be a necessary and appropriate way to combat school violence.

Perhaps the best example of coalition building among professional groups is the Voices vs. Violence campaign of the National Mental Health Association (1994). This campaign has brought together approximately 40 professional associations and community organizations, including the American Counseling Association, to conduct a variety of antiviolence activities, such as a community audit that assessed the extent to which one community was addressing the issue of violence. The result of this audit was a community blueprint for action. Counselors may want to consider forming such coalitions in their own communities to develop concrete action plans to deal with issues of violence.

SUPPORTING PUBLIC POLICY AND LEGISLATION

Counselors must find ways to influence public policy and legislation aimed at curbing interpersonal violence. This should include advocating for public policy and legislative initiatives at the local, state, and federal levels.

- At the local level, visit school boards and encourage them to develop and implement a coordinated systematic and developmentally culturally appropriate program for violence prevention beginning in the formative years and continuing throughout the secondary grades.
- Conduct letter-writing campaigns directed at public policymakers and community leaders on the impact of violence on human development. Exhort them to take action.
- At the state and national levels, organize personal visits to legislators. During these visits, underscore the mental health dimensions of interpersonal violence and call upon legislators to initiate and/ or support laws aimed at violence prevention. For example, advocate for block grants to combat interpersonal violence at the local level.
- Testify before legislative panels about the culture, etiology, impact, and prevention of violence.

Developing Prevention Programs

Counselors committed to action against violence should focus attention on preventative initiatives. They should become involved in a consultant capacity in initiatives developed by municipal governments, police departments, schools, social agencies, and civic or religious groups in their own communities. Such efforts might involve targeting at-risk populations, promoting family and community action, and initiating multidisciplinary education efforts.

- Take part in establishing youth programs such as Midnight Basketball. A program such as this takes young people off the streets and engages them in a constructive activity, thus hopefully decreasing the likelihood of juvenile violence.
- Take part in designing community initiatives that include public information campaigns and programs to change the physical environment of a community. This could involve Take Back the Night activities that help families and neighborhoods send a message to would-be offenders that violent crime will not be tolerated. The intent of such an event is to convey that the night belongs

to the neighborhood's families and not to those who wish to engage in violent activities. Still another programmatic initiative might include supporting the efforts of community organizations to enrich family life. This might mean consulting with agencies and parent organizations as they develop programs for helping families recognize substance abuse, gang affiliations, or the stress that can lead to domestic violence.

- Take part in the development of interdisciplinary teams of professionals to sponsor educational programs directed at specific populations. An example of such a program is the Youth Violence Project initiated by the University of Virginia's Curry School of Education ("Curry addresses," 1997). This graduate-level educational experience examines the incidence, causes, response strategies, and prevention techniques for working with violent youth. Designed for school personnel and those who routinely work with adolescents, it covers such areas as the characteristics of violent youth, restraint and behavior management, school law, crises response, conflict mediation, and issues of culture, community, and ethnicity. Faculty for this educational experience represent a multidisciplinary team of scholars, law enforcement personnel, lawyers, counselors, psychologists, and urban planners.

CONCLUSION

This chapter has explored American society's culture of violence and provided actions and strategies that counselors can use to challenge violence effectively at all levels. The destructive impact of interpersonal violence on quality of life and psychosocial development is disturbing, but the course of violent behavior is neither inevitable nor irreversible. However, eradicating interpersonal violence presents a formidable challenge to professional counselors.

Those who are committed to preventing violence and promoting a safe environment for optimal psychosocial growth and development must play an integral role as social advocates and systemic change agents. Challenging interpersonal violence requires counselors to move beyond traditional roles and be able to perceive accurately environmental influences that promote violent behavior. They must decide to intercede at a systemic level to challenge those dynamics that perpetuate the culture of violence. Counselors who consciously work to combat violence on a systemic level can be in the forefront of establishing an alternative culture that fosters respect for human life and mitigates against violence. In this way current members of the counseling profession can leave a legacy of nonviolence to future generations.

REFERENCES

Anderson, W., & Bauer, B. (1987). Law enforcement officers: The consequences of exposure to violence. *Journal of Counseling and Development, 65,* 381-384.

Andrews, B., & Brewin, C. R. (1990). Attributions of blame for marital violence: A study of antecedents and consequences. *Journal of Marriage and the Family, 52,* 757-767.

Aizenman, M., & Kelley, G. (1988). The incidence of violence and acquaintance rape in dating relationships among college men and women. *Journal of College Student Development, 29,* 305-311.

Brown, D. (1996). Counseling the victims of violence who develop posttraumatic stress disorder. *Elementary School Guidance and Counseling, 30,* 218-227.

Constable, P. (1996, September 14). Rapper dies of wounds from shooting. *The Washington Post,* pp. A1, A14.

Curry addresses violence in our schools. (1997, Spring). *Curry, University of Virginia,* 2-3.

Donnerstein, E., Slaby, R. G., & Eron, L. D. (1994). The mass media and youth aggression. In L. D. Eron, J. H. Gentry, & P. Schlegel (Eds.), *Reason to hope: A psychological perspective on violence and youth* (pp. 219-250). Washington, DC: American Psychological Association.

Emde, R. N. (1993). Horror! The horror! Reflections on our culture of violence and its implications for early development and morality. In D. Reiss, J. E. Richters, M. Radke-Warrow, & D. Scharff (Eds.), *Children and violence* (pp. 119-123). New York: Guilford Press.

Goldstein, P., Hunt D., Des Jarlais, D.C., & Deren, S. (1987). Drug dependence and abuse. In R. W. Amler & H. B. Dull (Eds.), *Closing the gap: The burden of unnecessary illness* (pp. 89-101). New York: Oxford University Press.

Harwood, H., Napolitano, D., Kristiansen, P., & Collins, J. (1984). *Economic cost to society of alcohol and drug abuse and mental illness, Final report.* Unpublished manuscript. Rockville, MD: ADAMHA.

Herek, G. M. (1989). Hate crime against lesbians and gay men. *American Psychologist, 44,* 948-955.

Improving America's Schools Act of 1994, Pub. L. No. 103-382.

Kazdin, A. E. (1985). *Treatment of antisocial behavior in children and adolescents.* Homewood, IL: Dorsey Press.

LH Research, Inc. (1993). *A survey of experiences, perceptions, and apprehensions about guns among young people in America.* Report to the Harvard School of Public Health under a grant from the Joyce Foundation.

Lung, C. T., & Daro, D. (1996). *Current trends in child abuse reporting and fatalities: The results of the 1995 annual 50-state survey.* Chicago, IL: National Committee to Prevent Child Abuse.

National Committee for Injury Prevention and Control. (1989). *Injury prevention: Meeting the challenge.* New York: Oxford University Press.

National Mental Health Association. (1994). *Voices vs. violence.* Alexandria, VA: National Mental Health Association.

Page, R. M., Kitchin-Becker, S., Solovan, D., Golec, T. L., & Hebert D. L. (1992). Interpersonal violence: A priority issue for health education. *Journal of Health Education, 23,* 286-292.

Prothrow-Stith, D. (1991). *Deadly consequences: How violence is destroying our teenage population and a plan to begin solving the problem.* New York: Harper Collins.

Rajgopal, P. R. (1987). *Social change and violence: The Indian experience.* New Delhi: Uppal.

Robbins, L. N. (1991). Conduct disorder. *Journal of Child Psychology and Psychiatry, 32.* 193-212.

Rutter, M., & Giller, H. (1983). *Juvenile delinquency: Trends and perspectives.* New York: Penguin Books.

U.S. Department of Justice (1994). *Violent crime: National crime victimization survey.* Annapolis Junction, MD: Bureau of Justice Statistics Clearinghouse.

U.S. Department of Justice (1995). *Violence against women: Estimates from the redesigned survey.* Washington, DC: U.S. Government Printing Office.

Waxman, S., & Iverem, E. (1997, March 10). "Gangsta" rap singer slain in L.A. *The Washington Post,* pp. A1, A10.

5

Gay and Lesbian Activism: A Frontier in Social Advocacy

Bob Barret

Gay and lesbian people are perhaps the most misunderstood minority in our country. Children of other marginalized groups mature with the support of an extended community that includes parents, grandparents, neighbors, and even teachers and religious figures. For gay and lesbian youth, identity development takes place in the absence of family support and in the presence of almost universal stigma. As a result these youth learn to hide who they are, and many gay male and lesbian adults master the art of passing as members of the majority. They date and may even marry persons of the opposite sex. Some hide their sexual orientation even from themselves; others may create fictive lives, changing the pronouns of friends and lovers so their family members and coworkers will not know they are gay. The loneliness of such an experience is enormous and can be very destructive to healthy personality development.

This chapter provides a brief overview of some of the issues that gay men and lesbians face in their experience, including language, visibility, and the role of the mental health profession. The chapter next explores the recruitment and choice myths about homosexuality. The chapter concludes with a discussion of the ways counselors may become involved in working for social justice for sexual minorities, first by increasing awareness, becoming informed, and finding support and then by seeking out and taking advantage of the many opportunities in the community to promote the well-being of gay men and lesbians.

ISSUES

For counselors, understanding the gay and lesbian experience is difficult. Few counselors receive formal training that includes sound information about this community. Important for the counselors to remember is that the bewilderment experienced by most nongay people as they confront the stereotypes of homosexuality is minute compared to that of the man or woman who is trying to understand himself or herself as gay or lesbian. Important issues for both gay and nongay counselors and clients include the language used, the increased visibility of gays and lesbians, and the role of the mental health profession in this increased visibility.

LANGUAGE

The problem of language is a basic consideration:

- The term *homosexual* suggests that this community is just about sex. In fact, sexuality plays the same role in all of our lives regardless of sexual orientation. Gay men and lesbians are no more sexual than nongay persons.
- The words *gay* and *lesbian* suggest there are two groups within the larger community of sexual minorities, but bisexual and transgendered people also are represented in the gay community. Although they exist in smaller numbers, the kind of discrimination and oppression they experience is like that of gay men and lesbians.
- The term *gay community* is in many ways a myth; the community may be deeply divided, and various subgroups may have entirely opposite goals.
- The term *sexual preference,* commonly used by uninformed people, contains an offense. More correct is *sexual orientation* because preference suggests a choice that most sexual minorities do not recall making; gay persons like nongay persons discover their sexual orientations. Gay men and lesbians come out as a statement of integrity. They are simply being who they are. The only choice they make is how to integrate this part of their being into their lives.
- The term *homophobia,* a word that has been used to describe those who support the oppression of gay persons, is another language problem. Homophobia, or the fear of those whose sexual

orientation is different, does add momentum to the efforts to suppress this minority. Recently, Logan (1996) suggested that the more accurate word is, in fact, *homo-prejudice*. Understanding gay and lesbian oppression as a prejudice, rather than as a fear, assists all of us as we consider how to work toward greater inclusivity.

- Deciding the proper term to describe the person one loves also causes consternation. Is she my partner? That sounds like a business arrangement. Lover? Well, we are more than sex mates. How about significant other? Spouse? Life partner? This is often confusing both in and out of the gay community.

Language problems like these interfere with understanding and can make communication difficult. Just what is this gay, lesbian, bisexual, transgendered group of people and what is it they want? The sheer complexity of these names tells us the community is complex. Trying to understand it is not going to be easy for most. In this chapter, for the sake of clarity, the words *gay* and *lesbian* are used to represent all sexual minorities, and the term *gay community* likewise includes all those whose sexual orientation is different from that of the majority.

VISIBILITY

Until recently, gay men and lesbians pretty much stayed out of sight, denying the nongay community the opportunity to know who they were and how their lives were so like everyone else's. They lived primarily in a subculture that provided social support and protected them from having to be more visible. They had few role models and routinely encountered negative stereotyping in the news and entertainment media. They have been virtually absent even from professional literature.

Happily, that situation is changing rapidly. Gay liberation began in the 1960s when gay men and lesbians in New York City fought back against police who were harassing them. The Stonewall Riots marked the first time that the gay community stood up publicly and said, "We have had enough! We will no longer let fear force us into silence against oppression." In the past 30 years, this movement has grown and the community has become much more visible.

Role models now appear in the news and on popular television shows. There are organizations like PFLAG (Parents and Friends of Lesbians and Gays) that represent the needs of this misunderstood minority. Churches, bowling and softball leagues, outdoor clubs, reading groups, political groups, square dance clubs, and rodeos for gay men and lesbians provide opportunities to learn about the community, to socialize and have fun. Fueled in part by those who were forced to be public because of their HIV status, the gay community is emerging with much vitality and energy.

THE ROLE OF THE MENTAL HEALTH PROFESSION

The mental health profession has played both a positive and a negative role in the increased visibility of sexual minorities. In the 1950s and 1960s, psychological research began to challenge the notion that homosexuality was inherently pathological. In 1973, the American Psychiatric Association removed homosexuality as a mental disorder from their *Diagnostic and Statistical Manual of Mental Disorders* (*DSM*); soon after this move, psychologists, counselors, and social workers adopted more affirmative positions toward homosexuals. Nevertheless, research tells us that sexual minorities continue to experience discrimination as they seek mental health services.

Within 5 years of depathologizing homosexuality, researchers were reporting the continued negative attitudes of mental health practitioners toward gay and lesbian clients (Fassinger, 1991; Martin, 1982). Clients reported that their counselors seemed reluctant to assist them as they explored questions about their sexual orientation. Being told "you cannot be gay" or changing the subject when sexual orientation came up was not a rare experience. Even worse, many counselors insisted that clients work to change their sexual orientation. These experiences intensified rather than diminished the shame and guilt that sexual minorities had to overcome in order to create healthy and stable lives and probably did more harm than good.

Even decades later, the situation has not changed much. Garnets, Hancock, Cochran, Goodchilds, and Peplau (1991) reported that 99% of mental health practitioners provide services to gay men or lesbians, yet negative attitudes toward sexual minorities and practices persist. Fassinger (1991) identified studies that have revealed that mental health professionals are uninformed, work from heterosexist perspectives, and hold on to societal stereotypes about gay people. McHenry and Johnson (1993) spelled out ways that nongay counselors may unconsciously collude with their gay and lesbian clients' self-hate. Failing to congratulate the gay client who has decided to live with a partner or not appropriately supporting client distress when a coming out has resulted in rejection are just two of their examples. The overwhelming finding is that gay persons rarely find mental health professionals who are informed and affirming about their issues. Our profession has failed to provide accurate information and high-quality service delivery to sexual minorities.

Some of this bias and mistreatment is understandable. Few mental health professionals ever receive training in the unique needs of gay and lesbian clients. Graduate programs and accrediting agencies fail to include this population in their curricula or standards. Even programs at professional meetings are few and may not be well attended. The stigma attached to homosexuality prevents many of those who are curious or who see the need to improve their knowledge from learning about this often invisible group. The same shame and fear that make it difficult for many gay and lesbian persons to approach a clerk in a book store with questions about resources are also barriers for nongay persons. Today, however, there are some who appropriately encourage gay affirmative stances in counseling. Even among psychoanalysts the change is evident. Frommer (1994), for example, advocated, that "an affirmative stance that emotionally communicates to the patient that analyst's belief that homosexuality is a natural developmental end point for some individuals is viewed as the correct application of psychoanalytic technique with homosexual patients" (p. 215).

MYTHS ABOUT HOMOSEXUALITY

Resistance to the acceptance of homosexuality is widespread. Because of the complexity of understanding this community, oppression may be fueled by those who see homosexuality as a moral issue. These opponents use religious organizations to lobby against gay and lesbian rights. One of their tactics is to perpetuate myths about the so-called *gay lifestyle* in order to justify oppression.

Two principal myths about sexual minorities are most often used. In one, hate and fear of homosexuals are encouraged by trumpeting that the gay community "recruits" its members through the sexual abuse of children. In the second, prejudice against this community is supported by encouraging others to believe that homosexuality is a choice.

Although research studies could be assumed to refute such myths, research on homosexuality is not only extremely complex but also generates findings that are far from conclusive. Well-designed empirical studies of this population are complicated by a number of factors. One is that subjects are often difficult to find. Given the invisible nature of many gay and lesbian adults, locating what might be a representative sample is incredibly difficult. Another factor is that most gay persons who participate in research studies are self-selected, and most reports are based on self-administered inventories. Yet another factor is that sample sizes are generally small, and the demographic information that exists about the gay community is woefully incomplete. Even estimates of the population that is gay or lesbian may be in error. Percentages range from 3% to 15%, and the actual number may never be known. Given these complications, research studies should be seen as merely an indication of what we may find once the science becomes more exact.

The Myth of Recruitment and Molestation

Gay men and women grow up in heterosexual families with heterosexual parents, brothers, sisters, aunts, and uncles. Many report that they know they are different at an early age and eventually find ways to locate other gay people. They frequently state feeling as if they are the "only ones who are attracted to persons of the same sex" until they discover others who are like them. This discovery can come through news reports, television talk shows, or local gossip about gay bars or events. The incidence of homosexuality among children raised by gay and lesbian parents appears to mirror that of children who grow up in nongay households (Barret & Robinson, 1990). The myth that gay men and lesbians seek out unsuspecting children and lure them into destructive sexual relationships that result in a homosexual orientation has never been substantiated and defies common sense.

Equating homosexuality with child molestation is a myth that seems to be promoted primarily by conservative religious groups. The evidence shows that in more than 90% of the cases in law enforcement statistics, sexual abuse of children is a crime perpetuated by persons who are heterosexual (Voeller & Walters, 1978).

THE MYTH OF CHOICE

Is it *sexual preference* or *sexual orientation?* This question and the appropriate terminology is at the heart of the debate about extending civil rights to gay men and lesbians. Although the research on the causes of homosexuality is not definitive, most experts believe that sexual orientation is fixed at a relatively young age and cannot be changed. Research findings are inconclusive about the genetic bases of sexual orientation. However, as the science of genetics becomes more exact, many predict that homosexuality will in fact be proved to have a biological basis.

Some persons suggest that gay men and lesbians just need the correct kind of counseling in order to become heterosexual. However, respected professional organizations such as the American Psychiatric Association (1993), the American Psychological Association (1997), the National Association of Social Workers (1992), and the American Academy of Pediatrics (1994) have published position papers clearly stating that so-called *reparative* or *conversion* therapies that attempt to change sexual orientation from homosexual to heterosexual are ineffective and inappropriate. Although there may indeed be some short-term behavior change, real success in changing sexual orientation is ineffective (Edwards, 1996).

Many gay men and lesbians respond to the question of choice by reminding the questioner that the notion of deciding to join a minority that encounters daily discrimination, faces rejection from parents and friends, and creates enormous career conflicts could not be rational (Marcus, 1993). Most nongay persons are unable to recall when they "decided" to be heterosexual. The same is true for gay men and lesbians. Like all people, the choice that exists is how one will merge sexual orientation and sexual behavior into a sexual identity.

THE LESBIAN AND GAY RIGHTS MOVEMENT

By understanding the problems and myths, counselors may begin to understand that gay men and lesbians need and deserve the kind of social support that advocacy can create. The general absence of laws that protect this minority from discrimination in employment, housing, and public accommodation supports the prevailing negative attitude toward homosexuals and institutionalizes prejudice.

Still, in communities across the nation and in all kinds of organizations, gay men and lesbians are becoming more visible and demanding that discrimination end. Jamie Nabozny, for example, successfully sued school administrators and counselors who refused to protect him from antigay violence in the Ashland, Wisconsin, school system ("Lambda wins," 1997). He endured threats, intimidation, beatings, and humiliation from his classmates. He was trapped in bathrooms, kicked, and even urinated on while school officials took no disciplinary action. His and his parents' requests for assistance were ignored with the admonition that such action was only natural given his open homosexuality. But a federal jury thought otherwise and awarded him just under $1 million. This successful suit sends a clear message about the consequences of failing to extend civil protection to gay persons. Contrary to some public discourse, the gay rights movement does not seek special rights but rather equal protection under the law.

SOCIAL ACTION FOR GAY MEN AND LESBIANS

Counselors who seek to become advocates for gay men and lesbians have abundant choices. Activities on behalf of sexual minorities are not just opportunities to participate in the worldwide human rights movement, they also offer a unique chance to assist as this largely invisible minority becomes visible. Those who were active in the civil rights struggles of the 1950s and 1960s or who worked for women's rights in the 1970s were present during a similar time. Today the momentum of the gay and lesbian rights cause is increasing, and those who join in this effort can make a difference that will endure for generations. This truly is one of the cutting edges, both in our nation and in our profession.

A first step toward social action is to become more aware of individual biases and prejudices. The question is not, "Are you homo-prejudiced?" Rather, the proper orientation to this issue is, "How can I become more aware of my homo-prejudices and limit the ways they influence my behavior?" One starting point is to take a self-inventory to discover where individual prejudices are likely to influence action. Consider your feelings if others thought you might be lesbian or gay. Visit a gay bookstore in the city nearest you. Observe your feelings as you mingle with other customers. Check out your reactions to people, books, and other objects there. Discover your areas of discomfort and discuss them with a colleague. Understanding of self is essential for those who seek to join in the gay rights movement.

Another starting point is to take an inventory of heterosexual privilege. As with all prejudices, the majority is often unconscious about their privileges, and most people take heterosexual rights for granted. I recently asked a class to brainstorm heterosexual privilege, and they came up with a list of over 30 items, ranging from the right to marry to the right to hold hands in public. Class members used this list to examine their internal reactions if such privileges were extended to gay men and lesbians. Here, they stumbled upon some of their discomforts with equality for gay men and lesbians. Thinking of a same sex couple being married or publicly displaying their affection was uncomfortable for these students. These same discomforts certainly would influence their verbal and nonverbal responses to gay clients. Responding to the complex challenge of seeking out information and increasing their appreciation for the gay experience will help all who initiate social action for this community.

A second step toward social action is to become informed. The bottom line rests with improving counseling services, and far too many gay men and lesbians continue to access counseling service providers who are uninformed about their needs. Isay (1989) and Dworkin and Gutierrez (1992) provided useful starting points for understanding the unique mental health needs of sexual minorities. Workshops, journal readings, informal conversations with professional colleagues, and sound supervision will enhance service delivery and individual counseling skills.

Learning about gay and lesbian persons is not difficult. For those who are involved in clinical work, asking gay clients to become teachers is an easy and respectful method of learning more. Let them know you are not as informed as you want to be, and they will tell you a lot about resources in your community. Understanding of sexual minorities also can be enhanced through reading. Marcus (1992, 1993) has written two books that give basic information about the personal and political experiences of sexual minorities. Don Clark, one of the first psychologists to write about the gay experience, created a classic in *Loving Someone Gay* (1995). These three books are a useful foundation. And do not overlook the spiritual lives of gay men and lesbians; as for many, spiritual practices may be important sources of support (Barret & Barzan, 1996). It is also vital to recognize that the gay community, like all communities, is composed of various cultures. Learn the unique ways Native American, African American, and Asian American gay men and lesbians respond to their unique cultural backgrounds (Greene, 1997).

A third essential step toward social action is to find support for yourself. Clearly there are potential negative consequences for those who become connected to the gay rights movement. Emotional responses to homosexuality are deeply ingrained, and most people avoid examining topics that create discomfort. However, in all communities there are gay and nongay persons willing to get involved in social activism on behalf of sexual minorities. These individuals provide key support, but they never totally eliminate the threat of attack from groups or individuals who oppose gay rights. A man who directed an award-winning play that had gay characters was attacked by an elected official and called gay even though he is not. A teacher who listened to a young woman talk about her confusion about sexual orientation was admonished by her principal. Laws that forbid counselors from speaking with young people about sexual orientation without a parent being present are being considered by school boards and other legislative bodies around the country. Proceeding carefully and anticipating resistance are essential.

In my experience, the place to start building support is with the person with the most authority. For example, an intervention to encourage our local newspaper to expand its coverage of the gay and lesbian community began with a letter to the publisher. His encouragement set the tone for what became an ongoing dialogue with editors and reporters and has resulted in a much more realistic presentation of our gay community. For another example, an intervention to encourage a business to include sexual orientation among the protections for all employees began with speaking to the president of the firm and resulted in immediate success. If the person in charge is not afraid, those who work in other responsible positions are also likely not to be afraid.

Changing institutionalized homo-prejudice is just one place for activism. Fortunately, there are abundant opportunities within all communities that involve changing attitudes before policies. Among these are the following:

- Attend a training. At professional meetings, training on counseling interventions that are useful with gay and lesbian clients is becoming routine. These "starter" experiences enable the beginner to improve direct service delivery. Each summer, the Lesbian and Gay Health Conference, sponsored by George Washington University Medical School, is offered in different parts of the country and provides the most up-to-date mental health information on issues that range from HIV disease to political oppression.
- Teach others about gay, lesbian, bisexual, and transgendered issues. Become an advocate for the inclusion of gay and lesbian counseling in graduate programs. Ask program coordinators to see that this population is included in routine coursework on multiculturalism and diversity. Seek out the gay and lesbian students in your graduate program, ask them to discuss ways they need support, and invite them to speak to faculty and students about their experiences. If no one seems willing, put together a training program and offer it as a unit in formal or informal trainings. Help teachers and other school officials understand the unique needs of gay and lesbian parents as they interact with schools. Check to see if your library carries books that represent gay literature or subjects. If they do not, give them a list of titles. If they do, let them know that you appreciate it. Speak to church and civic groups about the need for more inclusive policies.
- HIV disease has had a major role in the emergence of the gay community. Learn about HIV and the many ways that gay and nongay persons who are influenced by this disease need support. Also, work to make sure others understand that gay and HIV are

not interchangeable. HIV is not a gay disease. Equating the two does a disservice to both.

- Join AGLBIC. The Association for Gay, Lesbian, and Bisexual Issues in Counseling is the newest and fastest growing division within the American Counseling Association. Members are gay-affirming counselors who work in various settings. This is a good source of information and a networking opportunity through which you can learn about social activism for gay men and lesbians around the country.

- Contact your local gay community. Many larger communities have a gay and lesbian switchboard that fields telephone calls. These organizations are an excellent source of information and resources. Contact the one nearest you. If there is not one, look into getting one organized. Find the gay newspaper that covers your town. Some may be statewide and others may be local. They are a valuable source of information and resources.

- Work in your community. There are an endless number of issues that will enhance the lives of gay men and women. Encourage your employer to add sexual orientation as one of the protected classes in employment nondiscrimination policies. Speak to your coworkers about their experience with gay and lesbian clients. See if there are ways to improve service delivery. How about advertising in local gay community newspapers about the availability of gay-positive counseling services? Or contact gay and lesbian mental health professionals and ask them to conduct a training session in your workplace. Is there a youth group for sexual minorities in your community? If so, seek ways you can lend support. If not, consider starting one. Gay and lesbian youth need all the support and advocacy that they can find in order to make it through adolescence with a healthy sense of their identity.

- Speak to political/religious figures. Becoming an advocate for human rights for all persons is one way you can speak up on behalf of gay and lesbian citizens. Contact local elected officials and state your availability to serve as a resource when gay-related issues come up. Encourage school boards to include issues of sexual orientation in human sexuality training and in health education curricula. Write letters to members of your state legislature and/or Congress. In the summer of 1996, at both the state and federal levels, laws were passed that protected heterosexual marriage from the threat posed by the Hawaii Supreme Court to legitimize homosexual marriage. A federal Employment Nondiscrimination Act that would have outlawed discrimination on the basis of sexual orientation in the workplace failed to pass the U.S. Senate by one vote. This bill will be reintroduced. Educate your community about why it is needed and encourage your representative to vote for it.

- Understand the diversity within the gay community. Throughout all your activism, understand that, like all communities, the gay and lesbian community is diverse. There are subgroups based on race, particular interests, and even parental status, and these groups often disagree about what needs to be done. Broaden your understanding of these issues. Realize that older gay men and women often experience isolation within their own culture, and that many gay professionals believe that choosing a career that involves working with children is totally inappropriate. Even political groups within the community may be at odds with each other. In spite of all the commotion, there is no "homosexual agenda" that the community as a whole would support.

- Start a support group. In many medium- and small-sized cities there are few places for gay men and women to gather and have serious conversations about their lives. Consider starting a support or therapy group that might assist in reducing isolation. Advertise your group so the larger community understands that gay persons are present and need support services.

- Contact PFLAG. Parents and Friends of Lesbians and Gays is an international organization that seeks to provide support. Many of these groups meet regularly in mainline churches and are invaluable as they assist parents and friends who are trying to understand ways homosexuality is impacting their lives. If there is no chapter in your community, start one.

- Speak at city, county, and state official meetings when antigay issues come up. In many cities and towns antigay legislation is passed without much discussion. Speaking up against discrimination at meetings where these laws are presented is one of the most effective ways to be gay positive. If you are uncomfortable being so public in your advocacy, call your local officials or take them to lunch and let them know that you support the gay community. Encourage local law enforcement officials to gather data on hate crimes against gay men and lesbians. Offer to teach a unit on gay and lesbian issues in police academy training programs.

- March in gay pride marches or participate in public protests about antigay efforts. Know that across the nation June is Gay Pride month, and in all larger communities there will be marches and other celebrations of gay and lesbian freedom. Pay attention on National Coming Out Day (October 11) and congratulate those you see coming out or come out more fully yourself. Last year on National Coming Out Day, I put *The Advocate,* an award-winning biweekly magazine about the gay community, in my waiting room. Certainly my gay and lesbian clients have the right to see their publications there along with other reading material.

- Put books with gay and lesbian titles on your office bookshelf. Clients will see these books and understand that you are interested in gay issues. Gay and lesbian clients are likely to feel safer and more willing to talk about their lives.

CONCLUSION

There are unlimited opportunities for persons to promote the well-being of the gay men and lesbians who live as neighbors, co-workers, family members, or fellow citizens. Most of us grew up without much accurate information about homosexuality, and the general invisibility of the gay community does not encourage the public to look beyond the negative stereotype that is so prevalent. One day, the stigma about being gay or lesbian will be less of a barrier. The communities that truly seek diversity will understand that tolerance is several steps away from the ideal in which persons are prized because of their differences and all people enrich our life experience because of their differences.

Among the many opportunities for counselors to become activists for social change, perhaps the most daunting lies in assisting the gay and lesbian community as it attempts to gain social justice. Discrimination and homo-prejudice exist in virtually every community as well as within the mental health profession. Counselors are in an ideal situation to assist all of us as we come to a fuller understanding of sexual minorities and an appreciation for the unique contributions that gay men and lesbians make to enriching our culture.

The time for social action on behalf of gay men and lesbians is now. As the gay and lesbian community steps more fully into the light, this movement offers all of us the chance to participate in making our communities more inclusive and stronger because of our diversity. A rare opportunity exists today to further a movement that will make a difference in the way all of us live our lives. As more and more people become familiar with the unique needs of lesbian and gay people, the American spirit of fairness will lead most institutions to change their policies so that all persons are more equal. Get involved in the gay rights movement. Your life and that of others will be better because of your contribution.

REFERENCES

American Academy of Pediatrics. (1994). Homosexuality and adolescence. *Pediatrics, 92,* 631.

American Psychiatric Association. (1993). *Gay and lesbian fact sheet.* Washington, DC: American Psychiatric Association.

American Psychological Association. (1997). *A statement on the effectiveness of reparative therapy for homosexuals.* Washington, DC: American Psychological Association.

Barret, R., & Barzan, R. (1996). Spiritual experiences of gay men and lesbians. *Counseling and Values, 41*(1), 4-15.

Barret, R. L., & Robinson, B. E. (1990). Gay fathers. Boston: Lexington Books.

Clark, D. (1995). *Loving someone gay.* Berkeley, CA: Celestial Arts.

Dworkin, S., & Gutierrez, F. (1992). *Counseling gay men and lesbians: Journey to the end of the rainbow.* Alexandria, VA: American Association for Counseling and Development.

Edwards, R. (1996). Can sexual orientation change with therapy? *APA Monitor, 27*(9), 49.

Fassinger, R.E. (1991). The hidden minority: Issues and challenges in working with lesbian women and gay men. *The Counseling Psychologist, 19,* 151-176.

Frommer, M.S. (1994). Homosexuality and psychoanalysis: Technical considerations revisited. *Psychoanalytic Dialogues, 4,* 215-233.

Garnets, L., Hancock, K. A., Cochran, S. D., Goodchilds, J., & Peplau, L. A. (1991). Issues in psychotherapy with lesbians and gay men: A survey of psychologists. *American Psychologist, 46,* 964-972.

Greene, B. (1997). *Ethnic and cultural diversity among lesbians and gay men.* Thousand Oaks, CA: Sage.

Isay, R. A. (1989). *Being homosexual: Gay men and their development.* New York: Avon Books.

Lambda wins Nobozny case. (1997, Fall/Winter). *The Lambda Update, 14*(1), 1-2.

Logan, C. (1996). Homophobia? No. Homo-prejudice. Yes. *Journal of Homosexuality, 31,* 31-53.

Marcus, E. (1992). *Making history: The struggle for gay and lesbian equal rights, 1945-1990.* New York: Harper Collins.

Marcus, E. (1993). *Is it a choice?* San Francisco: Harper San Francisco.

Martin, A. (1982). Some issues in treatment of gay and lesbian patients. *Psychotherapy: Theory, Research, and Practice, 19,* 341-348.

McHenry, S. S., & Johnson, J. W. (1993). Homophobia in the therapist and gay or lesbian client: Conscious and unconscious collusion in self-hate. *Psychotherapy: Theory, Research, and Practice, 30*(1), 141-151.

National Association of Social Workers. (1992). Position Statement: "Reparative" or "conversion" therapies for lesbians and gay men. Washington, DC: National Association of Social Workers' National Committee on Lesbian and Gay Issues.

Voeller, B., & Walters, P. (1978). Gay fathers. *The Family Coordinator, 27,* 149-157.

6

Addressing the Needs of At-Risk Youth: Early Prevention and Systemic Intervention

David Capuzzi

As the number of children and adolescents who engage in at-risk behaviors (e.g., abuse of alcohol and other drugs, unprotected sex, abnormal eating patterns, suicide attempts, gang membership) increases and as the likelihood of exposure to adverse environmental factors escalates (e.g., physical and sexual abuse, homelessness, violence), more and more youth are experiencing physical, behavioral, and emotional impairments. Because the impairments that youth experience can persist and increase in severity across the life span, the importance of early prevention and intervention efforts has increased in significance (Capuzzi & Gross, 1996). Robert Conyne (1994) drew attention to the importance of early prevention by offering examples of some of the issues and trends that are occurring in the United States:

- There are at least 20 million illiterate adults.
- About 19% of the population have been diagnosed as experiencing some type of mental illness or emotional disturbance.
- Nearly 25% of the students enrolled in K-12 settings drop out each year.
- AIDS has become one of the leading causes of death among the 15 to 24 year age group.
- Each year 5,000 infants are born with fetal alcohol syndrome.
- Adolescent suicide ranks second or third in most reports of the leading causes of death in the 11 to 24 year age group.
- About 50% of first-time marriages end in divorce.
- From 50% to 75% of child mental health referrals are for children affected by divorce.

- About 18.5 million Americans abuse alcohol, and over 100,000 alcohol-related deaths occur each year.
- Between 3 and 4 million women are physically assaulted by intimate male partners each year.

As noted by Horner and McElhaney (1993), the cost associated with these examples is staggering, with $273 billion spent in 1990 in treatment and social services for individuals involved in alcohol and drug abuse or experiencing mental illness. These dollar amounts do not include costs associated with, for example, teenage pregnancy, AIDS, eating disorders, suicide, homelessness, and school dropout. When such additional problems are taken into consideration, the estimated costs increase to incomprehensible levels. As imposing as these dollar amounts are (Capuzzi & Gross, 1996), they do not include the immeasurable costs associated with the loss, suffering, and grief of the family members and friends of vulnerable children, adolescents, and adults. The supply of counselors, social workers, psychiatric nurses, psychologists, and psychiatrists is swamped in the wake of the need for counseling and therapy (Conyne, 1994). Policies connected with managed care and understaffing of social service agencies further complicate the problems experienced by children, adolescents, and adults in need of assistance from licensed professional counselors and other helping professionals (Capuzzi & Gross, 1996). Given these facts and circumstances, early prevention and systemic intervention are of paramount importance.

Early prevention and systemic interventions are, however, based upon a different approach to helping than that associated with prevalent diagnostic/prescriptive approaches. Prevention and systemic intervention are not focused entirely on dysfunction and remediation; rather, they emphasize proactive approaches designed to empower the individual, change systemic variables, and forestall the emergence of dysfunction.

This chapter focuses first on early prevention efforts by listing the defining qualities of prevention and providing examples of prevention programming, such as developing life skills, enhancing interpersonal communication, learning strategies for cognitive change, achieving self-management and self-control, and coping with stress.

The chapter then explores systemic intervention efforts by describing impeding factors and presenting examples of systemic interventions, such as integrated service centers, partnerships, and accelerated schools. After a brief discussion of secondary and tertiary prevention, the chapter concludes with additional recommendations for actions and strategies to address the needs of at-risk youth more successfully.

EARLY PREVENTION EFFORTS

Because counselors and other mental health professionals may or may not have had the opportunity to work in settings that emphasized prevention efforts, it is important to describe the defining qualities of prevention. Conyne (1994), Gilliland and James (1993), and Janosik (1984) defined prevention efforts as focused on averting human dysfunction and promoting healthy functioning. The emphasis is on enhancing optimal functioning and well-being and on the development of competencies. This approach differs significantly from the identification and diagnosis of disorders and maladaptive behavioral patterns and the provision of treatment to lessen impairment.

THE DEFINING QUALITIES OF PREVENTION

Prevention efforts can be defined as follows:

1. *Prevention efforts are proactive.* Prevention initiatives address individual and systemic strengths and further develop these strengths so that future dysfunction either does not develop or does not occur at a level that could lead to impairment. The key word is *initiatives.* Prevention efforts are based on taking initiative—which contrasts with reactive approaches designed to intervene after problems have developed to the point that functioning is impaired.

2. *Prevention efforts focus on functional people and those who are at risk.* Prevention services, such as those offered by school counselors and child therapists, focus on those who are healthy and coping well so that strengths can be identified and enhanced and additional skills can be learned. Although prevention efforts are also directed to those known to be at risk, such

as children of divorce or children of alcoholics, they are not limited to such populations. The purpose is to provide proactive efforts across the population being served so that future difficulties are avoided.

3. *Prevention efforts are cumulative and transferable.* When counselors assist others through prevention, clients' interpersonal development and their hierarchy of skills are enhanced. Elementary children, for example, who have participated in groups designed to enhance self-esteem may, at a later date, feel good enough about themselves to learn about becoming more assertive. The ability to use assertive behavior may be the key to refusing drugs or resisting pressure to join a gang; these same behaviors may prevent an individual from being victimized in some other situation.

4. *Prevention efforts are used to reduce incidence.* Prevention efforts are put in place before problems develop that could lead to at-risk behaviors (e.g., drinking, truancy, stealing). They might also be used to reduce the incidence of a new dysfunction (e.g., depression in response to change).

5. *Prevention efforts promote peer helping.* When elementary, middle school, and high school youth learn to improve communication ability, assertive behavior, problem solving, decision making, and other related abilities, they are also better able to participate in supervised peer-helper programs. There are many instances in which the power of a peer member group outdistances that of a concerned adult, especially when it is important to direct a youth to seek professional assistance or to provide needed encouragement and support.

6. *Prevention efforts can be group based, population based, or individually based.* Many prevention efforts are focused upon at-risk populations (e.g., information and discussion about the HIV virus or hepatitis B may be shared with sexually active adolescents, or victims of abuse may be counseled so that they do not develop lifelong dysfunctional patterns). Prevention efforts may be entirely focused on an individual so that depression can be overcome or suicidal preoccupation can be eliminated. The point to keep in mind, however, is that when larger

populations are reached, it is possible to impact the lives of larger numbers of people.

7. *Prevention efforts can be used early in the life span.* Because we know that children who are homeless or who have been physically or sexually abused may develop traits and self-concepts that put them at risk during adolescence and adulthood, early prevention is essential. Prevention efforts that effect changes in self-esteem, behavior, feelings, and thinking are essential so that these children are not at risk for substance abuse, prostitution, depression, suicide, or battering.

8. *Prevention efforts target more than a single system.* Each of us must simultaneously interact in a variety of environments (family, school, community). Practitioners do not emphasize or focus efforts in one system to the exclusion of others. Functional individuals must learn to cope with the demands of several systems on a daily basis.

9. *Prevention efforts are sensitive to the demands of diverse populations.* It is unlikely that a single constellation of services or any one approach to prevention can make an equal impact on all groups. Diverse populations present unique challenges and demand a thorough understanding of cross-cultural and multicultural differences. What one population may find to be acceptable prevention programming may be intolerable to another. Counselors must be sensitive to the needs and traditions of diverse populations if they are to be successful with early prevention efforts.

10. *Prevention efforts are collaborative.* Prevention efforts can be complex and must be conducted in collaboration with professionals from a number of disciplines. For example, a school counselor working with a depressed adolescent may need the assistance of a psychiatrist, a nurse practitioner, or a nutritionist if medication is needed, or if diet must be addressed to control a chronic pattern of depression. Often the expertise required to assist an individual, a family, or a larger population may require input and teaming—as well as case management— involving professionals from several disciplines.

11. *Prevention efforts are applicable in more than one context.* Faculty and staff in a school setting, for example, may be able to apply

the principles of prevention to develop a crisis management plan for violent behavior, to another problem, or to an at-risk population. The planning process that is followed in implementing early prevention for problematic eating behaviors might also be applied to work with middle-school students susceptible to gang membership or drug abuse.

12. *Prevention efforts are empowering.* Empowerment should be the primary goal of all prevention efforts. This empowerment should apply not only to recipients of prevention efforts but also to the provider of prevention services. When individuals who receive assistance build on strengths and develop new coping skills, they feel better about themselves and their ability to make good decisions, and they lead a healthy lifestyle. When professionals increase their effectiveness and their ability to enhance the lives of others, they also feel productive, competent, and capable of helping individuals or systems change.

EXAMPLES OF EARLY PREVENTION EFFORT

Early prevention (often referred to as primary prevention) should be focused upon helping youth enhance their ability to communicate, problem solve, and manage stress, so that they do not make decisions or engage in behaviors that place them at risk sometime in the future. Counselors in all settings need to advocate for opportunities to spend time with young people in ways that help children develop the ability to function at an optimal level. (The human and economic costs of not doing so are addressed at the beginning of this chapter.) A number of experts in contemporary prevention strategies (Hadge, 1992; Janosik, 1984; McWhirter, McWhirter, McWhirter, & McWhirter, 1993; Roberts, 1991) have identified and described some early prevention efforts that should be extended to all children and adolescents. Examples provided by McWhirter et al. (1993) include developing life skills, enhancing interpersonal communication, learning strategies for cognitive change, achieving self-management and self-control, and coping with stress.

Developing Life Skills

Life skills can be defined as the ability to make use of personal resources for the purpose of expressing needs and constructively influencing the environment (Capuzzi & Gross, 1996). Such skills can influence the development of relationships and friendships, nonviolent conflict resolution, and the ability to talk with adults. Developing these life skills can be accomplished through education and training in life skills, school peer mediation, peer tutoring, and peer facilitation.

Education and training in life skills involves developing and incorporating modules into the curriculum at elementary, middle, and high school levels. Heavy emphasis should be placed at the elementary level. Such modules could be developed, and even taught, collaboratively by counselors, nurses, physicians, teachers, social workers, psychologists, and physical educators. The format for teaching any targeted skill should contain the following components: teach, model, role-play, provide feedback, and assign homework. Almost any skill (e.g., assertiveness) can be taught within this framework, and the fact that it is implemented within the classroom means that entire populations can be reached so that more and more young people can master the skills needed to avoid problems or involvement in at-risk behaviors.

School peer mediation, peer tutoring, and peer facilitation all involve teaching and supervising students to handle interpersonal helping. School peer mediation involves teaching peer mediators to work with other students so as to facilitate problem solving between disputing students. Peer tutors are students who teach other students in both formal and informal learning situations. Peer tutoring can provide a cost-effective way to meet individual needs, develop ownership of the value of education, and enhance self-esteem and motivation. Peer facilitation, sometimes called *peer helping*, is a process in which students are taught to listen, paraphrase, support, and provide feedback to other students. Peer facilitation is an effective way to empower children and adolescents and to provide adjunct support to the professional counselor.

Enhancing Interpersonal Communication

Interpersonal communication skills are primary factors in the development of mutually beneficial relationships. Programs developed to enhance interpersonal communication skills usually offer training in verbal and nonverbal communication, creation of constructive friendships, avoidance of misunderstanding and development of long-term relationships (McWhirter et al., 1993). Lack of ability to communicate well with others can lead to lowered self-esteem, isolation, and the development of future at-risk behaviors; enhancing interpersonal communications skills provides an excellent early intervention or primary prevention focus.

Learning Strategies for Cognitive Change

Because cognition mediates both behavior and affect, cognitive restructuring can be an effective early or primary prevention strategy. All children and adolescents have the potential to problem solve. As noted by McWhirter et al. (1993), there are times when the emotional components of a problem, the egocentric focus associated with the earlier years of life, and the lack of experience with systematic problem solving throw up barriers to effective decision making. Both school and agency counselors can teach children and adolescents the steps of effective problem solving and decision making. Their process enhances self-esteem and feelings of empowerment. McWhirter et al. suggested that the following components be taught:

1. *Define the problem*. The problem is defined as clearly as possible and is stated as a goal to be achieved. The goal is assessed: Does it meet the underlying needs? If it is attained, does it help the individual achieve satisfaction?
2. *Examine variables*. The specifics of the total situation are examined. Background issues and environmental factors are considered, and it may be necessary to gather and appraise additional information. It is particularly important to identify feelings and thoughts at this stage. Often earlier maladaptive responses must be modified. In both this step and step 1, questions and suggestions from other students in the classroom or the group are useful.
3. *Consider alternatives*. Various means of solving the problem are considered. The strengths and weaknesses of each possibility are evaluated. Again, the teacher or counselor may call for brainstorming to generate ideas from other students about alternatives and strategies.
4. *Isolate a plan*. The alternatives are gradually narrowed down until what seems like the best response or solution remains. A plan

for carrying out this alternative is prepared, and the potential consequences are considered in more detail.

5. *Do action steps.* After a plan is decided upon, action must be taken to implement it. Thus youth are systematically encouraged to follow through on the necessary steps to carry out their plan. They perform the behaviors that make up the solution plan.

6. *Evaluate effects.* Finally, youth need to evaluate the effectiveness of the solution. Teaching them to look for the effects of their thoughts and feelings is important. They analyze and evaluate the outcome, review the decision, and, if necessary, develop another plan to achieve their goal. (pp. 276-277)

Achieving Self-Management and Self-Control

Self-management means that self-control has been achieved and implies that individuals can develop the ability to control thoughts, feelings, and behavior. Teaching self-management and self-control involves teaching children and adolescents self-assessment, self-monitoring, and self-reinforcement. Self-assessment means that the child or adolescent learns to evaluate his or her behaviors against a personally meaningful standard in order to determine whether the behavior is adequate. Self-monitoring requires that the child or adolescent observe and record his or her own behavior. Record keeping may involve recording the contingencies in the environment prior to and immediately following the behavior. Self-reinforcement involves applying one's own consequences for a given behavior (e.g., self-praise, spending time in an enjoyable way, buying something of significance). Usually children and adolescents who master the techniques of self-management and self-control feel energized, motivated, and positive about themselves.

Coping With Stress

Because there are so many potential stressors encountered by each of us on a day-to-day basis, *coping with stress* is a particularly significant phrase in today's society. It behooves the adults in our society to teach children and adolescents as much as possible about stress and stress management. Numerous models, especially those that emphasize primary prevention programs that focus on identifying stressors and managing stress, can be developed for use by school and agency counselors. For an overview of the topic, ideas for primary prevention, and pertinent additional reading on the topic, see "Stress and Coping in Today's Society" (Miars, 1996).

SYSTEMIC INTERVENTION EFFORTS

The systemic approach focuses on changing the "system" to meet the needs of at-risk youth, instead of changing the individuals to meet the needs or requirements of the system. Kushman and Heariold-Kinney (1996) provided excellent examples of systemic intervention efforts as related to schools. Because high levels of commitment from the community, the school boards, the superintendent, principals, staff, parents, and students are required for the systemic approach to work, many schools and school districts are reticent to analyze and then change systemic elements that do not meet the needs of children and adolescents and escalate the probability of at-risk behaviors.

IMPEDING FACTORS

As noted by Kushman and Heariold-Kinney (1996), a number of factors within the school can impede student success and serve as obstructions for at-risk youth. One such factor has to do with the organizational structure of a school. Many urban schools, for example, are too large. Students who attend large schools with large classes often feel overwhelmed and may have little opportunity to experience the acceptance and involvement they need. (This may be especially crucial during transition periods such as moving from elementary to middle school or middle school to high school.) School hours are another aspect of organizational structure that can make it difficult for at-risk students who have to work as well as attend school. Because school hours are usually scheduled from about 8 a.m. until 3 p.m., there is little flexibility for students who must work. Class scheduling can also be problematic when set up in periods of approximately 50 minutes. Students are usually expected to learn concepts and make applications during this time frame. For some learners, this system works; for other students, it is problematic because before concepts can be understood, the students must rush to the next class during which there may be little or no connection or integration between subjects.

Procedural practices in schools may also impede student progress and constitute systemic barriers to student success. As noted by Kushman and Heariold-Kinney (1996), procedural practices are those practices and policies established to ensure that the school runs smoothly and that students, faculty, and staff are safe. At times, however, rules interfere with the education of youth. For example, it makes little sense to suspend a student who is skipping school or to give a failing grade to a student who for some understandable reason is having difficulty with a specific subject. The disciplinary actions do not solve the problems. Such rules not only fail to help a student but also convey the message that the adults do not care if the student does not succeed. There should be consequences for not following school rules, but rules should not be designed to interfere with educating a student. Usually, at-risk youth are the youth who suffer the most from policies regarding attendance, tardiness, and dress codes.

Instructional strategies and practice are also factors within the system that may negatively impact at-risk youth. Students vary in the way they learn. A curriculum that is designed to fit a single teaching style can be detrimental to many students, including those who are at risk. For example, a curriculum based on seat time rather than competence can be a barrier for those who work at faster or slower rates than time blocks provide. In addition, a curriculum that is meaningless for and disconnected from the student's out-of-school life can result in both boredom and disengagement. Some of the brightest at-risk students have dropped out of school due to boredom and lack of challenge.

In addition to changing within-school factors, the systemic approach challenges schools to consider the community as an asset instead of a potential problem and to "partner" with parents, businesses, and other community stakeholders. The goal is to cultivate partnerships with parents and the community as a whole because individuals in parental and community roles have a vested interest in students' success. These partnerships often take the form of parent involvement programs, school-business compacts, and restructured schools that give parents more of a presence in decisions regarding discipline, scheduling, curriculum instruction, and other areas that directly affect students.

EXAMPLES OF SYSTEMIC INTERVENTION EFFORTS

The Integrated Service Center Model

Some schools have experimented with becoming integrated service centers in which the school itself houses all services so that these services are readily accessible. In such centers, students not only receive their education but also have direct access to counseling and family services. Such schools attempt to eliminate the turf issues and red tape that often result when schools try to work with outside service agencies.

The Partnership Model

Several school reform models for at-risk students stress the idea of developing a partnership between the school and the community it serves. One such partnership is James Comer's School Development Program (Comer, 1980, 1988). The model focuses on being responsive to the child-development and relationship needs of poor and minority students that are usually not well addressed by schools and that can impede academic progress. This model stresses the importance of applying child-development principles to school decisions that are rendered on a collaborative basis by school faculty and staff and parents. (The school is also governed by a school planning and management team comprised of faculty, staff, and parents.) Another unique feature of this model is that the management team works closely with a mental health team that consists of a counselor, special educator, social worker, and psychologist. Because of this structure, mental health and child development experts are centrally involved in school matters rather than being relegated to the periphery in the decision-making process. This is a very promising model for systemic intervention on behalf of at-risk youth because it illustrates how counselors, teachers, administrators, and parents can work together in a partnership. This model makes it less likely that one group will blame another group when youth do not succeed; everyone becomes responsible for helping youth develop a success identity.

The Accelerated Schools Model

Another model for at-risk youth that is being implemented in many elementary and middle schools around the United States is Henry Levin's Accelerated Schools (Levin, 1987). At the core of Levin's model is the idea that students can be encouraged and empowered by building on their strengths. At-risk youth are viewed as having strengths, such as life experiences, culture, language, and leaning styles, and upon which a school can develop and plan its curricular and instructional programs. This model also stresses greater parent involvement, the empowerment of school faculty and staff and parents in school decision making, and the school's responsibility for accelerating the learning of all students. Again, the idea is to view the school community in broader terms than just faculty and staff and to involve parents and other community members in meaningful ways.

WHEN MORE THAN EARLY PREVENTION AND SYSTEMIC INTERVENTION ARE NECESSARY

Even the most competent and committed professionals may not succeed through the use of early or primary prevention efforts and systemic restructuring. Often, this is because prevention efforts or systemic changes were initiated when much of a school population had already reached early or middle adolescence or because there was an influx of young people who were already engaging in behaviors that placed them at risk. Although the focus of this chapter does not include secondary or tertiary prevention, these topics need to be briefly addressed because they are pertinent to successful efforts with at-risk youth.

Secondary prevention consists of intervention with individuals who are already in crisis for the purpose of restoring equilibrium as soon as possible and reducing the impact of the stress connected with a crisis situation. During a period of crisis, individuals are aware that the situation is out of control; they often feel helpless. Unless secondary prevention is made available, a crisis can escalate to the point at which it may be difficult to contain, and thus lead to irreversible consequences. For example, an adolescent at risk for suicide who does not obtain assistance may attempt suicide, survive, and then be left with a lifelong physical impairment as well as the emotional turmoil overlying the traits and characteristics precipitating the suicidal crisis in the first place.

Tertiary prevention attempts to reduce the amount of residual impairment that follows the resolution of a crisis. For example, adolescents who complete residential or outpatient programs for substance abuse may benefit through participation in weekly support groups for the purpose of providing the reinforcement and affirmation needed to prevent relapse. These same adolescents may also need to be concurrently involved in individual counseling or therapy to address the unmet needs that led to the use and abuse of a substance (emotional development and coping skills are usually arrested at about the age at which substance use began). Victims of sexual abuse may participate in either group or individual counseling or therapy long after the abuse has ceased for the purpose of repairing damaged self-esteem and rebuilding the capacity to trust and share intimacy with significant others.

The major implications of this discussion of secondary and tertiary prevention are that no matter how much early (primary) prevention and systemic intervention has been accomplished, professionals working with at-risk youth must be fully prepared to deliver crisis-management (secondary prevention) and post crisis (tertiary prevention) programs and services. Their secondary and tertiary efforts help complete the comprehensive constellation of services required to address the needs of youth at risk.

RECOMMENDED ACTIONS AND STRATEGIES

In addition to the actions and strategies discussed and described earlier in this chapter, there are additional steps that can be taken by counselor educators, the American Counseling Association, individuals connected with education in K-12 settings, and practicing counselors. Suggested steps include the following:

- **For the counselor educators:** One of the ways to change how counselors address the needs of youth at risk is to integrate a knowledge and skills base into counseling programs that will prepare counselors to work as effectively as possible with vulnerable young people. This will entail escalating student counselors' awareness of the diverse cultures in which many youth at risk must function so that the importance of early or primary prevention and systemic intervention can be more readily understood. Counselors will need to be thoroughly grounded in the principles and techniques of prevention and systemic change and have the self-esteem and advocacy skills to implement these changes. As noted earlier, there are going to be times when secondary prevention (crisis management) and tertiary prevention (postvention after a crisis has occurred) need to be implemented; therefore, counselors need to be trained to do both developmental counseling and preventive program planning as well as diagnosis and treatment planning. (This treatment planning may pertain to the individual and/or the system in which the individual must function.) Preparing counselors to be either developmentally/preventively focused or diagnostic/prescriptive focused will not equip practitioners to function effectively; a comprehensive knowledge and skills base must be delivered via every counselor education program in the country.

- **For the American Counseling Association:** The American Counseling Association must assume a leadership role and provide the position statements, publications, and training needed by members of the counseling profession to serve at-risk youth. When the American Counseling Association was founded in 1952 (then called the American Personnel and Guidance Association), the intention of the four organizations that joined together to form a larger, more powerful association was to provide the initiatives and leadership to help counselors provide a high standard of care. The impact a professional association can have on an entire profession is tremendous. During the last two decades, the focus of some of the leaders of the association has shifted from interest in increasing the expertise of the professional counselor to one centered on name changes, bylaw revisions, and internal organizational structure. Although all organizations or associations must change as the needs of society change, and hence the needs of the members who comprise the association, it behooves our association to get back to its roots and to focus on helping members meet the changing needs of those who comprise our schools and communities.

- **For education and counseling in K-12 settings:** Reform in education is being discussed and acted upon in schools and communities across the country. It is of paramount importance that the role of the counselor in K-12 settings undergoes a corresponding transformative change. Many school counselors are engaged in preventive work, systemic change, and collaboration with parents and other community members. By the same token, many school counselors are attempting to function in school counseling or guidance departments that hearken back to the 1950s and early 1960s and that do not address the needs of the youth of today. This transformative process will not take place unless administrators, teachers, parents, and other members of the community outside the school are involved. Many counselors either do not see themselves as empowered enough to engage in broad-based prevention and systemic change or do not have the skills to do so. Counselor educators and the American Counseling Association have much to do in this regard.

- **For practicing counselors:** The profession of counseling and human development and the needs of clients who come to professional counselors for assistance have changed dramatically during the past 10 years. There are many counselors, in a variety of settings, who have kept up with the changes in the profession and in the clients they serve. There are also counselors who completed coursework and degree requirements 10, 20, or 30 years ago who do not attend continuing education seminars and workshops, who do not pursue postmasters and postdoctoral coursework or training opportunities, and who do not keep up with new publications connected with their specialization or practice setting. Members of the profession should do everything possible to encourage colleagues to pursue education and training experiences and to arrange for supervision on a regular basis.

CONCLUSION

Addressing the needs of at-risk youth requires members of the profession to place more emphasis on early prevention and systemic intervention. Prevention and systemic intervention are not focused entirely on dysfunction and remediation; they are focused on proactive approaches designed to empower the individual, change systemic variables, and forestall the emergence of dysfunction. Because counseling and other mental health professionals may not have had the opportunity to work in settings in which their role responsibilities focused on prevention and systemic intervention, it is important to heighten awareness of the qualities of prevention programming and of the aspects of systemic intervention efforts. Examples of early or primary intervention efforts and strategies include life skills training, the development of interpersonal communication skills, learning strategies for cognitive change, enhancing self-management and self-control, and increasing ability to cope with stress. Examples of systemic intervention efforts and strategies include school/community reform initiatives such as the integrated service center model, the partnership model, and the accelerated schools model. When counselors discover that youth need more assistance than that already provided through early prevention and systemic intervention, they must also be prepared to engage in secondary prevention (crisis management) and tertiary intervention (postvention after a crisis has occurred).

In addition to strategies that can be employed in conjunction with early prevention and systemic interventions, counselor educators, the American Counseling Association, educators and counselors in K-12 settings, and practicing counselors who completed degree requirements in the past can implement proactive change efforts on behalf of youth at risk.

Counselors and other mental health professionals must begin delivering a new constellation of services designed to empower and equip young people to cope in a complex society. The cost of remedial services and the toll connected with grief, loss, and life-long impairment are too great to ignore. Counselors must also learn to see themselves as change agents and advocates; they must develop the knowledge and skills base to precipitate systemic change effectively.

REFERENCES

Capuzzi, D., & Gross, D. (Eds.). (1996). *Youth at risk: A prevention resource for counselors, teachers, and parents* (2nd ed.). Alexandria, VA: American Counseling Association.

Comer, J. P. (1980). *School power.* New York: Free Press.

Comer, J. P. (1988). Educating poor and minority children. *Scientific American, 259*(5), 28-34.

Conyne, R. K. (1994). Preventive counseling. *Counseling and Human Development, 27*(1), 1-10.

Gilliland, B. E., & James, R. K. (1993). *Crisis intervention strategies.* Pacific Grove, CA: Brooks/Cole.

Hadge, C. (1992). *School-based prevention and intervention programs: Clearinghouse fact sheet* (Report No. CG025631). Piscataway, NJ: Center of Alcohol Studies, Rutgers University. (ERIC Document Reproduction Service No. ED 372329).

Horner, J., & McElhaney, S. (1993). Building forces. *American Counselor, 2*, 17-21, 30.

Janosik, E. H. (1984). *Crisis counseling: A contemporary approach.* Monterey, CA: Wadsworth Health Sciences.

Kushman, J. W., & Heariold-Kinney, P. (1996). *Understanding and preventing school dropout.* In D. Cappuzzi & D. Gross (Eds.), *Youth at-risk: A prevention resource for counselors, teachers, and parents* (2nd ed., pp. 353-381). Alexandria, VA: American Counseling Association.

Levin, H. M. (1987). Accelerated schools for disadvantaged students, *Educational Leadership, 44*(6), 19-21.

McWhirter, J. J., McWhirter, B. T., McWhirter, A. M., & McWhirter, E. H. (1993). *At-risk youth: A comprehensive response.* Pacific Grove, CA: Brooks/Cole.

Miars, R. (1996). Stress and coping in today's society. In D. Capuzzi & D. Gross (Eds.), *Youth at-risk: A prevention resource for counselors, teachers, and parents* (2nd ed., pp. 129-147). Alexandria, VA: American Counseling Association.

Roberts, A. R. (Ed.). (1991). *Contemporary perspectives on crisis intervention and prevention.* Englewood Cliffs, NJ: Center of Alcohol Studies, Rutgers University.

7

Career: Social Action in Behalf of Purpose, Productivity, and Hope

EDWIN L. HERR AND SPENCER G. NILES

The call for counselors to engage in social action on behalf of various client populations has long been part of the mission and bylaws of the American Counseling Association and its predecessors. Indeed, professional counselors representing the American Counseling Association and its divisions have testified before the United States Congress and various state legislatures in support of legislation and funding directed at the elimination of child abuse, violence in schools, and chemical dependence. Likewise, they have testified in support of (a) greater student aid and career services in higher education, (b) more comprehensive forms of career guidance, (c) accessible and high-quality mental health services and counselor licensure, (d) and better education, counseling, and health services for migrant children, immigrants, and minority populations. These examples suggest that counselors, as members of professional organization committees on government relations or human affairs or task forces on professional counseling issues (e.g., counselor licensure), do participate effectively in social action. Counselors do serve as advocates for, or give voice to, client needs—especially those clients who have little political capital or who have no forum in which to speak for themselves.

Outside of the professional organizational context, however, there is little evidence or literature that suggests that individual counselors envision, articulate, or perform their role as a form of social action. Even though articles in the professional literature periodically challenge the counselor to be a change agent, to be a conscience of educational or institutional policy, and/or to be an advocate for clients (all roles directed at the client's environment), the reality seems to be that counselors are trained primarily to provide direct service to individual students or adult clients, not to consult about and otherwise work to transform their clients' environment. Like all generalizations, this one has exceptions that occur as counselors in different specialties and settings discharge their responsibilities. But aside from such examples as school counselors who provide parent effectiveness training and who consult directly with teachers on positive classroom climates for children, rehabilitation counselors who work with employers on job design tailored to the specific needs of a person with disabilities, marriage and family counselors who work with the family unit as a system of interacting parts that need to be helped to communicate and interact more effectively and with more respect, or the career counselor who works with middle managers or employers to help them to be more responsive to the career development needs of their employees, most counselors work with individual clients, not their environments. In this sense, counselors see their role as focused on individual change, not social action; as assisting persons to clarify their beliefs about their options and their environments; as helping clients adopt actions by which to cope more effectively with the expectations or requirements imposed upon them by the environment, whether the environment at issue is the family, the school, or the workplace. These are important functions, but without a sense of how they interact with social action, they may be incomplete.

This chapter, before turning to the more specific example of social action in the area of career development of students or adult clients, first explores further the concept of social action per se. The chapter then considers how the application of career counseling and career guidance can be seen in relation to social action in the contexts of the school-to-work transition, induction and adjustment of the worker in the workplace, and unemployment. The chapter concludes with a discussion of activities and arenas for social action, such as social policy and legislation, the career counseling process, and counselor training programs.

SOCIAL ACTION

At a rather fundamental level, the rationale for social action implies that neither counselors, nor the problems people bring to counselors, exist in a vacuum.

The content of counseling, the dilemmas people experience, and the substance of the problems with which they have to cope do not typically arise without external triggering events. In large measure, the personal questions for which people seek help are really functions of how they view current social or occupational expectations and opportunities for personal choice, achievement, social interaction, self-initiative, prestige, role differentiation, autonomy, and many other matters. The resulting anxieties, information deficits, or indecisiveness people experience is the content that concerns counselors and related professionals. (Herr, 1989, p. 3)

Such a view suggests that to understand human behavior and the potential, indeed the importance, of counseling as an intervention in human behavior is to acknowledge that people live, negotiate their identity, and activate their behavior in response to specific social, cultural, political, and economic environments. Such environments exert influences, positive or negative; apply limits, restrictive or wide-ranging; offer information, minimally or comprehensively; and provide opportunities, open or closed, with which people transact their individual behavior. Such environments are not static. They are constantly changing, in subtle or dramatic ways, and individuals are under constant pressure to receive, interpret, and act upon messages, covert or overt, related to their personal behavior, self-efficacy, and worthiness. Sometimes persons react to these influences with purposefulness and productivity; at other times, they react with irrational beliefs, or violence, or chemical dependency, or with anxiety and depression.

Thus, in thinking of the counselor's role in relation to social action, several emphases emerge. One is that in virtually all counseling the focus of intervention is both on intrapsychic and interpsychic issues. The individual's psychological resources, skills, and maturity—as well as such issues as support systems; quality of interactions with others in the individual's environments; and the conflicts and barriers that have arisen for the individual in the family, the school, the workplace, in social relationships, and in the beliefs and actions about these that the individual client has developed—are all examined.

A second emphasis has to do with the question of counseling goals and interventions in relation to both the individual client and his or her transactions with the environment. Most problems a client brings to a counselor are multidimensional. In this sense, it is unlikely that one intervention alone will resolve the client's problems. For example, clients may have problems of poor self-efficacy and irrational beliefs that require individual counseling; but clients also may have problems of loneliness, child care concerns, financial problems, and a lack of information, which may require referral, securing information from community sources, and, indeed, social action to create or identify a relevant support group or network of child care providers among persons who share mutual needs for such provisions. Within such contexts, social action by the counselor may not be as dramatic as influencing some form of national policy; it may mean being creative at the local level to stimulate the development of opportunities and support systems, or perhaps taking a role in heightening sensitivity to individual needs in the school, the workplace and the community, a role that ultimately will make the client's environment more mentally healthy and affirming.

A third emphasis is that in both historical and contemporary terms, the existence of counseling is a function of sanctioned social action. Counseling in the schools and in community settings arose at the end of the 19th century because of the dynamics in the society associated with a major transition from an agricultural to an industrial society. As large numbers of people sought better economic and personal opportunities, the industrializing of the United States was fed by massive immigration from abroad and a large migration from the farms to the cities. These patterns of population movement created questions on how to distribute persons among the rapidly diversifying occupational structure, how to provide adequate education for children, and how to reduce the number of young children working many hours in the mines and factories of the nation as well as on how to bridge the gap between the school and the realities of the adult world. Parallel to these economic motives for the rise of counseling were those concerned with the rising concern for human rights. At the beginning of the 20th century, the social reformers, the settlement house workers, and others working with the poor, the displaced, and the immigrant populations of the country were making strong efforts to have these persons and, indeed, the entire working population be viewed not as chattels of industry but as persons of dignity with a right to determine their own destinies. Out of this mix of economic, educational, and human rights issues, counseling and, particularly, vocational guidance emerged as individualized responses to needs for social action. In this sense, for most of the last 100 years, whether or not it has been explicit, counseling and, in particular, career counseling and career guidance have become sociopolitical instruments, identified by legislation at the federal level, to deal with emerging social concerns such as equity and excellence in educational and occupational opportunities, unemployment, human capital development, persons with disabilities, child abuse, AIDS, teenage pregnancy, substance abuse, career decision making relative to the preparation for entrance into emerging skilled occupations, and the identification and encouragement of students with high academic potential to enter higher education in science and mathematics. These legislative initiatives—in which school, mental health, and rehabilitation counseling as well as career counseling or career guidance have been identified as either primary treatments of preference or vital elements of a program of interventions—have varied in their sources of social action: national defense, educational reform, economic development, support for equity and affirmative action, and human rights. In each of these instances, the support for the implementation of counseling as a mechanism designed to facilitate such national goals suggests that counseling in its various emphases is seen by federal policy and legislation as synonymous with social action.

CAREER COUNSELING AND CAREER GUIDANCE AS SOCIAL ACTION

Given the definitions of social action just described, it is useful to consider how the application of career counseling and career guidance in various contexts can be seen in terms of their implications for social action. In this section, three contexts are addressed: the school-to-work transition, induction and adjustment of the worker in the workplace, and reduction of unemployment.

The School-to-Work Transition

One of the most important recent national issues has been that of the school-to-work transition. As the United States has begun to come to terms with its place in the global economy, it has become more conscious of how other economic competitor nations prepare their students for the workplace and how they facilitate that transition. A number of national reports have addressed the issue in less than positive terms. For example, the Commission on Skills of the American Workforce (1991) stated that "the lack of any clear, direct connection between education and employment opportunities for most young people is one of the most devastating aspects of the existing system" (p. 72). Similarly, Berlin and Sum (1988), in a paper prepared for the Ford Foundation, in speaking about the United States, indicated that

> . . . we have the least well-articulated system of school-to-work transition in the industrialized world. Japanese students move directly into extensive company-based training programs, and European students often participate in closely interconnected schooling and apprenticeship training programs. . . . In Austria, Sweden, the former West Germany, and Switzerland, it is virtually impossible to leave school without moving into some form of apprenticeship or other vocational training. (p 1)

Furthermore, the Educational Testing Service (1990), in their important monograph, *From School-to-Work*, suggested that there are two difficult lifetime transition points: into the workforce for young people and out of the workforce for older people. In this perspective, the Education Testing Service goes on to state that

> the U. S. record in assisting these transitions is among the worst in the entire industrial world. . . . School counselors are overburdened and helping with job placement is low on their agenda. The U. S. Employment Service has virtually eliminated its school-based programs. Our society spends practically nothing to assist job successes among those who do not go directly to college. . . . Most developed countries have highly structured institutional arrangements to help young people make this transition; it is not a matter left to chance. West Germany does it through the

apprenticeship system, combining classroom work and on-the-job instruction. In Japan, the schools themselves select students for referrals to employers under agreements with employers. In other countries, there is either a strong employment counseling and job placement function within the school system or this function is carried out for the student by a labor market authority of some type, working cooperatively with the schools. (pp. 3, 22)

These reports each suggest that the issue of the school-to-work transition is a national problem that deserves social action by school counselors and others. To that end, in 1994 the U. S. Congress made the School-to-Work Opportunities Act a law of the land. The School-to-Work Opportunities Act provides for a school-based learning component, a work-based learning component, and a connecting activities component. The contributions of school counselors and their provision of career guidance and counseling are seen as major elements of the school-to-work transition, both in terms of the school-based learning and the connecting activities components. *Career guidance and counseling*, as the term is used in the Act, means programs that (a) pertain to subject matter and related techniques and methods organized for the development in individuals of local, state, and national occupational, educational, and labor market needs, trends, and opportunities; (b) assist individuals in making and implementing informed educational and occupational choices; and (c) aid students to develop career options with attention to surmounting gender, race, ethnicity, disability, language, or socioeconomic impediments to career options and encouraging careers in nontraditional employment. When the connecting activities component is examined, many activities in which school counselors have roles are revealed. Examples include

- matching students with work-based learning opportunities of employers;
- providing technical assistance and services to employers in designing school-based learning components and counseling and case management services;
- helping schools and employers integrate school-based and work-based learning and integrate academic and occupational learning into the program; and

- providing assistance to participants who have completed the program in finding an appropriate job, continuing their education, or entering into an additional training program as well as linking the participants with other community services that may be necessary to assure a successful transition from school to work.

Although there is much more to say about the counselor's role in the school-to-work transition and in implementing the provisions of the School-to-Work Opportunities Act, suffice it to say here that such counselor involvement clearly constitutes social action. Such a statement is true for several reasons. One is that the effective transition of high school graduates and other school leavers from the secondary school to successful placement in the workforce is a national goal. Without its achievement, the economic development of the nation in a highly competitive global environment will be diminished and the career development of young persons will be random; many young people will be figuratively set adrift at the conclusion of their high school experience, rather than having a seamless, systematic transition from school to work.

Another reason that the school-to-work transition constitutes social action for counselors is that its complexity belies the simple provision of individual career guidance, counseling, or assessment within the confines of the school. Rather, to achieve a positive school-to-work transition following the secondary school experience requires counselors to be in direct dialogue with employers and other community sources, to know the opportunity structure of the local community, to help bridge the language and content of the school and the workplace, and to provide technical assistance to employers so that they implement the types of induction, orientation, and on-the-job training programs that can integrate high school learners into the workplace with a minimum of stress and adjustment difficulty. In such roles, counselors can engage in the most positive social action as they promote and support the effective movement of students through this critical transition from the secondary school classroom to paid employment. In such roles, they can help teachers and school administrators take the instructional and curricular steps necessary to enhance the attitudes, knowledge, and skills of students preparing to enter the workplace, and they can work with employers to create more jobs that provide creative and challenging career ladders for the workforce. They can facilitate the sharing of information among government, industry, and schools to improve program planning and student choice. Such information stimulates employers and schools to work together to take a long view of education and training related to the creation and maintenance of a workforce that is flexible, teachable, and equipped with basic academic and vocational skills that allow students to be successfully employed in learning-intensive workplaces (Herr, 1995).

Induction and Adjustment of the Worker in the Workplace

Within the school, counselors may be the primary actors in working with students, school personnel, and teachers in creating an effective school-to-work transition process. The roots of these processes begin in elementary school as students begin to develop career awareness, and continue in junior high school and high school as they make informed choices about courses and curricula that stretch them and prepare them for entrance into the workforce or postsecondary education. School counselors have important roles at each of these educational levels—elementary, junior high, and senior high school—in working directly with students and in trying to facilitate positive school and work environments.

Counselors in community settings and in independent practice also offer their own forms of social action as reflected in the career counseling and career guidance they provide for persons with and without disabilities who must deal with the issues of induction and adjustment to the workplace and mobility within it. Further, these issues of purpose and productivity are issues of social action for counselors who are engaged in career counseling in business and industry, in private practice, in postsecondary institutions, and in diverse community settings. These counseling roles have to do with workforce development, and they may be implemented by counselors who provide direct services to employees, to employers, or both. When consulting with employees, the counselor's role in workforce development may have to do with the smoothness or jaggedness of individual career development—including the subset of issues that occurs as an individual anticipates, is inducted into, and progresses through the specific transitions required of persons in particular organizations. These are questions of person-situation fit as well as of employability skills. In these contexts, the focus of the interventions that counselors provide vary: they include assisting young workers to facilitate their induction and adjustment to work; helping plateaued workers to clarify their behavioral options in their current workplace or out of it as they consider career change; providing information and support to women who reenter the workforce or who are part of dual career families; coaching workers who select training and education programs; assisting workers to identify and progress through career ladders and career paths of interest to them; identifying referral sources for persons experiencing substance abuse problems; promoting physical and mental wellness among workers; conducting outplacement counseling; teaching seminars on retirement planning; and helping employees and their family members plan for geographic or international transfers.

Just as in the school-to-work transition, the counselor engaged in issues of workforce development, induction, and adjustment to work is also engaged in social action. He or she is dealing with issues of individual purpose and productivity that are vital to the national interest just as these issues are vital to individual feelings of self-efficacy, worth, and competence.

REDUCTION OF UNEMPLOYMENT

Perhaps the ultimate context in which counselors who practice career counseling engage in social action is in their role with those who experience unemployment. It is here that career development and mental health overlap; it is also here that individual action and social action come together. In such contexts, career counseling becomes a source of hope and empowerment for persons often undergoing a time of despair.

As research on unemployment, job stress, and work adjustment problems has grown over the past quarter century, it has become clear that worker distress about work is associated with a range of social and personal problems. As Millar (1992), director of the National Institute of Occupational Safety and Health, has reported, "there is no doubt that job-related stress and other psychological disorders are rapidly becoming one of the most pressing occupational safety and health problems in the country today" (p. 5). Job satisfaction is linked to a variety of important psychological constructs such as self-esteem, job involvement, work alienation, organizational commitment, morale, and life satisfaction; these linkages can be positive or negative depending upon whether or not there is job satisfaction. Dawis (1984) contended that job satisfaction has behavioral consequences. "On the positive side are tenure, longevity, physical health, mental health, and productivity; on the negative side, turnover, absenteeism, accidents, and mental health problems" (p. 289). Fundamental to the issues of social action inherent in the job satisfaction and job stress literature is the matter of person-job fit, its implications for individual commitment to work, and how counselors facilitate person-job fit through measures such as individual counseling and assessment as well as through collaborating with the client on values clarification about work, confronting irrational beliefs about the client's interaction with the workplace and the workplace itself, and helping employers create work environments that are less stressful, more accommodating of workers needs, and more attuned to job designs by which person-job fit can be made as positive as possible.

But as difficult as job stress, job dissatisfaction, and work adjustment problems are, persons dealing with these issues still have a workplace to go to and a work identity, however fragile, by which to orient their life. Those who are unemployed are likely to have none of these. Unemployment, particularly extended unemployment, is a phenomenon that carries with it significant individual and social costs and, as a result, is an area to which most national governments are willing to allocate resources for career counseling or career guidance in the hope that such processes can help to prevent or to reduce the social costs of unemployment. Unemployment costs money, money that governments typically prefer to allocate to other purposes. Unemployment costs to governments fluctuate with rates of unemployment, but whatever the level of unemployment, the results are reduced taxes, productivity, and revenues; increased costs to governments for their social security and social service systems, such as the safety nets that must be put in place to provide a financial floor for those who are out of work, discouraged, and without resources to sustain themselves or their family; costs for medical treatment, mental health, and psychiatric services; and costs for increases in imprisonments, mortality rates, violence and abuse, suicides, and other physiological, behavioral, emotional, and stress-related disorders that have been found in cross-national studies to correlate significantly with rates of unemployment. Such findings have illustrated that although unemployment is complex and difficult for the individuals affected, unemployment is also a major social and economic issue that is increasingly global in its impact (Herr & Cramer, 1996).

However important in social, economic, and governmental terms unemployment is, it is at its roots an individual problem. Regardless of the official statistical rate of unemployment in a particular nation (5%, 8%, 15%), for the individual who is unemployed the rate is 100%. In such a context, unemployment is virtually always a personal crisis for the person experiencing it. In addition to its economic consequences for the individual and his or her family, research of the last 25 years in the United States and other nations has clearly defined that unemployment is also a process with psychological, emotional, physiological, and behavioral corollaries. Although there are individual differences in coping with unemployment, the virtually predictable emotional and cognitive consequences include boredom, identity diffusion, lowered self-esteem, guilt and shame, anxiety and fear, anger and depression (Levine, 1979). Schlossberg and Leibowitz (1980) and Herr (1993) have supported the observations of other researchers that prolonged unemployment often is manifested in periods of apathy, alternating with anger, sadness, sporadic optimism, few habits of regularly structured activities, few meaningful personal contacts, ominous feelings of victimization, lack of personal power, and low self-worth. Borgen and Amundson's (1984) major studies of unemployed persons in Canada suggested that the experience of unemployment depicts an emotional roller coaster that is compatible in its impact and stages to those found in victims of rape, incest, disease, and crime: shock, confusion, helplessness, anxiety, fear, and depression (Janoff-Bulman & Friese, 1983).

Such studies, and many others that can only be summarized here, have suggested that some people react to unemployment with physical manifestations (e.g., rises in cardiovascular disease, hypertension, cirrhosis, early death, chemical dependency), others in behavioral terms (e.g., aggressiveness, violence, spouse or child abuse), and others in psychological terms (e.g., depression, anxiety). Research has suggested that the unemployment of a parent is frequently reflected in changed behavior of children in schools (e.g., greater distractibility, digestive upsets, irritability). Thus the effects of unemployment are wide-ranging, and counselors in any setting— the school, community agencies, independent practice—are likely to encounter either the direct or the ripple effects of unemployment as it touches clients, family members, or children in its economic, psychological, physiological, or behavioral impact on these persons.

Counselors, then, in any setting are likely to engage in direct or indirect social action as they confront the multidimensional implications of unemployment. As they work to restore the dignity, self-esteem, sense of structure, predictability, and social support of unemployed persons, and as they help them find their way back to employment, counselors offer hope, a renewed sense of purpose, and optimism to clients and their families. Whether or not the counselor also advocates for clients to employers and seeks to encourage job creation and other community actions that will decrease the problems of unemployment that exist, the counselor is engaging in social action either directly or indirectly.

ACTIVITIES AND ARENAS FOR SOCIAL ACTION

In order to instill hope and to help clients acquire the skills necessary to manage their careers effectively, counselors must use different social action strategies to address their clients' concerns and to alter the contexts in which they are involved.

As a counselor contemplates any intervention, being sensitive to a client's context is especially important because career identities are shaped by a person's physical, social, political, and economic environments. Thus effective social action requires counselors to understand how their clients' environments interact with and influence the interpretations and meanings clients attach to work and occupational opportunities. Additionally, effective social action requires counselors to develop the knowledge, skills, and awareness necessary for responding effectively to environments that artificially restrict opportunities and access to information.

These requirements for effective social action influence the activities of the career counselor. In essence, these requirements are a type of call to action for career counselors. Specifically, counselors are called to act within three arenas in order both to instill hope in their clients and to help clients acquire career management skills. These arenas are social policy and legislation, the career counseling process, and counselor training programs.

Social Policy and Legislation: Learning, Informing, and Implementing

To have an impact on social policy and legislation, counselors must first learn about existing legislation that addresses career-related issues (e.g., school-to work transitions, family leave, and Americans with disabilities). Learning about the degree to which legislators support the underlying issues and possible initiatives related to such career-related concerns is important. Of importance, as well, is counselor participation in lobbying efforts to voice support for initial and continued funding of pro-career-development legislation. Although face-to-face meetings are often most effective, counselors can communicate directly with governmental representatives via the Internet, E-mail, or fax; the growth of user-friendly communication technologies permits little justification for counselors not to voice their support for career development initiatives.

Learning about career development initiatives and legislation is also important because research findings show that clients underutilize the services to which they are entitled (Orndorff & Herr, 1996). Counselors can not assume that parents, students, and clients are knowledgeable about their rights vis-à-vis career services. Thus counselors must take an active role in informing their clients about the opportunities and resources resulting from career development social policy initiatives.

Beyond learning about existing legislation and informing clients about available resources, counselors need to take the lead in implementing the career development programs emerging from legislative initiatives. Unfortunately, research findings have shown that counselors are often not at the forefront of these activities. For example, findings from a multistate survey of public high schools indicated a lack of commitment to career development programs for diverse student groups (Bloch, 1996). Bloch noted that this lack of commitment is due, in part, to the academic-rationalist approach to curriculum development embedded in most public high schools in the United States (i.e., an approach that emphasizes academic disciplines taught in college and that conceptualizes such disciplines as academic "silos" rigidly separated from each other). Furthermore, overburdened school counselors often lose their connection to that part of their professional role that focuses on preparing students for the world of work. Clearly, the effective implementation of career development social policies requires counselors to develop strategies for changing practices and curricula that are not supportive of career development initiatives.

Change strategies must also be used when counselors identify discriminatory employment practices. In such instances, counselors must act as "career development advocates for disenfranchised clients by actively challenging policies and traditions that stand in the way of equity in the workplace" (Lee, 1989, p. 219). In fact, advocacy is the primary process required of counselors in the social policy and legislative arena. Thus counselors who are seeking to instill hope in their clients and who wish to help clients acquire career management skills must be actively involved in shaping and implementing relevant career development policies in the United States.

THE CAREER COUNSELING PROCESS

Counselors engage in social action by providing multifaceted career interventions and by expanding their roles beyond traditional career counseling practices. Specifically, counselors who are engaged in social action integrate the roles of advocate, facilitator, and community counselor into the career counseling process. Using each of these roles effectively requires counselors to possess the knowledge, skills, and attitudes necessary for practicing competent multicultural career counseling (Bowman, 1993). Multicultural career counseling competencies are essential for understanding and responding to clients' concerns and contexts and for reassuring clients that they have the information and support to make good decisions. And although multicultural career counseling theories are relatively new, a growing body of literature has identified career interventions for a wide array of client concerns and contexts (e.g., Bowman, 1993; Leong, 1993).

Career counselors engaged in social action must also have a thorough knowledge of the career resources that are available in the community. There are several reasons why this is important. The first is that having this knowledge enables counselors to play the role of facilitator by providing clients with access to important information related to their career concerns (Enright, Conyers, & Szymanski, 1996). Playing this role effectively requires counselors to maintain files of useful resources, including names of potential mentors who represent a diversity of backgrounds (e.g., African American, Asian American, Latino, individuals with disabilities, gay, lesbian, and bisexual men and women), information on accommodations for disabled individuals with different functional limitations, names of employers willing to provide opportunities for job shadowing and internship experiences, and names of individuals willing to participate in informational interviewing and mentoring experiences (Enright et al., 1996).

The second reason is that knowing about the career resources available in the community facilitates appropriate referrals to other mental health, career, and social services. Such referrals obviously increase the probability that clients will access important information and resources for resolving their career dilemmas (e.g., employment offices, one-stop career shops, support groups). A third reason is that knowing which resources are available helps counselors identify areas where services are lacking. In these instances, counselors can again take on a strong advocacy role and thus seek to rectify service deficiencies in their communities (Lee, 1989).

Advocacy is also important when clients' career concerns are the result of external factors, such as the large-scale downsizing of jobs and of workers in local firms. In these instances, counselors concerned with social action address not only the career concerns of individual clients but also the career concerns of the community at-large (Cahill & Martland, 1996). This is accomplished by integrating individual career counseling skills with community counseling skills. Combining career counseling and community counseling strategies is critical in rural communities where economic restructuring can threaten the very existence of the community.

Community career counseling builds on the strength of individual career counseling and offers assistance to people in their struggle to maintain their communities, even as opportunities for career development are created and selected. Thus, in addition to individual career counseling skills, counselors need skills in facilitating group problem solving and consensus building as well as an understanding of social and economic development processes.

Essentially, career counselors who instill hope in their clients and empower them to manage their careers are multiculturally competent, act as facilitators of information and referrals, advocate for their clients when employment practices and community traditions stand in the way of equity in the workplace, and integrate individual career counseling skills with community counseling when the causes of clients' career concerns are community based. Combining these skills expands traditional approaches to career counseling and equips counselors for effective social action aimed at facilitating career development in clients.

COUNSELOR TRAINING PROGRAMS

Training career counselors for social action presents two issues for counselor training programs. The first is that counseling programs need to respond to the fact that, in general, students in training to be counselors have little interest in career counseling, and they report negative training experiences (e.g., poor teaching, inadequate clinical training and supervision) related to career counseling (Heppner, O'Brien, Hinkelman, & Flores, 1996). Obviously, this tendency highlights the need to bring career courses and career counseling to life and to help students understand the ways in which career and personal issues are inextricably intertwined across the life span (Blustein, 1992). Emphasizing the application of career interventions for diverse client concerns and discussing the importance of contextual factors (e.g., family, culture, economics, politics) in career development can also help in this regard.

A second and related issue is that, traditionally, the content of career counseling courses does not address social action. (Indeed, there may even be some controversy among faculty in training programs as to whether it is the counselor's responsibility to engage in social action activity and thus the program's responsibility to provide such training.) Ideally, however, a rationale for and techniques of social activism are integrated into the overall mission of the counselor training program.

Regardless of the degree to which social action is an accepted part of the overall mission of the training program, counselor educators incorporate social action into career courses in a number of ways: they teach students about important career development legislation and the need to engage in lobbying efforts to muster legislative support for such initiatives; they teach students how to participate in such lobbying efforts; and they expose students to the impact of contextual factors on career development. This sensitizes students to the psychological ripple effects of issues such as unemployment, job loss, and inequities in access to work and educational opportunities. Students can then be exposed to strategies for intervening in instances when external barriers artificially limit access to the world of work. Additional suggestions related to counselor training in the area of career development are provided by Swanson (1993).

A major point embedded within both of these issues concerning counselor training is that counselors must understand the importance of career counseling and the ways in which intrapersonal and contextual factors influence career development if they are to engage in social action to instill hope in their clients and empower them to manage their careers effectively.

CONCLUSION

In sum, counselors involved in career intervention are engaged in social action in much of what they do, whether or not they label their actions in this manner. Such an assertion is true because as counselors help individuals to find purpose and hope and the skills to manage their careers effectively and productively, they also are engaged in achieving outcomes that have an impact beyond the individual client. Successful career interventions with a particular client are likely also to result in economic and psychological benefits that accrue to a spouse, children, an employer, and a community. Successful career interventions in support of effective school-to-work transitions, the positive induction and adjustment to work, and the reduction of unemployment are actions that benefit the individual and society. As such, these interventions respond directly or indirectly to policies and legislative statutes that validate the importance of career guidance and counseling as important sociopolitical instruments in achieving national goals of nonbiased access to opportunities, individual purpose, and achievement.

Counselors engaged in career development activities, at either individual or contextual levels, can make more visible and more direct their roles in social action as they conceptualize more broadly the impact of their actions in individual career counseling, community counseling, and advocacy. Such an outcome will add to the importance and the vitality of counselors as facilitators of hope and opportunity in the 21st century.

REFERENCES

Berlin, G., & Sum, A. (1988). *Toward a more perfect union: Basic skills, poor families, and our economic future* (Occasional Paper No. 3). New York: Ford Foundation.

Bloch, D. P. (1996). Career development and workforce preparation: Educational policy. *Career Development Quarterly, 45*, 20-40.

Blustein, D. L. (1992). Applying current theory and research in career exploration to practice. *Career Development Quarterly, 41*, 174-184.

Borgen, W. A., & Amundson, N. (1984). *The experience of unemployment, implications for counseling the unemployed.* Scarborough, Ontario: Nelson Canada.

Bowman, S. L. (1993). Career intervention strategies for ethnic minorities. *Career Development Quarterly, 42*, 14-25.

Cahill, M., & Martland, S. (1996). Community career counselling for rural transition. *Canadian Journal of Counselling, 30*, 155-164.

Commission on Skills of the American Workforce. (1991). *America's choice: High skills or low wages.* Rochester, NY: Center on Education and the Economy.

Dawis, R. V. (1984). Job satisfaction: Workers' aspirations, attitudes, and behavior. In N. C. Gysbers (Ed.), *Designing careers. Counseling to enhance education, work, and leisure* (pp. 275-302). San Francisco: Jossey-Bass.

Educational Testing Service. (1990). *From school-to-work.* Princeton, NJ: The Anchor.

Enright, M. S., Conyers, L. M., & Szymanski, E. M. (1996). Career and career-related educational concerns of college students with disabilities. *Journal of Counseling and Development, 75*, 103-114.

Heppner, M. J., O'Brien, K. M., Hinkelman, J. M., & Flores, L. Y. (1996). Training counseling psychologists in career development: Are we our own worst enemies? *The Counseling Psychologist, 24*, 105-125.

Herr, E. L. (1989). Career development and mental health. *Journal of Career Development, 16* (1), 5-18.

Herr, E. L. (1993, October). *The crisis of unemployment.* Plenary paper presented at the International Conference on Unemployment and Counseling, Eötvös Loránd University, Budapest, Hungary.

Herr, E. L. (1995). *Counseling employment bound youth* (ERIC/CASS Publication). University of North Carolina at Greensboro, School of Education.

Herr, E. L., & Cramer, S. H. (1996). *Career guidance and counseling through the life span: Systematic approaches* (5th ed.). New York: Harper Collins.

Janoff-Bulman, R., & Friese, I. (1983). A theoretical perspective in understanding reactions to victimization. *Journal of Social Issues, 39,* 1-17.

Lee, C. C. (1989). Needed: A career development advocate. *Career Development Quarterly, 37,* 218-220.

Leong, F. T. L. (1993). The career counseling process with racial-ethnic minorities: The case of Asian Americans. *Career Development Quarterly, 42,* 26-40.

Levine, S. V. (1979). The psychological and social effects of youth unemployment. *Children Today,* 8(6), 6-9, 40.

Millar, J. D. (1992). Public enlightenment and mental health in the workplace. In G. P. Keita & S. L. Sauter (Eds.). *Work and well-being: An agenda for the 1990s.* Washington, DC: American Psychological Association.

Orndorff, R. M., & Herr, E. L. (1996). A comparative study of declared and undeclared college students on career uncertainty and involvement in career development activities. *Journal of Counseling and Development, 74,* 632-639.

Schlossberg, N. K., & Leibowitz, Z. (1980). Organizational support systems as buffers to job loss. *Journal of Vocational Behavior, 17,* 204-217.

School-to-Work Opportunities Act of 1994, Pub. L. No. 103-239.

Swanson, J. L. (1993). Integrating a multicultural perspective into training for career counseling: Programmatic and individual interventions. *Career Development Quarterly, 42,* 41-49.

8

Combating Ageism: The Rights of Older Persons

JANE E. MYERS

The *graying of America* is a term often used to describe demographic changes in the 20th century. At the same time, popular use of the term *gray-out* suggests a fading into the background that occurs as one *grays*. These statements suggest two important issues for exploration: our population is growing older, and growing older may not be a fully positive experience. It is important for counselors to understand these changing demographics from a macro or societal perspective as well as from a micro or individual perspective.

This chapter first states the problem by exploring demographic changes in the United States with a focus on the aging of our population, counselors' responses to the graying of America, and the consequences of these responses to the needs of older persons. The chapter then discusses the phenomenon of ageism, an unreasonable prejudice against persons based on chronological age, in relation to what, where, when, how, and why as well as in relation to its personal impact on older individuals. The chapter concludes with a consideration from both macro and micro perspectives of recommended strategies and actions for counselors, and with suggestions for counselor advocacy and empowerment.

STATEMENT OF THE PROBLEM: DEMOGRAPHIC CHANGES, COUNSELORS' RESPONSES, CONSEQUENCES

DEMOGRAPHIC CHANGES

Only 4% of the population of the United States were over age 65 at the turn of the 20th century. In contrast, more than 13%

of the population will be in this age group as we enter the next millennium. By the year 2030, 20% of the population, or one in every five persons, will be over 65 (American Association of Retired Persons [AARP], 1996). As the population ages, the age structure of our society is changing as well. Earlier in this century that structure was diagrammed as a pyramid, with younger persons as the large base, adults in the middle, and older persons as the tapering top. Although an inverse pyramid is not an inevitable outcome, a structure with a bulge in the middle and smaller at both top and bottom is a more accurate picture of our society at present. The baby boomers have begun to reach midlife, and it is estimated that fully 50% of the population will be age 50 and over as the year 2000 begins.

Changes in the numbers of older persons are due to a variety of factors, the most obvious one being that people are living longer. Improved medical care, enhancements in our ability to treat chronic disease, the ability of persons with disabilities to live long and productive lives, the eradication of diseases such as polio, and decreased infant mortality are among the factors that have prolonged the life span in this century. In addition, increased affluence and better public health measures, including controlled water supplies, inspection of foods in grocery stores and restaurants, and universal inoculations against diseases such as tuberculosis and many varieties of the flu have resulted in a better and healthier standard of living for most persons.

Persons born in our country in 1900 could expect an average life span of only 47 years. Persons born in 1990 can expect to live to be more than 75 years of age. Interestingly, a survivorship phenomenon exists in regard to aging, such that the longer a person lives, the longer a person can expect to live. A person reaching age 65 in 1990 could expect to live an additional 17.3 years, for a total of more than 82 years of life. Gender differences in life expectancy change this figure significantly, in that women reaching age 65 may expect to live another 19 years while men can expect another 15.3 years. Persons of minority races have shorter life spans, with Native Americans living on reservations still expecting a life span of about 47 years.

Currently, only 8% of the older population are African Americans, compared to approximately 12% of persons under age 65. Over 85% of older Americans are Caucasian. Slightly less than 4% are Hispanic, and 3% consist of persons from other ethnic backgrounds. Although the reasons for these differences are complex, a history of poverty, lower socioeconomic status, a lifetime of low-paying employment, lack of access to health care, and poor nutrition are among the reasons for shorter life spans among minority populations. The results of institutional racism do not disappear in the later years, but rather are compounded by the stigma associated with advancing age.

Ageism, similar in nature to racism, sexism, disabilityism, and other -isms, refers to an unreasonable prejudice toward persons based on their advanced age. This stigma connected to aging is quite interesting. An individual can be, for example, a nonethnic minority, a nonfemale, a nonhomosexual, or nondisabled, but that individual has only two choices related to aging: growing old or dying young. Aging is thus a normative life experience. With persons today living three fourths or more of their lives as adults and one third to one half as older adults, counselors are in a position in which some of their clients, or the families of their clients, will inevitably be older individuals. In addition, counselors who do not die young may expect to experience aging as a personal process as well. Given these facts, how have counselors responded to aging?

COUNSELORS' RESPONSES

Richard Blake, writing in 1975 after a careful study of counselors' responses to aging, stated the situation briefly and unequivocally: "Older people are the forgotten and ignored of [the counseling profession]" (Blake & Kaplan, 1975, p. 176). Blake's challenge was accepted by the American Counseling Association, which subsequently contracted with the U.S. Administration on Aging for five grant projects designed to impact counseling training, counseling research, and counseling practice with older persons. Over a span of 14 years, and with funding in excess of $1.2 million, these projects were designed to develop curriculum and training materials as well as provide counseling services to older persons (Myers, 1995; Myers & Schwiebert, 1996).

The first two national projects on counseling older persons developed curriculum resources for graduate-level training and for training paraprofessional service providers to older persons. The third used a train-the-trainers approach that resulted in more than 3,200 practicing professional counselors receiving training in basic aspects of aging and gerontological counseling. The fourth project stressed the need for all counselors to graduate with some knowledge of aging and the needs of older persons and thus developed curriculum modules for infusion into each of the core areas of counseling preparation specified in the standards of the Council for Accreditation of Counseling and Related Educational Programs (CACREP, 1994). In addition to a curriculum manual, a series of training videotapes also were developed and disseminated through the American Counseling Association.

The final national aging project targeted counselor training at the pre- and in-service levels through the development of competency statements. Two sets of statements were developed, the first set addressing the minimum competencies required of all counselors for work with older persons and their families, in both individual and group sessions. The second set of competencies formed the basis for a proposal to the National Board for Certified Counselors (NBCC), which resulted in the National Certified Gerontological Counselor (NCGC) credential. An additional proposal to the board of CACREP resulted in the implementation of a new set of standards for a specialty in gerontological counseling training. As an aside, dissemination was a major component of these projects. A continuing series of articles in the newsletters of the American Counseling Association and all of its divisions, NBCC, CACREP, and other organizations were designed to assure that counselors were informed of available resource materials to help them work effectively with older clients. One copy of each set of curriculum materials (except the videotapes) was distributed free of charge to each of the more than 450 counselor education training programs in the nation. The Association of Adult Development and Aging, a division of ACA, was established (and now has more than 2,000 members) to keep these concerns in the minds of counselors and counselor educators.

By 1997, about 200 persons had achieved certification as a NCGC, and two counselor training programs had achieved accreditation for their gerontological counseling specialty. These numbers were far fewer than those expected, as determined by multiple national surveys of professional counselors as well as of counselor training programs (see Myers, 1995, for a description of these studies). In short, counselors' responses to the aging of our population indicated disinterest.

As an example of this disinterest, it is helpful to look at enrollments in counselor education courses that emphasize gerontological issues. Although studies of these courses have not been conducted, anecdotal evidence gathered at annual meetings of groups, such as the Association for Adult Development and Aging, especially the Committee on Standards, and the Association for Counselor Education and Supervision, especially the Adult Development, Aging, and Counseling Interest Network, suggests that enrollments in such courses are uniformly small. The author struggles annually with university enrollment expectations and the threat of course cancellation for low enrollments. For the past 3 years, no more than 3 to 4 counseling students out of 120 in the counselor education program have enrolled in the course entitled "Counseling the Older Adult." As a consequence, instructors such as myself are forced to open enrollment to persons with various backgrounds who are majoring in a variety of academic disciplines. The result is a need to modify the curriculum and teach a broad-based course focusing on basic gerontology, with counseling interventions taught primarily at the paraprofessional level. Thus even those few students who choose to specialize in gerontological counseling are being shortchanged in the education received for this specialty. It may be "good enough" to achieve national certification in the specialty, but is this good enough when the quality of lives of older persons and their families is at stake? I think not.

THE CONSEQUENCES

The lack of interest in issues of aging among professional counselors and counselor educators has significant consequences, professional and personal, both large and small. For counselors to assume that the ageism so pervasive in our society either does not affect them or does not apply to them represents a very serious form of denial and makes us all contributors to the problems faced by older persons. Denial of aging, until one actually experiences the aging process during the midlife decades and beyond, seems to be the norm.

Two excellent examples of denial are found in the work of two major theorists in our field: Donald Super and Erik Erikson. Super's early and widely used career development theory incorporated five stages of career development: fantasy, exploration, establishment, maintenance, and decline. As Super neared the age of 60, his theory underwent significant changes. What emerged was a "life-career rainbow," in which a variety of life roles (e.g., student, parent, worker, leisurite) were defined and shown to be active throughout the life span. In talking with Super about these changes over dinner one evening, he indicated to me the importance of what we learn about life as we grow older. At the time we were celebrating his 80th birthday, and he was planning a series of speaking engagements in the United States and abroad, and a trip to the Soviet Union with his son. Erik Erikson described eight psychosocial stages of life span development, ending with the challenge of ego integrity versus despair. He described this last stage as a time when healthy older persons look back on their lives and gain a sense of well-being with the life they have lived. In recent years, research with older persons has suggested that the struggle for integrity is largely resolved in the late 60s and early 70s, which was the end of the life span during the time that Erikson first wrote his theory. When he reached his 7th, 8th, and 9th decades, Erikson began to reconceptualize the later stages of life, suggesting that a stage beyond that of integrity in fact existed.

Recently I received a call from an experienced professional counselor who had, early into her retirement years, become greatly concerned about the problems of aging. She was certain that counselors needed to respond, and that the way to get this response was to provide training in how to work with older persons. Curriculum materials and videotapes were badly needed. When I expressed my agreement with her, along with the fact that this very rationale was used, successfully, between 1977 and 1990 to gain grant funding to develop training materials and projects for counselors, and that all of the materials were disseminated to counselor education programs in the country, her response did not surprise me. Two of the things she said were "I never heard of your work," and "Isn't that wonderful—but you were ahead of your time. I think people are ready to listen now."

Crose (1991) alerted us to an important issue in work with older persons: that counselors respond from a personal knowledge base. As a consequence, we may fail to recognize our own stereotypes and misconceptions as they affect our older clients; we may fail to meet effectively the mental health and counseling needs of older persons and their families, and we may, and often will, fail to recognize or actualize opportunities to advocate for the needs of older persons. Can we afford to wait until we ourselves grow older to begin to recognize and deal with these concerns? I suggest that we cannot. Ageism affects all of us *now*, if we recognize that aging is a part of the life span, not apart from the life span.

AGEISM: WHAT, WHERE, WHEN, HOW, AND WHY?

Ageism was defined earlier as an unreasonable prejudice against persons simply because of their chronological age, or perceived chronological age. It is important for counselors to understand what ageism is, as well as where, when, how, and why it occurs, as a first step in combating this phenomenon.

AGEISM: WHAT?

Robert Butler first described ageism in his 1975 Pulitzer-Prize-winning book, *Why Survive? Being Old in America*. Numerous studies since that time have confirmed the pervasiveness of negative attitudes toward older people. These attitudes have been identified in persons of all ages, including children, adolescents, young and midlife adults, and older persons themselves. Ageism has been found among a variety of health care providers, including nurses, psychologists, psychiatrists, and counselors.

Old age is viewed as a time of undesirable physical, emotional, social, and financial losses. Older persons are viewed as a group living with poverty, disability, and depression. In spite of abundant research establishing that four out of five older persons are living above the poverty level, that over 95% of older persons are living in the community and less than 5% in institutional settings, and that rates of depression peak in middle rather than later life, these stereotypes persist. Older persons are mistakenly viewed as emotional and financial drains on their adult children (most support their adult children emotionally as well as financially), as wanting to live with their adult children (what adult wants to give up his or her independence after a lifetime of being in charge?), as being disinterested in sex (there is no age limit to sexuality), and as chronically ill (86% of older persons experience one or more chronic physical impairments, yet most are able to live actively and independently).

An interesting and widely held stereotype, supported by cliches such as "you can't teach an old dog new tricks," is that older persons are set in their ways. Research reveals that reaction time slows with age, but that intelligence does not decline. Older persons can learn equally well, although the pace of learning and learning styles may need to be modified. After all, sorting through a lifetime of accumulated knowledge in the process of assimilating new information certainly requires more time than sorting through only a few years of information. How great is the fund of knowledge in a person 70 years of age, and how many neurons are involved in information processing for such an individual, compared to the fund of knowledge for a person 50 years younger? We lack research in this area, but the possibilities are intriguing.

Research is available to support the perspective that change is unlikely to occur in later life. A front-page headline in my local newspaper that attracted my attention in this regard read "If You're 30, You're Finished" (1992). In the article, Dr. Paul Costa of the National Institute on Aging, a well-known and certainly reputable research organization, reported that "by the time people reach 30, their basic personality traits—anxiety, assertiveness, or openness—are virtually 'set like plaster'." This somewhat pessimistic view of development seems to argue against the prospects of continued development throughout the life span. If people do not change, what role is there for counselors in working with adults over the age of 30? Certainly change is difficult at any age, so the basic question that must be asked is whether change is more difficult in later life. I think that as we get older, we become more and more like ourselves and less and less like anyone else. If we are set in our ways when we are younger, chances are excellent that we will be perceived this way when we are older. The preponderance of research suggests that personality is consistent with aging, not discontinuous.

The developmental perspective suggests that individuals are capable of change and growth across the life span, even if that change means becoming more firmly who they are. In the process of coping with changing life circumstances, personal change and growth can certainly be an asset. Those who fail to cope, or who continue to try to resolve new problems with old, tried-and-true-but-no-longer-effective coping resources, are likely to be among the older persons who could benefit most from counseling interventions. From an ageist perspective, believing that older persons cannot change relieves service providers of the challenge of trying to help them change. However, multiple studies of mental health interventions reveal that older persons have the capacity for change and continued growth, regardless of chronological age factors (see Myers & Schwiebert, 1996, for a more extended discussion of the research in this area).

Ageism: Where, When, How?

Ageism is both formal and informal, obvious and subtle. Formal aspects of ageism, such as mandatory retirement ages in some professions, are easier to identify. The author is a private pilot who frequently attends aviation training seminars and reads aviation publications. One of the most important characteristics of a safe pilot is good judgment in dealing with the aviation environment, from weather to mechanical systems to navigation to air traffic control. Judgment, from all accounts, is gained only through experience. Thus it remains an enigma why federal legislation requires airline pilots, whose reflexes may have slowed a tiny bit from the aging process but whose competence as defined by judgment is at an all-time career high, to retire at the age of 60—with an estimated 19 years of useful life remaining! Quick arithmetic here reveals that these pilots are expected to not work for the remaining 25% of their life span, like it or not.

How many counselors are aware of and responsive to legislation concerning child abuse in their state? The answer should be 100%. Among these same counselors, how many are familiar with the mandatory laws regarding elder abuse, which also exist in each state? How about the laws concerning grandparent visitation rights, or age discrimination in employment (which extends to persons between the age of 40 and 70)? The fact that our mental health system gives far greater attention to the needs of younger persons, rather than older, reflects our pervasive lack of public awareness and support for programs for our older population. This is a form of ageism.

The prejudices held by health care providers likewise limit the choices of older persons. Managed care is a particular case in point because medical treatment and hospital-stay limitations are based on studies with younger persons, who are known to heal more quickly and require larger doses of medication. Many of the medical problems and "dementias" of older persons are thus iatrogenic, or physician-induced, such as when prescriptions calibrated for use with young persons, usually males in their 20s, are prescribed for older persons. Fortunately, these problems can be alleviated or reversed with proper medical care, especially under the treatment of trained geriatric physicians.

Family, friends, and neighbors of older persons—the informal support network—also are a source of ageism that acts to limit the lives of older people. Family members often are among the first to suggest to an older person that "you can't do that!" at your age. Well-meaning loved ones overprotect, interpret the thoughts of older persons, expect them to accept the "facts of aging," and charge them with "getting old" if they cannot remember a name or forget where they placed their keys. The same actions of a younger person cause few if any reactions from the same family members. When younger persons express a legitimate distaste for life when circumstances are undesirable, friends may suggest counseling or offer empathy. With older persons, the same behavior often results in a label of *cranky*.

I recently overheard a conversation between a retired father and his 30-something daughter. Dad was dealing with a difficult situation over home repairs and was trying to work with several builders and insurance agency representatives. He had several conversations in which he tried to accommodate their schedules and restrictions while still trying to make the point of what he needed to have accomplished and when. When daughter heard about the situation, her suggestion (made forcefully and aggressively) was that he immediately obtain an attorney and a backup statement from a builder she knew to "make" them do what was needed. Dad, a competent and effective problem solver throughout his 57 years of life, indicated he would probably continue on the path he had started. Daughter's response shocked all within earshot: "What's the matter Dad? Does aging mean you stop producing testosterone?" This statement was clearly ageist, not to mention offensive. However, it was not uncharacteristic of what many younger persons think about in relation to aging and older persons, though fortunately most are not quite as outspoken as this young woman was with her father. By the way, Dad's method resulted not only in resolution of all of the problems but also multiple follow-up calls from supervisors to ensure that he was satisfied with the work.

Ageism is reflected in words, deeds, and actions. It is reflected in the things we do for older persons (e.g., speaking louder or slower than normal to be sure we are heard and/or understood), our responses to older persons (e.g., becoming visibly frustrated when standing behind them in the grocery line, even though we may experience the same wait behind a mother with small children but not feel annoyed), and the things we fail to do with regard to older persons (e.g., consider them for paid tasks, not just volunteer work opportunities). Whenever we make choices and perform actions based on age, we may have succumbed to ageism.

A special note is necessary concerning the use of language to instill ageist attitudes, beliefs, and behaviors. This is a subtle and extremely pervasive means for the perpetuation of negative stereotypes about older persons. The first and most prominent example of the use of language in this manner is found in the frequently used term *the elderly*. *The elderly* implies that all persons who are elderly share some common characteristic or characteristics, usually with negative connotations as discussed earlier. The elderly are often seen as frail, ill, rigid, slow, boring, forgetful, and depressed. In actuality, there are almost 30 million persons in this age category, and what they share in common is largely a function of chronological age. It could be said that the elderly population is comprised of persons aged 65 and over, or aged 60 and over, or whatever

chronological age, and that statement would be correct. Other statements concerning the elderly run the risk of being accurate for only
a portion of the older population. Thus use of the term *the elderly*
functions to stereotype, label, categorize, and, in many instances,
denigrate the lives of older persons.

Johnson (1996) found the word *elderly* to be

> dangerous in the sense that armies of elders can ingest the word
> and start thinking of themselves as 'the elderly' rather than as
> potent, respectful, and quite independent persons of worth . . .
> costly as well as dangerous . . . by relegating perfectly good elders
> to the ranks of something less than useful; dependent and gener-
> ally incapable. Such imputations subvert one's sense of self and
> contribute to the flight toward a legitimate, but most dependent
> social role, the role of patient. (pp. 9, 13)

The power of language cannot be overemphasized. The point has
been made that many negative attributes are associated with terms
such as *aged*, *elderly*, and *old*. It is noteworthy that older persons
who perceive themselves to be younger than their chronological
age, either physically or mentally, report that they feel better and
perceive their health status to be better than persons of the same
age who self-identify as old.

Ageism: Why?

Perhaps it is only human nature that results in ageism. We tend
to fear what we do not understand, and the processes of aging are
not well understood. We also know most about older persons in
institutional settings because those who are independent are far
more difficult to access and to study. Those in institutional environments tend to be the most frail older persons, and those who
experience the most serious and disabling conditions. Not surprisingly, the association of *aged* and *disabled* results in fears of aging
being equated with fears of disability. Thus most studies of older
persons reveal that fear of loss of independence is the greatest fear
associated with aging. In addition, although death may be denied
as a relatively remote prospect in the younger years, for older persons
it becomes an increasing reality. Fears of death contribute to fears
of aging, the aging process, and being old.

Predominant social values that place a high priority on full-time, paid employment also contribute to ageism. Retirement constitutes a loss of employment, and retired persons are viewed, often unconsciously, as unemployed. Thus the retired role, although not well defined, is also not highly valued.

Competition for resources and roles between persons of different ages or generations contributes to ageism. For example, the media frequently remind us that the Social Security system is running out of money, so that younger persons who are paying Social Security taxes today are unlikely to benefit in terms of pensions from this fund in their later years. At the same time, the media remind us that today's older persons, who are living longer than was expected, are drawing a disproportionate share of Social Security funds. Younger persons reading this information cannot help but reflect on the implication that they are paying for the lifestyles of the older generation while facing an uncertain future in regard to the funding of their own later years of life.

SELF-FULFILLING PROPHECIES: THE PERSONAL IMPACT OF AGEISM

Although it is important to understand the dynamics of negative social attitudes toward older persons, any discussion of ageism is incomplete without consideration of the personal impact of social devaluation. Pedersen (1991), Sue and Sue (1990), Lee (1996), and others have explained in detail the processes of minority identity development. These authors have postulated that persons who belong to minority groups tend to internalize the predominant social perceptions of their group. Older persons are members of a minority group and are also members of our society. It is normal for them to internalize the predominant views of aging, often holding these views for a lifetime before growing older.

The consequences of internalizing negative attitudes include both a dislike of their peers and lower self-esteem. Older persons may fail to develop relationships with their age peers and may become isolated because they prefer not to associate with "those old people." When they internalize negative societal beliefs about older persons, a sense of personal devaluation, vulnerability, and decreased sense of self-efficacy is likely to result. When they begin to question their abilities, withdrawal from normal activities and associations followed by an increased sense of lowered self-esteem can result. This process can become cyclical and devastating, and has been described as *social breakdown* (Kuypers & Bengtson, 1973).

The social breakdown process explains how ageism creates a climate in which older persons *can* be devalued, and where normal responses result in social and psychological withdrawal and decline. At the same time, this process implies a variety of interventions that have the potential to interrupt, to halt, or even reverse this process. Ultimately, prevention efforts, undertaken from both individual and societal perspectives and across the life span, offer the potential for a better quality of life for older people.

RECOMMENDED ACTIONS AND STRATEGIES FOR COUNSELORS

Counselors are uniquely positioned to have a positive impact on the lives of older persons. As developmentalists, we recognize and support the possibility of positive growth across the life span. We also recognize and are able to respond to the needs of all individuals for assistance in coping with the normal circumstances of life, such as career entry, career change, retirement, second careers, marriage, divorce, remarriage, parenting, grandparenting—the list could go on for pages. What is important is the arena in which we choose to apply these skills. What is recommended here is a dual approach that includes both a macro or societal perspective, with the counselor as an agent for social change, and an individual approach that includes the counselor as an individual and the counselor as a change agent for other individuals.

THE MACRO PERSPECTIVE: ADVOCACY AND EMPOWERMENT

Empowerment refers to actions intended to help people help themselves, or to create personal power, while *advocacy*, as used here, refers to actions taken on behalf of others to assure that empowerment does, in fact, occur. What is important in bringing these two actions together is the intended outcome: to create environments in which individuals are able to live their lives effectively and with a sense of well-being, in which they can choose to change themselves and/or their life circumstances to achieve their goals to live life more fully. Three aspects of environmental change that counselors can directly affect are policies, services, and accurate information.

Empowerment and Advocacy Through Policies

Laws and policies at all levels—international, federal, state, county, local, agency, business and industry, caregiver—can affect the quality of life of older persons. Examples were provided earlier of mandatory retirement laws, elder abuse laws, and grandparent visitation laws. Numerous other examples could be provided. Counselors need to examine laws and policies in all settings with consideration for the needs of persons across the life span. Where laws are restrictive, outdated, or nonexistent, advocacy for change is needed. Working with policy makers and legislators at all levels must be a priority. Counselors have statements to make about job sharing, second career training, phased retirement, older worker skills, and a variety of additional issues that can be incorporated into the development of policies and laws—and that affect quality of life and opportunities for older persons—if we make ourselves part of the decision-making process.

We need to support legislation and policies that enhance the rights of older persons and help to defeat or replace policies that limit the rights of older persons. Those rights, first identified with the passage of the Older Americans' Act (OAA) in the 1960s, are relevant today (see Appendix A). That Act continues to set national policy for older Americans. We need to have presence with lawmakers when the OAA is reauthorized. Although the OAA includes provisions for counseling, the counseling specified is specific to legal counseling, nutrition counseling, and health counseling. Professional counseling can and should be added.

In 1977, the ACA introduced a set of proposed revisions to the OAA, entitled the "Older Persons Comprehensive Counseling Assistance Act of 1977." This Act proposed, among other things, the development of a national clearinghouse of information on the provision of counseling services to older persons, the development of a plan in each state for providing comprehensive counseling services to older persons, grants to states to provide counseling assistance to older people, grants for training and retraining counselors to work with older people, and research and demonstration projects to identify and develop effective services, interventions, and programs to meet the mental health and counseling needs of a broad array of older people. The Act was neither approved nor funded (unfortunately). It was reintroduced several times during congressional sessions in the early 1980s, each time with little success. I use the term *little* here intentionally. Although the amendments were never approved, the repeated introduction of the legislation did serve as a means of information and advocacy both for professional counselors and for the counseling needs of the older population. Perhaps at some point this legislation could be reintroduced, with the most likelihood of success coming through coalitions with other mental health service providers.

Empowerment and Advocacy Through Services

If older persons are to experience the benefits of preventive and remedial mental health services, counselors need to be trained and available to work with them. In the absence of federal legislation, which mandates and funds gerontological counselor training and counseling services for older persons, it is up to us to assure that these things occur.

Training opportunities for counselors in gerontological issues are limited. Infusion of gerontological counseling into counselor preparation has not uniformly been implemented. If the current status of training for counselors to work with older persons is to change, we need to approach decision makers in the educational arena—counselor educators and educational administrators. Any time we get a chance to fill out a professional development needs assessment form, or comment on the quality of education we received from our alma mater, we are presented with an opportunity to say we need more training to work with older persons.

Counselor educators are in a unique position from which to advocate for training for counselors to work with older persons. Educators can revise existing curricula to include more courses and curricular units specific to life-span and later-life issues. In addition, to promote the infusion model, counselor educators can take care in choosing texts for core courses that include issues of aging in the contents. To do so will send messages to publishers and textbook authors that life-span concerns must be incorporated if training effective counselors is to result.

Although it is important to train counselors to be effective in working with older persons, and also important to encourage accreditation of training programs for specialty training and certification of gerontological counselors, these measures will result in discouraged counselor education program graduates if the job market does not provide opportunities for employment commensurate with their training. Social services for older persons grew out of welfare programs for older and disabled persons. These programs traditionally were staffed by social workers. Hence, it is not surprising that many jobs in the aging network list social work training and credentials as prerequisites, and many of these positions are legislatively mandated or enabled. For example, each state has laws relating to long-term-care facilities, formerly known as nursing homes. These laws uniformly require that these facilities employ social workers. Accreditation agencies ensure that these staff are in place. Unfortunately, counselors are not included in this legislation.

Counselors, especially gerontological counselors, are relative newcomers to the field of services for older persons. We cannot expect automatic acceptance, especially when positions are legislatively controlled. Again, the need for advocacy with state and federal job classification systems to assure that counselors are included in position descriptions is clear. We also need to advocate with employers in the community, such as community mental health centers, to assure that counselors are hired in positions earmarked for geriatric mental health providers. The cross-over between training, credentialing, and advocacy is increasingly evident here: we cannot present counselors as the best trained professionals for such positions in the absence of strong training programs, accreditation, and certification to document our claims. Of course, we must also provide effective mental health interventions for older persons and their families, which requires a comprehensive knowledge base relative to this population.

Empowerment and Advocacy Through Accurate Information

The fact that all older persons are not alike has been established; but what are older persons like? We know enough about this population to have defined at least three subsets of older persons: young-old, middle-old, and old-old, with some lifestyle and health issues marking the differences between the three groups. We know that ethnic and cultural differences within the older population are significant, and that many of the problems of ageism are less apparent or not relevant for older minority individuals *within the family and cultural environment* (Adelman, 1994; Bahr, 1994; Strom, Collinsworth, Strom, & Griswold, 1992-93). But minority individuals who also are old are placed in a situation of double jeopardy, being subject simultaneously to the effects of -isms related to age as well as race. The addition of disabling conditions, gender, and sexual orientation as factors increases the potential negative effects of discrimination.

If counseling practice is to be informed, it must be informed with accurate information. Support for research on effective interventions and outcomes for a variety of circumstances experienced by older persons is essential. To the extent that older persons are like persons of other ages, counseling research will inform work with this population. However, there is some indication that strategies and techniques vary in effectiveness with older people, and that some interventions may be more effective at certain times and with certain older persons (see Myers & Schwiebert, 1996, for a discussion of outcome research with older persons). Outcome research studies are essential if we are to learn what works, when, with which older persons experiencing which conditions, and under what circumstances. We also need to develop interventions that help older persons conceptualize and develop lifestyles oriented toward health and wellness in their later years.

THE MICRO PERSPECTIVE: THE COUNSELOR AS CHANGE AGENT

Someone has to implement those strategies for reducing the effects of ageism just discussed, and that someone could be a professional counselor. To be effective as advocates for social change, counselors must first determine their own needs for attitudinal change. Then, in addition to receiving training to prepare them for work with older individuals and groups, counselors may find opportunities to advocate on an individual basis for older persons.

Counselor: Know Thyself

As members of an ageist society, counselors are likely to hold negative views of older persons, or negative perceptions of the potential of older clients for growth and change. It is imperative that we explore those attitudes prior to beginning work with older clients. Awareness training can be obtained at professional conferences as well as in graduate coursework. This training needs to include adequate opportunity for personal exploration and discussion in a safe environment, with group members available to challenge gently each other's mistaken beliefs and perceptions about older clients. Counselors need also to explore their own fears and feelings about the processes of growing older and death and dying. Again, this may occur in professional training settings or through individual or group counseling.

Those who work with older persons need to examine their motivations so as to ensure that our goal is to empower, rather than to patronize or to "do for" older people what they seemingly cannot accomplish for themselves. If we find that we feel sorry for our older clients, it will be hard to help them. If transference is an issue, in that many of our older clients remind us of an older relative or friend, then we are likely to be unable to accept our clients as individuals, and to respect them enough to confront their issues caringly and challenge them to continue to grow. Do we discriminate between older relatives and older clients, between older friends and older persons in general? If we find that we tend to treat all older persons alike, then we may be experiencing transference. If we find that we think all older persons are like the ones we know best, then we are likely to be engaging in stereotyping and ageism—for better or for worse. As part of our professional development as counselors, we should meet, learn about, and work with a variety of older persons, those who are independent as well as those who are frail or ill.

Finally, we need to examine our language when we speak with and about older persons. The words we use, the phrases we choose, and the intonations we unconsciously employ reflect the real meaning behind what we say. We need to become more aware of what we say, how we say it, and what we really mean, that is, what are truly our attitudes toward our older clients. Some suggestions for revising our language so as to avoid stereotyping older persons are found in Appendix B. These suggestions require and can result in significant attitudinal changes, thus helping to reduce ageist beliefs and attitudes for the counselor and for those with whom we interact when speaking with and about older persons.

Advocacy: Daily Opportunities to Be an Agent for Change

We each have opportunities on a daily basis to be advocates for change. We need to become more aware of these opportunities and take advantage of them on behalf of ourselves and our older clients. When faced with recommending persons for positions—paid as well as volunteer—or recommending members of advisory and governing boards, we have a choice to recommend only those who are younger or to include those who are older. When we decide for older persons that they "would not be interested," "would not want to use their time in a particular manner," "would not have the energy," or "would not be able to present new and creative ideas," then we must catch ourselves being ageist and take a different approach. Perhaps it is the older persons we know who are not appropriate choices. If so, the problem could be that we don't know enough older persons to make such choices. We may need to broaden our social and professional networks and actively create opportunities to interact with a variety of older people. To do so will enrich our lives as well as theirs.

CONCLUSION

The effects of ageism, or prejudice against older persons, are pervasive. Negative attitudes and stereotypes function to deny older persons the right to engage fully in the benefits of life in our country, demeaning their sense of self-efficacy and resulting in a lower overall quality of life. Ageism is perpetuated by individuals as well as organizations.

Counselors have vital roles to play as change agents working both with and on behalf of older persons. They need to view themselves as advocates who can effect change in laws, policies, and society. At the same time, we can help older persons live more effective lives through developmental interventions aimed at helping each person live life more fully throughout the life span. To be effective agents of change, we first need to examine our personal beliefs and biases, and develop healthy, respectful, positive, wellness-enhancing attitudes toward older persons. Because aging is a universal experience, all our efforts to assist this population will result in significant personal as well as professional gains. We will realize the ultimate benefits both vicariously as we watch our clients change and grow and personally as we ourselves experience the joys and challenges of the processes of aging.

REFERENCES

Adelman, P. K. (1994). Multiple roles and physical health among older adults. *Research on aging, 16*(2), 142-166.

American Association of Retired Persons. (1996). *A profile of older Americans.* Washington, DC: Author.

Bahr, K. (1994). The strengths of Apache grandmothers: Observations on commitment, culture, and caretaking. *Journal of Comparative Family Studies, 25*(2), 233-248.

Blake, R., & Kaplan, L. S. (1975). Counseling the elderly: An emerging area for counselor education and supervision. *Counselor Education and Supervision, 15,* 156-157.

Butler, R. (1975). *Why survive? Being old in America.* New York: Harper and Row.

Council for Accreditation of Counseling and Related Educational Programs. (1994). *Accreditation standards and procedures manual.* Alexandria, VA: Author.

Crose, R. (1991). What's special about counseling older women? *Canadian Journal of Counselling, 25*(4), 617-623.

If you're 30, you're finished. (1992). *Greensboro News & Record* (NC), p. 1.

Johnson, R. (1996, Winter). Chronologically endowed vs. elderly: One gerontological counselor's pet peeve. *Adultspan,* pp. 9, 13.

Kuypers, J. A., & Bengtson, V. L. (1973). Competence and social breakdown: A social-psychological view of aging. *Human Development, 16,* 37-49.

Lee, C. (1996). *Multicultural counseling.* Alexandria, VA: American Counseling Association.

Myers, J. E. (1995). From "forgotten and ignored" to standards and certification: Gerontological counseling comes of age. *Journal of Counseling and Development, 74*(2), 143-149.

Myers, J. E., & Schwiebert, V. (1996). *Competencies for gerontological counseling.* Alexandria, VA: American Counseling Association.

Older Americans' Act of 1965. Pub. L. No. 89-73.

Pedersen, P. (1991). Multiculturalism as a fourth force in counseling [Special issue]. *Journal of Counseling and Development, 20.*

Strom, R., Collinsworth, P., Strom, S., & Griswold, D. (1992-93). Strengths and needs of Black grandparents. *International Journal of Aging and Human Development, 36*(4), 255-268.

Sue, D., & Sue, S. (1990). *Counseling the culturally different* (2nd ed.). Englewood Cliffs, NJ: Prentice-Hall.

Appendix A

Rights and Obligations of Older Americans: 1961 White House Conference on Aging

RIGHTS OF SENIOR CITIZENS

Each of our senior citizens, regardless of race, color, or creed, is entitled to

1. the right to be useful;
2. the right to obtain employment, based on merit;
3. the right to freedom from want in old age;
4. the right to a fair share of the community's recreational, educational, and medical resources;
5. the right to obtain decent housing suited to needs of later years;
6. the right to the moral and financial support of one's family so far as is consistent with the best interest of the family;
7. the right to live independently, as one chooses;
8. the right to live and die with dignity; and
9. the right of access to all knowledge as available on how to improve the later years of life.

OBLIGATIONS OF AGING

The aging, by availing themselves of educational opportunities, should endeavor to assume the following obligations to the best of their ability:

1. the obligation of each citizen to prepare himself or herself to become and resolve to remain active, alert, capable, self-supporting, and useful so long as health and circumstances permit and to plan for ultimate retirement;
2. the obligation to learn and apply sound principles of physical and mental health;
3. the obligation to seek and develop potential avenues of service in the years after retirement;
4. the obligation to make available the benefits of his or her experience and knowledge;

5. the obligation to endeavor to make himself or herself adaptable to the changes added years will bring; and
6. the obligation to attempt to maintain such relationships with family, neighbors, and friends as will make him or her a respected and valued counselor throughout his or her later years.

Appendix B
Changing Our Ageist Language

Strategies for changing our ageist language include attention to vocabulary and phrases and statements. The following suggestions are taken from AARP's *Truth About Aging: Guidelines for Publishers*, 1979 (Washington, DC: Author).

Avoid words and phrases which

- demean—such as old maid, old codger, old fool, over-the-hill, has-been;
- patronize—such as cute, sweet, dear, and little;
- stereotype older persons—such as passive, dependent, nagging, and shrewish as applied to older women, and dirty old men and leches as applied to older men; or
- are negative physical descriptors—such as deaf, dentured, fragile, frail, withered, doddering.

Replace ageist statements with nonageist statements. For example:

- Ageist: At 72, she is confused, apathetic, withdrawn, taking no interest in anything.
- Nonageist: All her life she has been confused, apathetic, withdrawn, taking no interest in anything. No wonder she's that way at 72.

- Ageist: What does an old man like that want with a sports car?
- Nonageist: Now that his children are on their own, he can have that sports car he has always wanted.

- Ageist: That man she's with must be half her age!
- Nonageist: Men of all ages find her attractive.

- Ageist: Ask my grandmother. I'm sure she'll do it. She always has plenty of time!
- Nonageist: Ask my grandmother. She always tries to make time to help others.

9

Spirituality as a Force for Social Change

JUDITH G. MIRANTI AND MARY THOMAS BURKE

The United States is in the throes of major challenges to its long-established institutions, namely, the family, the church, and the educational system. The values that governed these institutions were questioned, and many discarded, in the turbulent 1960s and 1970s. A values vacuum resulted, and today, uncertainty and anxiety seem to pervade the lives and families of the baby boomers. As we review the statistics on violence, suicide, addiction, homelessness, discrimination, and related symptoms of alienation and antipathy among the people of the wealthiest country in the world, we are forced to ask the question, Why is there such discouragement and such emptiness in the lives of so many? The need for counselors and counseling skills to help a generation find a sense of meaning and purpose is evident. But given the dramatic changes in the social milieu of this nation, how do counselors intervene and impact the system in order to provide a more fulfilling and meaningful life for its citizens?

The United States is experiencing a resurgence of interest in spirituality, yet little work has been done in the field of counseling that operationalizes definitions or descriptions of spirituality or that discusses the relationship between counseling and social action. There is also an absence of literature addressing how counselors work with spiritual issues. Some authors see counselors as hesitant to embrace the concept of spirituality as part of their working knowledge base (Maher & Hunt, 1993), and therefore, clients are referred to ministers or rabbis to have their needs met.

A concern for this lack of research on the topic prompted the convening of a Summit on Spirituality in 1995. Participants in the summit agreed upon the following working definition and description of spirituality:

> Spirituality may be defined as the animating force, represented by such images as breath, wind, vigor, and courage. Spirituality is the infusion and drawing out of spirit in one's life. It is experienced as an active and a passive process.
>
> Spirituality is also described as a capacity and tendency that is innate and unique to all persons. This spiritual tendency moves the individual toward knowledge, love, meaning, hope, transcendence, connectedness, compassion, wellness, and wholeness. Spirituality includes one's capacity for creativity, growth, and the development of a value system. Spirituality encompasses a variety of phenomena, including experiences, beliefs, and practices. Spirituality is approached from a variety of perspectives, including psychospiritual, religious, and transpersonal. ("Summit on Spirituality," 1995)

This chapter uses the description of spirituality agreed upon by summit participants. If spirituality in this sense moves individuals toward knowledge, love, meaning, hope, connectedness, compassion, wellness, and wholeness, then persons who accept spirituality as a value in their lives will feel compelled to respond proactively to societal needs. Because dignity of the human person is the criterion against which all aspects of life must be measured, this dignity can only be realized in relationship and solidarity with others. If society is to function in a way that respects human dignity, then it must enable persons to find self-realization in their work; it must permit persons to fulfill their material needs through adequate remuneration; and it must enhance unity and solidarity within the family, the nation, and the world community.

This chapter first examines how counselors can respond to the need to include a spiritual dimension in counseling and take responsibility for social change. It then discusses our responsibility in preparing counselors to include spirituality in their training. The chapter next explores ways to incorporate and integrate the spiritual dimension of counseling into the practice of counseling so as to meet the challenges of addiction, AIDS, and prejudice against the mentally ill. The chapter concludes by considering how counselors can act as agents for social change through incorporating the spiritual dimension and by suggesting concrete ways in which counselors can use this dimension to act as creative architects and agents of social change.

RESPONDING TO THE NEED

In its relatively short history, the United States has made impressive strides in providing material necessities and economic prosperity for many of its people. The country has moved from an agricultural to a technological society, and in the wake of this move, sweeping social changes have taken place. The experiment in political democracy carried out by American founders did a great deal to ensure the protection of civil and political rights of our nation. However, major problems and injustices that infringe upon human dignity remain, including homelessness, hunger, unemployment, racial and ethnic discrimination, feminization of poverty, the lack of quality health care and child care, and inadequate education for the poor. Counseling as a profession must respond to these needs if counselors are to become a force for social change. These are the issues that touch the heart and soul of our nation.

Dealing effectively with these issues requires specialized training, especially in the spiritual dimension of counseling. Hinterkopf (1994) has asserted that without the necessary training in this spiritual dimension, counselors run the risk of being insensitive to the spiritual concerns of their clients. Counselors who lack the required competencies in the spiritual dimension can miss opportunities for fostering growth and development in their clients. Some possible reasons why counselors hesitate either to address the spiritual dimension or to empower social change in their clients' lives are that (a) counselors may fear imposing their own values on their clients; (b) counselors themselves may hold negative attitudes toward spirituality and organized religions; (c) counselors may lack specific in-depth knowledge of spiritual concerns; or (d) counselors may lack a facilitative theoretical model (Burke & Miranti, 1995).

In order to address the spiritual dimension adequately and empower social change in their clients' lives, counselors must first examine their own biases and prejudices. They need to be familiar and comfortable with their own spirituality so that they can encourage and support this dimension in the lives of their clients. Mandatory ethics require that counselors respect diversity. However, aspirational ethics inspire counselors to look beyond the immediacy of the particular situation and encourage client growth and development in ways that foster the clients' interest and welfare (Herlihy & Corey, 1995).

Counselors meeting the aspirational dimension of the ACA Code of Ethics have an opportunity to make a significant contribution to the profession. Currently, there is a growing awareness and a willingness to explore spiritual and religious matters within the context of counseling and counselor education preparation programs. Kelly's (1994) and Pate and High's (1995) survey of counselor education programs found that counselor educators have a generally positive attitude toward religion and spirituality as a legitimate aspect of counselor training.

The interest and awareness of spirituality across cultural environments, the accepting nature of spiritual issues in self-help groups, and the movement toward wellness models have stimulated efforts to incorporate the spiritual dimension into the counseling process. According to Bergin (1988), it is imperative to scrutinize the implications that incorporation of a spiritual perspective will have for counseling and behavior change. The perspectives advanced by Bergin seem to provide an appropriate base for professionals to begin a conceptualization of spirituality for therapeutic practice and for addressing the social condition.

If we accept the premise proposed by Ingersoll (1997) that spirituality is an organismic element possible for all people to develop in their lives, counselors will embrace the challenge to prepare themselves for this phase of their work. Counselors need training in this realm in order to be able to weave dialogue about the spiritual dimension of a client's life into standard counseling approaches and especially to understand and appreciate the varied cultural expressions of spirituality. Basic to all of this is the need for counselors to articulate an understanding of their own spirituality and its development throughout their lives (Ingersoll, 1997).

Counselors need to be prepared to help clients when religious beliefs reflect an unhealthy or dysfunctional family system or personal belief system (Chandler, Holden, & Kolander, 1992; Heise & Steitz, 1991). Often passivity and overdependence (upon a higher power) may represent an avoidance in taking responsibility for self or a reason to judge self or others as good or bad. Such thinking often inhibits the client from self-development and from allowing other persons to grow and develop into the fullness of personhood.

Research has shown that a counselor's spiritual and religious values influence goals, interventions, and topics explored during counseling sessions (Grimm, 1994). For counselors to be change agents, they must first be aware of the impact of their values on their clients in particular, and on the outcome of counseling in general. Religious and spiritual value orientations can make three important contributions to the counseling process (Bergin, 1988, 1991). First, the counselor can agree conceptually that spiritual and religious realities exist and that they affect behavior. Second, spiritual and religious values can provide a moral frame of reference. Third, religious and spiritual views can provide a set of techniques for counseling. Corey, Corey, and Callanan (1998) cautioned counselors who choose to practice from a spiritual and religious framework that they have an ethical responsibility to be aware of how their beliefs affect their clients and work to make sure that they do not bring harm to their clients.

As counselors formulate their own position on the place of spiritual and religious values in the counseling process, Corey et al. (1998) recommended that they reflect on the following questions:

1. Are you imposing your values on your client when you decide what topics can be discussed?
2. Is it appropriate to deal with religious and spiritual issues in an open and forthright manner as clients' needs arise?
3. Do clients have the right to have their religious and spiritual issues explored in counseling?

Even if issues of a spiritual or religious nature are not the expressed focus of a client's presenting concerns, these issues may enter indirectly as the client explores moral conflicts or as she or he struggles with a lack of meaning or purpose in his or her life.

Consider briefly the case of Ben who comes seeking relief from guilt and his shame for having passed on the AIDS virus to his wife of 20 years. Exploring with Ben the source of his guilt and shame may seem apparent. However, to assume that Ben was unfaithful and thus the consequence of his infidelity was a life-threatening condition is much too simplistic. Helping Ben embrace the complexity of this situation may enable Ben to express his helplessness and despair that could be grounded in his religious beliefs. If the counselor reframes Ben's thinking according to his or her religious belief system, we have cause for concern. Imposing values is not only unethical but the course of counseling could prove counterproductive.

Counseling does not need to be devoid of religious talk or expression. If religious issues are directly or indirectly brought up by the client, skillful and competent counselors are able to deal professionally with these issues just as they are able to handle other problems and issues of a secular nature. A client's religiosity need not be feared, but rather should be used in formulating therapeutic goals in the counseling process. How can this be achieved?

PREPARING COUNSELORS: OUR RESPONSIBILITY

In academic settings, students need to be exposed to religious and spiritual issues and they need help in understanding how to address these issues, just as we prepare them to address other issues that present themselves (Mattson, 1994). Pate and Bondi (1992) argued that the importance of religion in counseling implies that "counselor education students need to be taught the importance of religious beliefs in the lives of many of their potential clients and the relevance of religion in the counseling process" (pp. 109, 112).

Several recent studies of counselor education programs (Kelly, 1994; Pate & High, 1995) have indicated that in fewer than 25% of the programs, religious and spiritual issues occur as a course component. A substantial number of state-affiliated programs in the Kelly (1994) study gave little or no attention to religious and spiritual issues. Although religious beliefs of clients were reported to be of some importance in the curriculum of 84% of CACREP-accredited education programs (Pate & High, 1995), only 16% reported that these beliefs were of more than some importance. CACREP-accredited programs do report more attention to clients' religious beliefs and practices than Kelly's (1994) respondents. But students in 30% of the accredited counselor education programs can graduate and begin their professional counseling careers without a curricular introduction to the important role that religious beliefs and values might have in the lives of their clients (Pate & High, 1995).

The question then becomes Would the profession of counseling be satisfied if a survey found that over one third of the programs judged to meet program accreditation standards ignored issues such as race, gender bias, and sexual orientation in the curriculum component in which client diversity is addressed? Likewise, would we in the counseling profession accept as appropriate a finding that only 15% of the responding program heads indicated that counselor awareness of any other aspect of client diversity was very important (Pate & High, 1995)?

Bergin (1991), as part of a discussion about the discrepancy between personal investment in religion and consideration of religion in counseling, concluded that "this discrepancy probably reflects the fact that such matters have not been incorporated into clinical training as have other modern issues such as gender, ethnicity, race, etc." (p. 396).

Sensitivity toward client diversity and all that this implies necessitate that all aspects of a client's world view be considered important in the counseling process. Counselor education programs will be remiss if they fail to train counselors to explore effectively and to facilitate with clients the spiritual and religious issues presented either directly or indirectly in the counseling process. The counseling profession and counselor educators need to engage more deeply in professional dialogue about ways to incorporate the religious and spiritual dimensions into the counseling process in order to meet client needs.

Training programs must be willing to revaluate their philosophies in light of societal needs, and they must adopt curricular components that expose students to techniques and strategies that incorporate and integrate the spiritual dimensions into the counseling process. This includes developing materials and resources for practical application of the spiritual perspective in practicums and internships, engaging students in serious dialogue about their own spiritual development, and being willing as counselor educators and practitioners to share our own personal spiritual journeys.

A major focus of counselor training programs needs to be developing and upgrading skills to intervene effectively in the lives of clients from a variety of cultural backgrounds, including the religious and spiritual components, as well as incorporating into the training models holistic approaches that help clients to view their lives from a transcendent point of view (Lee & Sirch, 1994).

TAKING ACTION TO MEET THE CHALLENGE

The need for skilled counselors who can efficiently facilitate life-enhancing change is becoming increasingly apparent as we prepare to meet the modern issues facing our society. The social system is vulnerable to the escalating violence as seen in gang warfare, drug trafficking, and the spread of AIDS. Unless we as counseling professionals can help the at-risk, disenfranchised, handicapped, and disadvantaged populations find meaning in their lives, the problems will only escalate.

As the counseling profession approaches a new millennium, opportunities exist to reach beyond the safe confines of practice to a more global, inclusive interconnectedness with others of similar and different values. Now, more than ever, the emphases on purpose and meaning, the essence of spirituality, are within the grasp and scope of the helping professional.

Counselors can become more proactive in helping to shape a new society, one in which people realize the importance of the mind, body, spirit connection, and in which spirituality, the essence of meaning in our lives, emerges from the confines of religious doctrine and becomes the driving force that truly binds the human family together (Lee & Sirch, 1994). Then, and only then, will the counseling profession be a force for change. Through the incorporation of the religious and spiritual dimensions, counselors can become socially active in, for example, addiction recovery and supporting AIDS and mentally ill patients.

Action for Addiction Recovery

During the past 65 years, addiction has moved from a little understood category of human behavior to a recognized and acceptable diagnosable disorder (Chapman, 1996). Many counselors who work in addiction recovery accept the importance of the spiritual dimension in a client's life. The well-established and accepted Alcoholics Anonymous (AA) programs form the basis for the treatment not only of alcoholism but also of other debilitating addictions. The basic premise for AA is the 12-step program mandating that the client must acknowledge his or her dependence on a higher power before recovery can begin. By acknowledging this reliance on the higher power, the client begins the journey toward recovery. The counselor is free to invite the client to explore the importance of this spiritual presence. It is by addressing the spiritual issues that a solid base, which enables the person with an addiction to reach recovery, is created. This recovery involves the body and the mind as well as the spirit. (Alcoholics Anonymous, 1976). Dyer (1995) described this process as "an inward journey of enlightenment . . . expanding the godlike qualities of love, forgiveness, kindness, and bliss with ourselves." He describes this journey as "free of dogma" (p. 5). This enables the person with no religious background to embrace the broader considerations of spirituality rather than the specific tenets of a perceived theistic theology. In this context, the term *spirit* refers to the contribution made to recovery by the client's harmonious connectedness with the environment (Johnson, 1980). More specific applications of the spiritual dimension in counseling have come from authors in family therapy and in addictions recovery. Recalling how the issue of spirituality has been addressed from a systems perspective, a unique understanding of spirituality can aid any system. Within the field of addiction recovery, the 12-step program has consistently maintained a primary focus on spirituality (Mack, 1994).

ACTION FOR AIDS PATIENTS

When serious illness strikes, a person needs all the support that is humanly possible, and this has never been more true than it is today with the AIDS epidemic. When clients hear the verdict "You have tested positive for the AIDS virus," many experience a feeling akin to receiving a death sentence. They do not know where to turn, and they are often referred to counselors who are recognized for their skills and sensitivity to client needs. It is most important that counselors be prepared to address the meaning of life with these AIDS patients. Often these clients find that life's meaning is the only sustaining force during their time of loneliness and fear. They often do not share this verdict with family and friends because they fear rejection and condemnation. Therefore, the support of a competent counselor is of utmost importance at this crucial time. Asking clients to share their fears often brings to the surface their greatest fear, namely, their fear of God. This is particularly true if the client is a homosexual who has already experienced alienation from an organized religion.

Recognizing the AIDS patient's vulnerability, counselors must guard against preaching or proselytizing while helping the client get in touch with his or her spiritual essence and find peace in the relationship with self (Barret & Barzan, 1996). Patients diagnosed with any serious illness, such as cancer, stroke, or heart disease, have an overwhelming feeling of hopelessness, but none more than AIDS patients because of the societal stigma associated with the disease.

Counselors with a spiritual orientation in their practice will have a commitment to reach out in a special way to the lepers of our day. These counselors will feel compelled to speak out against the prejudice they see and become advocates on behalf not only of their own clients but also of this population in such great need of physical and spiritual healing.

Action for Mentally Ill Patients

Another population that is spurned by society is that of the mentally ill. Physical illness is often accepted in families and openly discussed, whereas mental illness is covered up and hidden. A sense of shame is attached to having a family member who has been diagnosed, for example, as manic depressive.

Many of these patients, when dismissed from the hospital, often find themselves homeless and are looked upon as the dregs of society. Counselors have an obligation to act on behalf of those who are unable to speak for themselves and to advocate for appropriate care for this suffering segment of society. According to Herr (1991), most of the problems of psychological vulnerability experienced by these clients are multidimensional. They trigger a ripple effect that touches the lives of the families of which they are a part. That is, when a family member becomes mentally ill, his or her condition impacts others with whom they interact. The result is that many family members turn to counselors in their time of need.

ACTING AS AGENTS FOR SOCIAL CHANGE

Considering the modern issues that call for social action—racism, physical and sexual abuse, family violence, divorce, AIDS, hopelessness, poverty, elder abuse, the plight of immigrants and migrant workers—the search for meaning can be a start toward affecting a change in the social conditions of our day. Commitment on the part of counselors to be change agents and to take social action through incorporating the spiritual dimension can be a powerful step toward dealing with the pain brought on by these social ills. In today's society, counselors must decide whether to accept existing conditions or to be creative architects of a new world. Counselors who are committed to their spiritual beliefs have no choice but to recreate society and bear witness to their transcendent beliefs. There is not, nor can there ever be, any reason or excuse for these counselors to be resigned to the persistent injustice, dehumanizing poverty, and humiliating domination of certain segments of our society. To resist these structural conditions and to replace them with others that promote greater justice and dignity in the access to goods and services is a major goal of these counselors.

Is there a way for counselors to achieve these goals? The answer is Yes. Counselors must do this first and foremost by being—that is, by modeling rather than telling and by actions rather than words. Nothing can excuse counselors who are committed to the spiritual dimension of life from the responsibility of loving their neighbors as themselves and from reaching out to their neighbors in time of need.

To struggle to change society with a view toward achieving humane forms of life for all is the central way that these counselors can combat "man's inhumanity to man." A look back at recent history demonstrates that the true makers of history were not the successful politicians but rather the prophets who resisted the enticements of power for commitment to their convictions. People such as Martin Luther King, Gandhi, Dorothy Day, and Mother

Teresa are examples. Counselors can do no less. They cannot allow themselves to be infatuated by established power and the hope of influencing policy makers. Rather they must take their cue from the struggling "deviants" who are often their clients and summon power by setting an example, by taking upon their shoulders the vulnerability of the oppressed.

Counselors cannot remain passive in the face of the prevailing injustices and inequalities of homelessness, joblessness, and hopelessness in our society. Counselors must instead see that because there needs to be a social upheaval, they should be at the center of the movement.

The greatest threat to these committed counselors is clearly the magnitude of the task and the loss of hope when progress is not seen immediately. Many prophets of doom preach the message that generous attempts to build a better world lead to more suffering than deliverance. Such pessimism seems to be a malady that afflicts mainly intellectuals in rich countries. The oppressed masses themselves, those who experience in the flesh the sting and stigma of poverty, disease, and political oppression, cannot afford the luxury of indulging in despair, as the buoyancy, hope, and continuing struggles of the peasants of Rwanda, the Native Americans of North America, and the courageous and triumphant people of South Africa so strikingly illustrate. Counselors, therefore, must see each client as a potential change agent and each situation as an opportunity to enter the client's worldview and to give leadership in the fight for a new world order.

Concrete ways that counselors can become creative architects and agents of social change include the following:

1. Initiate an awareness of the social issues through current mechanisms such as the American Counseling Association's World Conference; regional, state, and local conferences; the Summit on Spirituality; and the Multicultural/Diversity Agenda.
2. Challenge divisions such as the Association for Spiritual, Ethical, and Religious and Value Issues in Counseling (ASERVIC), Association for Humanistic Education and Development (AHEAD), and Association for Multicultural Counseling and Development (AMCD), whose missions address social issues, to take responsibility for leadership in this movement.

3. Join with social action groups such as Habitat for Humanity to combat poor housing. Get the commitment of local religious institutions to see this as their moral responsibility.

4. Provide leadership in the fight against homelessness by joining in efforts of grassroots organizations that minister to the homeless. Be willing to volunteer with the United Way and other such organizations and give time, talents, and treasures.

5. Stand in solidarity with minority groups that are being discriminated against by society. Speak out against this injustice and become known as a group of concerned citizens who make their voices heard. Develop position papers that can be presented to community leaders.

6. Approach the press and use the influence of the media to highlight the injustices that prevail in our society. Provide accurate data and documentation before initiating the contacts. Be prepared to speak openly and knowledgeably on the issues.

7. Enlist the aid of local agencies to identify the needs of migrant workers and their families. Contact local religious institutions to solicit their collaboration and to provide a welcoming, supportive, and nurturing environment for these migrant people.

8. Champion the needs of women and children. As counseling professionals, most of whom are women, we have a primary obligation to speak out on behalf of battered women, physically and sexually abused women and children, abandoned women and children, women who suffer injustices in the workplace, and legislation that discriminates against women. Focus energy by joining with established groups and by using the influence of our profession to lobby for more facilities and services for this segment of our society. Provide training and counseling for these women and mentor them in order to help them develop the skills necessary to change their lives. Also become involved in soliciting grants that will support training and counseling for women and children.

9. Raise awareness of the plight of the older poor and of the elder abuse that exists in our society. Support the efforts that are in place but expand them by volunteering to make needs known.

10. Influence counselor training programs so that the emerging professionals will have the skills to continue the cause for social justice by

- making sure that the spiritual dimension of counseling is included in counselor training;
- using references to different religious/spiritual traditions for case examples used in teaching;
- emphasizing religious/spiritual sensitivity in all counseling sessions;
- including religious/spiritual diversity in multicultural courses;
- preparing students to become social activists;
- guarding against the promulgation of only the Judeo/Christian perspectives in ethics concerns;
- making sure that all religious/spiritual traditions are acknowledged in discussions;
- encouraging students to become active in the fight against injustice; and
- requiring students to undertake service projects in the community as part of their clinical training.

Counselors must position themselves to be proactive in dealing with social issues and, through knowledge, skills, and training, be willing to take risks so that change can take place.

CONCLUSION

Many social issues call for social action on the part of the counseling profession. Taking responsibility for social change is a mandate for counselors. One way to approach this change is to incorporate the spiritual dimension of counseling into the practice of counseling; and the impetus for incorporating spirituality into the counseling process is today being widely discussed in the literature. A spiritual philosophy of life influences counselors and propels them to reach beyond the safe confines of individual and group counseling to a more global, inclusive interconnectedness with others of similar and different values.

If counselors are going to be a force for social change, they must make their voices heard and take risks to stand up for their convictions. They must actively advocate against the social injustices in our society—in which cultural diversity and spiritual pluralism are accepted as norms. A willingness by counselors to be creative architects, to bear witness to their transcendent beliefs, will help to change the persistent structures of injustice, poverty, and domination. As the counseling profession approaches a new millennium, the emphases on purpose and meaning, the essence of spirituality, are within the grasp and scope of helping professionals.

REFERENCES

Alcoholics Anonymous. (1976). *Alcoholics Anonymous* (3rd ed.). New York: Alcoholic Anonymous World Services.

Barret, R. L., & Barzan, B. E. (1996). Spiritual experiences of gay men and lesbians. *Counseling and Values, 41*, 4-15.

Bergin, A. E. (1988). Three contributions of a spiritual perspective to counseling and psychotherapy and behavior change. *Counseling and Values, 33*, 21-31.

Bergin, A. E. (1991). Values and religious issues in psychotherapy and mental health. *American Psychologist, 46*, 394-403.

Burke, M. T., & Miranti, J. G. (1995). *Counseling the spiritual dimension.* Alexandria, VA: American Counseling Association.

Chandler, C. K., Holden, J. M., & Kolander, C. A. (1992). Counseling for spiritual wellness: Theory and practice. *Journal of Counseling and Development, 21*, 168-175.

Chapman, R. J. (1996). Spirituality in the treatment of alcoholism: A world view approach. *Counseling and Values, 41*, 39-50

Corey, G., Corey, M. S., & Callanan, P. (1998). *Issues and ethics in the helping professions* (5th ed.). Pacific Grove, CA: Brooks/Cole.

Dyer, W. W. (1995). *Your sacred self: Making the decision to be free.* New York: Harper Collins.

Grimm, D. W. (1994). Therapist spiritual and religious values in psychotherapy. *Counseling and Values, 38*, 154-163.

Heise, R. G., & Steitz, J. A. (1991). Religious perfectionism and spiritual growth. *Counseling and Values, 36*, 11-23.

Herlihy, B., & Corey, G. (Eds.). (1995). *ACA ethical standards casebook* (5th ed.). Alexandria, VA: American Counseling Association.

Herr, E. L. (1991). Challenges to mental health counselors in a dynamic society: Macrostrategies in the profession. *Journal of Mental Health Counseling, 13*, 6-20.

Hinterkopf, E. (1994). Integrating spiritual experiences in counseling. *Counseling and Values, 38*, 165-175.

Ingersoll, R. E. (1997). Teaching a course on counseling and spirituality. *Counselor Education and Supervision, 36*, 224-232.

Johnson, V. E. (1980). *I'll quit tomorrow.* San Francisco: Harper and Row.

Kelly, E. W. (1994). Counselor preparation: The role of religion and spirituality in counselor education: A national survey. *Counselor Education and Supervision, 33*, 227-237.

Lee, C. C., & Sirch, M. L. (1994). Counseling in an enlightened society: Values for a new millennium. *Counseling and Values, 38*, 90-97.

Mack, M. L. (1994). Understanding spirituality in counseling psychology: Considerations for research, training, and practice. *Counseling and Values, 39*, 15-31.

Maher, M. H., & Hunt, T. K. (1993). Spirituality reconsidered. *Counseling and Values, 38*, 21-28.

Mattson, D. L. (1994). Religious counseling: To be used not feared. *Counseling and Values, 38,* 187-191.

Pate, R. H., Jr., & Bondi, A. M. (1992). Religious beliefs and practices: An integral aspect of multicultural awareness. *Counselor Education and Supervision, 32,* 108-115.

Pate, R. H., Jr., & High, H. T. (1995). The importance of client religious beliefs and practices in the education of counselors in CACREP-accredited programs. *Counseling and Values, 40,* 2-5.

Summit on spirituality. (1995). *Counseling Today, 38,* 6, 30.

PART TWO

Social Action: A Focus on Assessment,
Research, and Technology

10

Fair Access to Assessment Instruments and the Use of Assessment in Counseling

NICHOLAS A. VACC

How, if at all, are certified and licensed counselors addressing assessment issues? These issues impact client well-being in contemporary society, particularly those clients who have diverse cultural backgrounds, and so we must ask who is qualified to select, administer, score, and interpret assessment instruments and for what purpose (e.g., diagnose and treat clients)? If these questions, which are critical to certified and licensed counselors, are not addressed seriously and quickly by the profession, we will be doing a disservice to the public. Furthermore, not addressing them may cause counselors eventually to hold permanent second-class status among other human-service professionals.

Certified and licensed counselors need to establish a clear direction for how assessment practices can be socially responsible as well as socially responsive, particularly as these practices influence services for diverse populations. Counselor use of assessment, tests, and diagnoses, in serving diverse groups needs to be well-defined and well understood. Counselors need to be educated in how a client's social environment affects assessment practices. Clinical assessment, test usage, and diagnoses do not take place in isolation. Rather, they are linked with knowledge of cultural differences. To be adequately prepared, counselors need to understand (a) the effect of changes in our population on assessment practice in order to be socially responsive, (b) issues surrounding access to assessment instruments and practices in order to ensure fair access, and (c) the place of assessment in counseling as it impacts client well-being in order to be socially responsible. These three areas of understanding are explored in this chapter's first three sections. The chapter then presents a model for the assessment process that is responsive both to cultural diversity and theoretical variations, and provides a figure to illustrate the model. The chapter concludes with a look at training considerations in assessment.

SOCIALLY RESPONSIVE ASSESSMENT

Contemporary society in the United States is undergoing a great change in its racial composition. A report cited in *The Wall Street Journal* ("Capital Journal," 1997) estimated that in 50 years the United States will be 51% White, and the largest minority group will be Latinos. Currently, the three dominant minority groups— African Americans, Latinos, and Asians—comprise 49.1 million of the nation's 248.7 million people ("Makeup of Minorities," 1991). Latinos and Asians in the United States have each increased in number by 50% during the past 10 years. In essence, the United States enjoys an ethnically and culturally diverse population. We are a pluralistic society, and counselors' assessment practices need to be responsive to these differences.

The changes in our population require a fresh look at assessment practices used by counselors and other professionals who do testing. Effective solutions to the challenges posed by an ethnically and culturally diverse population will not be found in new tests or through revisions of present tests. As Anastasi (1997) adroitly indicated, "No single test can be universally applicable or equally 'fair' to all cultures. . . . It is unlikely, moreover, that any test can be equally 'fair' to more than one cultural group" (p. 345). Rather, what is needed by counselors and other professionals are better assessment practices. Yet this is only part of an effective response to groups that have not been served by existing practices. Effective solutions are possible only through recognition of the larger problem, with the critical issue being the quality and effectiveness of professional services to those clients whose social environment does not represent that of the middle-class norm. Counselors need to examine the quality and usefulness of assessment activities that are available relative to how such assessments may negatively affect clients. Needed is a reorientation of assessment practices to promote the development of all human talent. When assessment practices disproportionately deny opportunities to minorities, counselors need to ensure that the assessment practices are relevant. A key element for good assessment practices for all individuals is the use of multiple sources of assessment information when making decisions about individuals, groups, or institutions. The single best axiom for counselors and other professionals to follow when involved in assessment is that all tests are biased; and provisions should be made to try to eliminate or, at a minimum, reduce the effects of the bias.

A variety of ways exist for considering the concepts that influence bias in tests. Of primary importance, however, are the concepts of fairness and social equity. As reported by Anastasi (1997), test bias is still being examined, and with the present state of knowledge, there exists an insufficient basis for correcting inequities. Yet counselors and other professions need to examine the degree of bias that exists. Panlagua (1994) reported that bias in assessment can be reduced through

- examining our own bias(es) and prejudice(s);
- becoming aware of the potential effects of racism on the diagnosis of mental disorders;
- using socioeconomic variables;
- reducing the sociocultural gap between the client and the therapist;
- considering culture-related syndromes;
- asking culturally appropriate questions;
- using the least biased assessment strategies first, including physiological measures, direct behavioral observations, self-monitoring, behavioral self-report rating scales, clinical interviews, trait measures such as the California Psychological Inventory, self-report of psychopathology measures such as the MMPI, and projective tests such as the Rorschach test;
- consulting paraprofessionals within the respective racial/ethnic group;
- avoiding the Mental Status Examination because, for example, clients may not be able to count, may know who the last president in their country was but not the last U.S. president, may be unable to show eye contact because it is not rewarded in their cultural group, or may dress carelessly because they cannot afford to dress nicely; and

- using Richard Dana's Assessment Model, which includes assessing acculturation, providing a culturally specific service-delivery style (i.e., behavioral etiquettes), using the client's native or preferred language, using the EMIC perspective of assessment (which includes an understanding of clients in their own culture), and describing findings to clients using a culturally specific strategy.

The demographic changes taking place in the United States challenge counselors to be aware, to understand, and to be knowledgeable of a variety of cultures. Increasingly, all counselors are working cross-culturally, and accordingly, they need to highlight the role of culture in assessment, human development, and behavior. This change, however, requires counselors to reconsider some of the basic assumptions underlying their past assessment practices. Counselors need to challenge existing "professional wisdom." They must decide how much of what has been considered to be good practice may apply only to the White middle class in the United States because what typically is viewed as normative or representative may be an expression of one culture only.

Counselors have to make some fundamental changes concerning assessment practices because the cultural experiences of a diverse public influences what is seen and what eludes attention. Assessment issues that need consideration by counselors in our increasingly diverse society include the (a) appropriate skills needed to work in a socially responsible and effective manner with various populations, (b) appropriate place of standardized assessment with individuals of culturally different backgrounds, (c) implications of acculturation and language differences when assessing performance, and (d) research questions concerning assessment that counselors need to ask in order to understand our diverse society.

FAIR ACCESS TO ASSESSMENT INSTRUMENTS

Critical to certified and licensed counselors is fair access to selecting, administering, scoring, and interpreting assessment instruments. Among numerous issues surrounding fair access, one of the most important is the core assumption that qualified counselors are able to do assessment, that master's-level counselors are fully functioning mental-health service providers able to select, administer, score, and interpret tests as well as diagnose. This core assumption fundamental to the structure of the American Counseling Association, in which fair access to assessment instruments and the use of assessment in counseling help define the scope of practice for certified and licensed counselors. Although this issue may be viewed as more self-serving for professional counselors because it addresses a professional concern, it clearly speaks to the broad social issue of the availability of clinical services and thus impacts client well-being.

Regrettably, some counselors perceive assessment and testing as a potpourri of activities that are not linked to their scope of practice as a counselor. Therefore, a clearer identity for assessment, test usage, and diagnoses within counseling is needed so that the harmful effects of any limitations on counselor access to assessment instruments can be minimized for both clients and counselors. To achieve this goal, the profession needs to commit itself to a clearer conceptualization of the purpose of assessment, test usage, and diagnoses, and the treatment methods to be used as a result of assessment.

External Events Affecting Fair Access

Most certified and licensed counselors are aware of initiatives by some state regulatory agencies and state psychological associations to limit access to educational and psychological tests. The leaders of the ACA and of the National Board for Certified Counselors (NBCC) recognize the seriousness of counselors' loss of access to assessment instruments. For example, counselor use of the Draw A Person Test, Woodcock-Johnson Psycho-Educational Battery Test of Achievement, and Incomplete Sentences Blank has been challenged by the State of Louisianna Through the Louisiana State Board of Examiners of Psychologists of the Department of Health and Human Services (1995). For another example, the California Board of Psychology during hearings discussed qualifications for use of the Strong Interest Inventory and the Myers-Briggs Type Indicator by mental health service providers other than psychologists. This issue of test-user qualifications has significant implications for certified and licensed counselors and for counselor training programs.

The American Psychological Association (APA) has established a committee that is charged with describing the set of knowledge and skills necessary for professionals to administer, score, and interpret assessment instruments in a "competent and responsible manner." This committee will also address the issues of (a) informing psychologists and other health service providers of the skills and knowledge required in the responsible conduct of assessment, (b) influencing the curriculum of graduate training programs, (c) assisting test publishers in determining appropriate qualifications for test users, (d) informing the public about appropriate test-user qualifications, and (e) informing regulatory, disciplinary, accrediting, and credentialing bodies about test-user qualifications in order to assist in their development of standards, regulations, or guidelines. Clearly, APA, with its long history of test usage, will have an influential effect on and will be an effective force in addressing access to and use of assessment instruments. The decisions of this committee will ultimately effect all counselors.

Of primary concern to certified and licensed counselors are events external to the profession that create more regulation through state statutes, more restrictions through limitations of scope of practice, and more control by other professional organizations. Curiously, these external events often are aided by civil rights advocate groups and antitest groups that are not interested in scope-of-practice issues. Rather, they are seeking a mechanism by which to assert control over assessment and its consequences (e.g., placement, labeling, and restricting access to colleges, universities, professions, and employment).

Standardized tests are reportedly administered annually to more than 40 million individuals (Camara, 1988). These tests determine, for example, who will gain admission to colleges and universities and who will become lawyers, physicians, and certified and licensed counselors. Assessment instruments are also routinely used to determine award recipients as well as who will be promoted to the next grade or placement in public schools. In addition, the use of assessment instruments by insurance companies and managed care organizations is increasing in employment settings and in the professional practice of mental health service providers, for reasons of greater accountability, increased productivity, and proof of competency, diagnosis, treatment, and payment. Testing affects the general public, which is also seeking to assert control over assessment and its consequences.

Because social and professional policy issues involve the effects of assessment on certified and licensed counselors, there is a need to promote responsible and appropriate testing practices from within the field in order to avoid external challenges such as those that are currently taking place. In summing up their research on test-user qualifications, Moreland, Eyde, Robertson, Primoff, and Most (1995) reported that educational efforts are more effective in promoting good testing practices than in limiting the use of tests. Their report is a product of the Joint Committee on Testing Practices, which contains representatives from ACA, APA, National Council of Measurement and Evaluation (NCME), National Association of School Psychologists (NASP), and American Speech and Hearing Association (ASHA). The report has not yet been adopted by any of the participating organizations, but it should and can offer the core focus for ACA in addressing the important issue of access to assessment instruments.

The current state of affairs concerning selecting, administering, scoring, and interpreting assessment instruments as well as test-users qualifications is inconclusive. This is mainly due to *The Standards for Educational and Psychological Tests* (1985), which represents the expert opinion of APA, the American Educational Research Association (AERA), and NCME, and which is frequently viewed as "the authoritative document on test development and use" and cited in litigation cases. Yet this document does not address user qualifications other than to state that responsibility for test use should be assumed only by those who are properly trained, and that test manuals should specify the qualifications required to administer and interpret a given test. However, because some test publishers will not permit certified and licensed counselors to purchase their assessment instruments, test-user qualifications are an issue that should be addressed long before getting to the test manual. That is, test publishers need to be informed by certified and licensed counselors of counselors' skills, knowledge, and responsible conduct in using assessment instruments. Test publisher decisions about access to assessment instruments should not occur in a vacuum.

Indeed, the decisions should be influenced by professional policies of the counseling profession, and the place of assessment should not be left to the discretion of those outside the counseling profession.

Actions by ACA and NBCC to Ensure Access

The APA, AERA, and NCME are not alone in addressing the issue of test-user qualifications and in defining who may select, administer, score, and interpret assessment instruments. The ACA and the NBCC are mobilizing themselves to inform the general public, counselors, and other professionals of the situation. They are also taking steps to prevent certified and licensed counselors from having limited access to assessment instruments, thus making counselors unable to assess, diagnose, and treat clients independently.

The Fair Access Coalition for Testing (FACT), a group recently formed to protect counselors from the loss of access to testing instruments, is a coalition of professional groups that primarily consists of master's-level practitioners. FACT has prepared a policy statement in which it seeks fairness in any restrictions on the access to and use of tests. The highest priority of the FACT Steering Committee is to address the issues of access to and use of tests by counselors. FACT's goals include (a) developing model legislation about access to and use of tests by counselors and serving as a clearinghouse for this legislation, (b) developing standards of practice for mental health assessment and persuading managed health care firms to reimburse qualified providers, (c) obtaining a legal definition of *psychological activities* in every state, (d) working with test publishers to clarify qualifications in test manuals for each test user, and (e) establishing core statements about informing other professionals about the use of tests. These goals will involve professional ethics, tests publishers, and scope-of-practice sections of state regulations and statutes.

Many important events and philosophical movements have shaped counseling as we know it today, but much remains to be done to answer the questions concerning fair access to assessment instruments by certified and licensed counselors that are currently being debated among professional groups. These questions undoubtedly will lead to significant court cases, legislation, and public policy decisions mandating certain practices. Note that practicing psychologists and other health service providers who traditionally have had the privilege of independent practice are understandably concerned over the increase in the independent status and vendorship of master's-level practitioners. Furthermore, these providers view master's-level practitioners as contributing to the lower fees offered by managed-care organizations.

One of the hallmarks of treatment is the necessity to diagnose through assessing a client's mental status. Assessment is not only integral to diagnoses and independent practice but is also a critical component of the counseling process (Vacc, 1991; Vacc & Loesch, 1994). Assessment allows counselors to make relevant decisions about interventions through diagnosing the status of the client's well-being. Some counselors downplay the importance of assessment, believing that time spent assessing could be better spent counseling. However, assessment is necessary if certified and licensed counselors desire the option of independent practice.

SOCIALLY RESPONSIBLE ASSESSMENT

Counselors should have a contextual understanding of the place of assessment as it speaks to the broad social issues that impact client well-being in contemporary society. A contextual understanding of assessment encompasses the counseling process as it relates to diagnosis and treatment. Confusion exists, however, about some of the semantics concerning assessment. The issue can be clarified by making the distinction between *assessment* and *measurement*. Assessment, which can be considered the data-gathering process or method in counseling (Vacc & Loesch, 1994), subsumes measurement, which is the assignment of numerical or categorical values to human attributes according to rules (Crocker & Algina, 1986). Accordingly, assessment is broader than measurement and requires the counselor to understand, among other things, the types and purposes of the various assessment procedures. For this perspective, the distinction is made between *assessment* and *testing*, with assessment being the broader concept or the gathering of information, and testing being a systematic procedure for comparing the behavior of two or more persons (Cronbach, 1970). Counselors do not just give tests; they perform assessments. Unfortunately, testing has been used as a synonym for assessment, measurement, and evaluation. Evaluation subsumes assessment and is considered to be the interpretation and application of assessment data. It is important to understand that the term *assessment* implies ways of gathering information about an individual and determining differences or making judgments, whereas testing is only one way of gathering assessment information. Other assessment procedures include interviews, observations of behavior in natural or structured settings, the recording of various physiological functions, and the use of paper-and-pencil instruments. Information gathered from these procedures can be understood best through an assessment model that helps provide a conceptual framework. Accordingly, assessment is much more than the simple administration of a test.

Assessment Practices

Because there is some disagreement concerning the use of assessment in counseling, perhaps what is needed at this time is not specific guidelines concerning the content of assessment in counseling but rather a focus on identifying what counselors are expected to do in their work. Specific information related to work behaviors provides the basis for classifying the importance of assessment practices performed by certified and licensed counselors.

Loesch and Vacc conducted an empirical occupational analysis of counselors for the National Board for Certified Counselors (1993) to determine the tasks counselors perform. Fitzgerald and Osipow (1986) conducted a similar job analysis of counseling psychologists, and another study of clinical psychologists was conducted by Norcoss and Prochaska (1982). The NBCC study investigated the type and frequency of counselor activities so as to clarify the tasks that counselors perform. Thus the emphasis was shifted from a focus on what others think is needed to a focus on the nature of activities used during counselors' day-to-day professional roles. One hundred fifty-one work behaviors were identified through a review of the literature and a critical review by experts in the counseling field, using three levels of item refinement. The frequency of counselors' involvement with a specific work behavior was based on responses by 722 certified counselors. Of the top 10% of work behaviors identified most frequently by these counselors, almost half were assessment activities: evaluating existing precounseling data, assessing psychosocial status, assessing potential for client to harm self or others, self-evaluating counseling effectiveness, evaluating need for client referral, and evaluating clients' movement toward counseling goals. Thus this work-behavior investigation documents clearly that assessment is integral to the counseling process, that assessment in counseling is both important and interrelated.

It is difficult to establish a universal context between counseling and assessment because of the diverse theoretical counseling approaches employed by the profession. Daniels and Altekruse (1982) reported that the relationship between counseling and assessment has not received clear, concise, and adequate coverage in the literature. This situation has not changed in almost two decades, in part due to the multitude of theoretical approaches used by counselors. Further, different emphases are placed on the importance of or need for assessment in these approaches. However, an inclusive model of assessment that moves counseling closer to scientific practice could overcome these discrepancies.

THE ASSESSMENT PROCESS: A PROPOSED MODEL

This section presents an approach to assessment in counseling that is sensitive both to variations in theoretical frameworks and to clients from diverse cultural groups and life circumstances. The model is designed to help certified and licensed counselors conceptualize assessment in a socially responsible manner and is intended to improve counseling effectiveness. It also accommodates diagnosis and uses the best of science and practice. At the foundation of mental health services, in general, and managed care, in particular, is the necessity of problem conceptualization and treatment planning based on valid diagnoses. Not all work settings for counselors require the establishment of valid diagnoses, and some counselors are uncomfortable assigning a label. Yet conceptualizing assessment and diagnosis as part of the counseling process is helpful in defining a counselor's scope of practice and in promoting client change.

As reported by Vacc and Loesch (1994), assessment is viewed within a scientific or empirical counseling perspective as gathering information to formulate the focus of, or purpose for, counseling. Involved with the empirical counseling perspective are the interview with the client and determining and specifying the purpose of counseling, all of which are done in the context of cross-cultural and cross-ethnic differences. The counselor can be viewed as a scientist who is continually assessing and conceptualizing the relationship among the information obtained, the cultural and ethnic context of the client, counseling goals, and counseling strategies. For example, to understand and be of assistance to Jane, a 33-year-old employee of an insurance company who is generally unhappy with her life, a counselor must understand the way Jane views her work and must learn about her interactions with family members and others. During assessment, the counselor also learns that Jane wants her boyfriend to be more understanding about her wishes to visit her family twice a week and is concerned about the future in her current job. Assessment, in Jane's situation, includes activities that focus on the selection of information for counseling, the data (information) collection process, and the interpretation of those data. Beginning the counseling process with assessment is characterized by identifying the purpose for counseling as it relates to situational, social, and psychological factors, and the goal(s) of intervention. Counselors are interested in helping their clients and themselves determine the focus or purpose of counseling and delineating intervention goal(s) within the context of the client's cultural background. Therefore, establishing the purpose of counseling is not an end in itself but rather a method for delineating (change) goals, determining and implementing strategies of intervention, and constructing a framework for the continuous assessment of progress within the context of the client's social framework. A similar model has been proposed by Vacc and Ritter (1995) for assessing preschool children.

ESTABLISHING THE PURPOSE

Establishing the purpose of counseling is the heart of empirical counseling within the context of the client's cultural and ethnic background. Without defining the purpose for counseling, the effect(s) of counseling cannot be assessed. Counseling, by definition, suggests some type of action (i.e., an action-oriented purpose). The counselor, however, must be able to identify the specific nature of the purpose of action for counseling within the client's situational and social contexts. The purpose of counseling should be defined in ways that make it as specific (i.e., concrete) and observable as possible in order to permit measurement of progress and change. To say that Jane is anxious is not a specific statement. Rather, it conveys a state of psychological being. However, if Jane is described as often absent from her work, having thoughts of failure, and yelling frequently at friends, the counselor has stated specific and observable indicators of Jane's situation. The counselor is also able to delineate what led him or her to label Jane as *being anxious*. It becomes readily apparent that specific and observable indicators also are measurable, at least potentially. For example, with Jane, absenteeism from work and yelling at friends can be readily observed and measured.

Ideally, the purpose and goals for counseling should be specific, observable, and potentially measurable by more than one person. Although some purposes for counseling are simply not easily specified, empirical counseling still strives to produce measurable data. For example, the counselor might request that Jane monitor the frequency with which she has thoughts of failure. This self-report method of assessment will not suffice as a sole criterion within the content of empirical counseling but is a helpful adjunct activity. Similarly, if a counselor determines that Tom, a fifth-grade student, has feelings of low self-esteem, the counselor still will be able to develop an informal scale or to use an existing scale to assess Tom's self-esteem. By recognizing the specific and observable purposes for counseling during assessment, the counselor has potentially measurable indicators that will aid in the next step of goal determination. Careful and prudent assessment is also necessary to communicate with other professionals and to meet the needs of some regulatory groups for payment. The latter needs typically involve the use of the *Diagnostic and Statistical Manual of Mental Disorders* (fourth edition) (APA, 1994), commonly referred to as the *DSM-IV*.

The *DSM-IV* is employed by counselors for purposes of psychodiagnosis and treatment planning, insurance reimbursement, and communication with other helping professionals. The *DSM-IV* provides a common denominator among professionals from a variety of disciplines. The *DSM-IV* includes 18 diagnostic categories that conceptualize behaviors as a pattern or syndrome associated with present distress (i.e., symptom), with disability (i.e., impairment in one or more areas of functioning), or with significantly increased risk of suffering. The *DSM-IV* contains specific diagnostic criteria, a clinical sketch of each disorder, diagnostic considerations, information about the onset and nature of a problem, and any predisposing factors. Behaviors classified using the *DSM-IV* are viewed as mental disorders rather than as expected responses to particular events. The language and tone of the *DSM-IV* is reflective of the medical profession's view of human behavior as being either free from symptoms or free from illness in a medical sense.

DELINEATING GOALS

It is not uncommon for some clients to express concern about a facet of their lives without being able to indicate what they might want to do differently. The counseling process often involves confounding information, and it is the dilemma of the counselor to help identify realistic goals. The goals, like the purpose for counseling, need to be specific and observable. The goals of counseling are the desirable changes the client and counselor seek to obtain; for obvious reasons, they are highly interrelated with the purpose for counseling. With Bill, a 28-year-old bachelor, the purpose for counseling was determined as alleviating his inability to engage in conversation with women of similar age. Therefore, a goal in counseling was to increase his frequency of conversations with female peers. Establishing goals such as this permits the counselor an opportunity to determine whether the purpose for counseling has been achieved.

Note that it is recommended that goals be stated in a positive orientation. The counselor concerned with Bill's difficulties in engaging in conversation with women of his own age could have focused on "stopping the avoidance of speaking (behaviors) with female peers" rather than increasing the positive behavior desired. The latter approach, however, is advantageous because it focuses on the positive aspects and potentials of intervention; it suggests what the future could be if the negative present situation could be minimized.

DETERMINING STRATEGY

During this phase, the counselor determines, in conjunction with the client, a framework for action (i.e., a plan). At some point early in the counseling process, the counselor needs to arrive at a course of action, meaning that he or she cannot always wait to know everything there is to know about the purpose for counseling. When deciding a course of action or intervention strategy, counselors judge the probability of the validity of their actions based on already acquired data, which include knowledge, experience (i.e., past history), and the personality attributes mentioned earlier. Intervention strategies selected depend on the counseling orientation of the counselor. Strategies, however, may change the course of counseling because the client's presenting purpose for counseling often is not the "real" purpose for which counseling was sought.

IMPLEMENTATING STRATEGY

The entire process of empirical counseling is built on specification, which is a tangible and focal orientation to the purpose of counseling. This enables counseling with specific techniques and purposes. Up to this point, the counselor has had only data that enable him or her to decide on a strategy; a focus for the counseling process exists but not the data to determine the effectiveness of the strategy. The counselor has, in a heuristic manner, planned for the sequencing of the counseling process or intervention activities. During this phase, the counselor engages in the process of the intervention. In a very real sense, the counselor is now engaged in a scientific method in which he or she determines the purpose and goal of counseling, makes a hypothesis through the determination of a strategy, implements and tests the strategy, and then makes changes based on the results and conclusions as new data become available.

CONSTRUCTING ASSESSMENT AS A CONTINUOUS PROCESS

When new purposes for counseling are determined or treatment strategies fail, it is necessary for the counselor to return to the first phase of the empirical counseling approach. Assessment, therefore, is a continuous process. Accordingly, the initial assessment, goal determination, and strategy selection are not ends in themselves. Nor do they provide the totality of counseling. Rather, the counselor needs to consider the cultural and ethnic background of the client.

Recent research has revealed that situational contexts play a critical role in performance (Miller-Jones, 1989), and that people of different backgrounds are indeed exposed to different experiences that can affect standardized test results (Williams, 1983). Although the populations that participate in testing are multicultural and diverse, the performance and competence assessment models in our society are monocultural (Williams, 1983). It is possible that the use of culturally loaded or monocultural assessment instruments with clients of other cultural backgrounds may result in unfair predictions, assumptions, or decisions. Counselors should strive for culture-reduced instruments; but counselors also must be aware of different values, languages, expectations, and customs that affect assessment in general and testing results in particular. Therefore, counselors must proceed with caution when attempting to assess, evaluate, and interpret performances of persons who are not represented in the norm group on which many instruments are standardized (i.e., typically middle-class Whites).

The flowchart in Figure 10-1 illustrates the constructs in continuous empirical counseling within a context of cross-cultural and cross-ethnic differences. The flowchart does not include the specific procedures that counselors use in each phase, but it is sufficiently complete for characterizing the process.

It is constructed as taking place within the context of the client's cultural and ethnic background, and it begins with the initial assessment by the counselor, which may be categorized as informal and tentative at the outset but which establishes purpose. The assessment process is described in specific and observable behaviors that lead to the establishment of goals and objectives in collaboration with the client. Next, based on the professional counselor's knowledge, experience, and personality attributes, the strategy is determined and then implemented. Once the strategy has been implemented, the goal(s) and objectives or the strategy may need to be changed or reformulated based on continuous empirical assessment. This is shown by the feedback arrow from the continuous assessment decision diamond containing the question "Has there been progress?" If no progress has been made, the professional counselor must decide whether to change the goals and objectives. If the decision is to not change the goals, then the strategy is reviewed

Figure 10-1.
A Socially Responsible Empirical-Counseling
Assessment Model

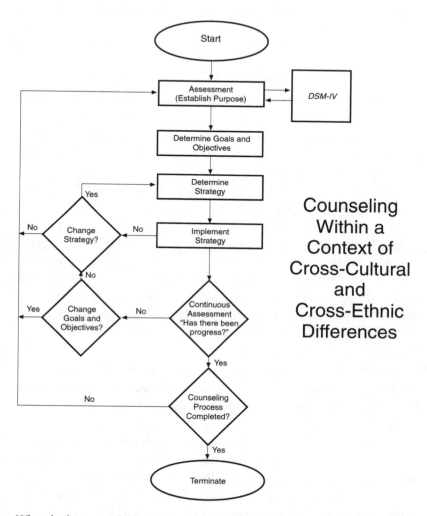

What the basic standard symbols—which convert narratives to graphics—in the flowchart mean:

- Ovals—represent the beginning and end point in the process.
- Lines with arrows—represent the flow of activities among functions.
- Rectangles—represent specific functions used at a particular step in the process.
- Squares—are occasionally connected to a rectangle and represent a concurrent behavior.
- Diamonds—represent decision-making activities.

and possibly redefined (as indicated by the feedback arrow), and counseling continues. Had the response to the change-goal decision been Yes, the counselor would formulate new goals based on continuous assessment. The flowchart thus displays empirical counseling with its continuous assessment and feedback procedure for the purpose of keeping counseling responsive to the client.

TRAINING CONSIDERATIONS IN ASSESSMENT

Training in assessment for counselors is important. Unfortunately, training in assessment for counselors is not uniform. In fact, considerable diversity exists among preparation programs. It thus becomes impossible to characterize the prototypical ACA member for purposes of classifying counselors' assessment skills.

The situation in ACA is paradoxical. The membership views assessment as germane to the standards for training and professional credentialing, as reflected by the CACREP and NBCC, but some of the theoretical counseling approaches embraced by ACA suggest a dichotomy between the literature on assessment and the literature on counseling. However, despite the current lack of integration between assessment and counseling, practical issues necessitate that counselors be knowledgeable and skilled in assessment. Accordingly, efforts need to be made to bring assessment and counseling together in training programs.

In order for counselors to engage in the assessment process, they should have course work and other acquired experiences that provide (a) a knowledge base that is derived largely from the social and behavioral sciences, (b) knowledge of diverse groups, (c) information on reliable and valid measures, methods, and techniques of assessment, (d) a conceptual framework of continuous assessment and sensitivity to cross-cultural and ethnic differences, and (e) skills to work with clients to affect change. Of particular concern is the continuation of assessment in practice because it has not been uniformly emphasized in counselor education training programs.

CONCLUSION

Assessment is a multidimensional continuous process for establishing a base of information about clients. In assessment, the focus needs to be on using information to help clients rather than to find a truth for placement selection. In working to improve assessment practices toward these ends, excellent resources for counselors include *Multicultural Assessment Standards: A Compilation for Counselors* (Prediger, 1994), which is available through the Association for Assessment in Counseling; *Code of Fair Testing Practices in Education* (Joint Committee on Testing Practices, 1988), which is available through APA; and *Responsibilities of Users of Standardized Tests* (AACD, 1989), which is available through ACA.

To be prepared to meet the needs of their clientele, counselors need to have knowledge of assessment and possess the skills necessary to provide effective assistance in a socially responsible manner for all U.S. populations. Relatedly, counselor educators need to provide the training in such a way that the public is assured that recent counseling graduates have at least a minimum level of competence in assessment. Counselors need to have not only contextual understanding of the lives of people with diverse cultural and ethnic backgrounds but also a conceptual framework for assessment that addresses the social issues impacting client well-being in contemporary society.

REFERENCES

American Association for Counseling and Development and Association for Measurement and Evaluation in Counseling and Development. (1989). *Responsibilities of users of standardized tests: RUST statement revised*. Alexandria, VA: Author.

American Psychiatric Association. (1994). *Diagnostic and statistical manual of mental disorders* (4th ed.). Washington, DC: Author.

Anastasi, A. (1997). *Psychological testing* (9th ed.). Upper Saddle River, NJ: Prentice-Hall.

Camara, W. J. (1988). *APA's role in fostering good testing practices*. Paper presented at the 96th Annual Convention of the American Psychologist Association, Atlanta, GA.

Capital journal. (1997, August 6). *The Wall Street Journal*, p. A12.

Crocker, L., & Algina, J. (1986). *Introduction to classical and modern test theory*. New York: CBS College Publishing.

Cronbach, L. J. (1970). *Essentials of psychological testing* (3rd ed.). New York: Harper and Row.

Daniels, M. H., & Altekruse, M. (1982). Preparation of counselors for assessment. *Measurement and Evaluation in Guidance, 15*, 74-81.

Fitzgerald, L. F., & Osipow, S. H. (1986). An occupational analysis of counseling psychology. *Journal of Counseling Psychology, 41*, 535-544.

Makeup of minorities in the U.S. is shifting. (1991, March 31). *Greensboro News and Record*, p. A4.

Miller-Jones, D. (1989). Culture and testing. *American Psychologist, 44*, 360-366.

Moreland, K. L., Eyde, L. D., Robertson, G. J., Primoff, E. S., & Most, R. B. (1995). Assessment of test user qualifications: A data-based measurement procedure. *American Psychologist, 50*, 14-21.

National Board for Certified Counselors. (1993). *A word behavior analysis of professional counselors*. Muncie, IN: Accelerated Development.

Norcross, J. C., & Prochaska, J. O. (1982). A national survey of clinical psychologists: Characteristics and activities. *The Clinical Psychologist, 35*, 1-8.

Panlagua, F. A. (1994). *Assessing and testing culturally diverse clients: A practical guide*. Newbury Park, CA: Sage.

Prediger, D. J. (1994). Multicultural assessment standards: A compilation for counselors. *Measurement and Evaluation in Counseling and Development, 27*, 68-73.

The standards for educational and psychological tests. (1995). Washington, DC: American Educational Research Association, American Psychological Association, and National Council of Measurement Evaluation.

State of Louisiana Through the Louisiana State Board of Examiners of Psychologists of the Department of Health and Human Services v. Boyd J. Atterberry, 95.CA.0391 (LA 1995).

Vacc, N. A. (1991). Changing times: Changing views about testing. *Journal of Humanistic Education and Development, 30*, 148-156.

Vacc, N. A., & Loesch, L. (1994). *A professional orientation to counseling*. New York: Taylor & Francis.

Vacc, N. A., & Ritter, S. (1995). Assessment of preschool children. In W. Schafer (Ed.), *Assessment in counseling and therapy* (ERIC/CASS Publication No. EO-CG 95-28). Greensboro: University of North Carolina at Greensboro, School of Education.

Williams, T. S. (1983). Some issues in the standardized testing of minority students. *Journal of Education, 165*(2), 192-208.

11

Technology: A Force for Social Action

JOHN A. CASEY

• *John Smith wakes up in his mountain chalet daily to breathe fresh air, enjoy a morning workout, eat a healthy breakfast, check the stock market and his E-mail messages via the Internet, download data from his personal digital assistant to his PC, purchase discount airfare tickets from the American Airlines web site on the World-Wide Web, and fax some updated information to his corporate clients in distant states before settling back to enjoy a new video in his home entertainment center with digital television and surround sound.*

• *Juanita Gonzales wakes up in her crowded inner-city tenement house to make sack lunches for her kids and herself, mass produces a few quick pieces of toast before rushing the kids to school with whatever clothes could be found in the laundry basket, and boards a city bus to her job at a small motel where she works the front desk. She used to have three times the number of coworkers at the motel, but when the company was sold and the union disbanded, two thirds of her colleagues were let go while she was taught how to use a headphone for being switchboard operator, a computer for handling reservations, and a credit card reader for customers checking in and checking out. At the end of her shift, she rides part way home but gets off the bus at a fast food restaurant for her second job where*

> *she dons headgear to take orders from the drive through*
> *and pushes buttons on the computerized cash register*
> *to handle the cash transactions and transmit orders to*
> *the monitors in the kitchen. When she finally returns*
> *home, she fixes a quick dinner for the family, super-*
> *vises homework when possible, and collapses into bed*
> *for a short night before starting over again tomorrow.*

Both of these individuals are fictitious; their activities are not. Similar routines are not uncommon in the present day United States. What John and Juanita have in common is an increased reliance on technology for their work; what separates them is who has the control. John decides when, where, and how to use his technological tools; Juanita is a prisoner, controlled by the technological tools someone else has placed upon her. And they are examples of the *technogap*.

This chapter begins by exploring the technogaps for adults and for students. It then discusses what counselors can do and provides ideas for community and school programs. The chapter concludes with a look at social implications—beyond hardware, software, and technical training.

THE TECHNOGAP FOR ADULTS

Michael and Linda Cohn (Cohn & Cohn, 1996) described the problems associated with increased demands to perform multiple tasks with rapid precision in their book *Technogap: Combating Stress at Work and Home in the 90s and Beyond.*

> People are cracking under the strain, and the number of people who can function under this system appears to be dwindling. Moreover, learned helplessness or depression may develop from the lack of control over one's work environment. Computers have increased our productivity, but have geometrically increased the expectations for productivity. The technologically disadvantaged are falling further and further behind in the productivity curve. While the "have's" are using technology to improve their lives, the "have not's" are falling prey to a lifestyle where the moving

sidewalk under them is speeding up faster and faster in the opposite direction.

The winners in the technology revolution have become the wealthiest people in the world today. In 1996, the average chief executive officer (CEO) made 290 times the pay of factory workers, up from 42 times as much in 1980, according to Holly Sklar (1997), the author of "Chaos or Community? Seeking Solutions, Not Scapegoats for Bad Economics." The average CEO salary and bonus in 1996 was $2.3 million, a rise of 39% from 1995. When long-term compensation, such as stock options, was added, the average was $5,781,300, a whopping 54% increase. That adds up to $15,839 a day, including weekends—more than many workers earn in a year!

Not only CEOs have benefited from the technology era. Workers in technology fields typically earn the highest salaries among college graduates annually. High salaries in Silicon Valley for workers led to a bidding war for homes in Silicon Valley, California; in 1996, multiple offers at full asking price were common, even though it was one of the most expensive home markets in the country. It should come as no surprise that this technologically intensive area receives over 30% of the venture capital invested in the United States despite having less than 5% of the country's population.

In contrast, technologically disadvantaged populations have suffered significant financial losses in today's world. While CEOs and technology workers enjoyed huge pay hikes (and the Fortune 500 company profits rose a record 23% in 1996), workers across all sectors received a raise of 3% in wages and benefits in the same period. Between 1989 and 1995, hourly wages dropped nearly 5% when adjusted for inflation in non-technology-related companies.

There are compelling reasons why technologically disadvantaged populations have not shared in the country's success. One reason is that technological skills are considered essential competencies for even entry-level jobs, as demonstrated in the U.S. Department of Labor's report of the Secretary's Commission on Achieving Necessary Skills (SCANS). In this report, information skills (using computers to process, acquire, evaluate, organize, maintain, interpret, and communicate information) and technology utilization skills (selecting technology, applying technology to a task, maintaining and troubleshooting technology) comprise two of the essential five skill domains.

Another reason is that, practically speaking, technologically disadvantaged populations do not have the same access to information, a key to knowledge and power in the technological age, as their technologically advantaged counterparts. They do not have the same access to databases for job searches. They do not have the same access to the E-mail chat groups that have become a formidable force in today's communication-oriented world. They do not have the same E-mail access to news groups that spread breaking news on a daily basis to subscribers who stay tuned to new developments. In work situations, they must accept the technology presented to them rather than design software and hardware for others to use.

THE TECHNOGAP FOR STUDENTS

Technologically disadvantaged populations are not limited to adults. Children, too, have fallen into a technogap primarily because of their school districts. Jonathan Kozol (1991) revealed the poverty of an East St. Louis school in an interview with a teacher:

> I don't know even where to begin. I have no materials with the exception of a single textbook given to each child. If I bring in anything else—books or tapes or magazines—I pay for it myself. The high school has no VCRs . . . The AV equipment in the building is so old that we are pressured not to use it. (1991, p. 29)

Kozol subsequently contrasted New Trier High School in suburban Chicago:

> New Trier's students have superior labs and up-to-date technology. One wing of the school, a physical education center that includes three separate gyms, also contains a fencing room, a wrestling room, and studios for dance instruction. In all, the school has seven gyms as well as an Olympic pool. (p. 65)

Since Kozol's book was published, the gap has continued to grow between wealthy school districts that have state-of-the-art computer hardware and software resources, including Internet access, and their poorer counterparts that use whatever is donated.

Technologically disadvantaged students suffer within school classrooms as well as across school districts, often because of family economic differences. While one student may turn in a final project utilizing multimedia (editing a video from a camcorder and adding special effects and sounds), another may be turning in a paper-and-pencil work that was prematurely terminated by a family trauma or a part-time job obligation.

The gap between rich and poor is growing rapidly across the United States, as illustrated by a chart entitled "Rich World, Poor World" (1996) in *USA Today*. Between 1980 and 1995, the income disparity surged, particularly in the South and Southwest. States with the greatest income disparity between rich and poor in 1995 were California, New York, Florida, Texas, South Carolina, Tennessee, West Virginia, New Mexico, Oklahoma, Louisiana, Mississippi, Alabama, and Kentucky.

Children in low-income families are five times more likely to drop out than their affluent counterparts, according to the Annie E. Casey Foundation's (1997) eighth annual study of U.S. children. Dropouts subsequently are 10 times more likely to live in poverty when compared to college graduates. Dropouts and even graduates with limited technological expertise from substandard schools typically cannot qualify for entry-level jobs. Even those with some technological aptitude are often placed in positions of high demand and stress, as typified by Juanita in the second vignette. College graduates with advanced technological training, however, such as John in the opening vignette, may find great opportunities with higher levels of income, responsibility, and autonomy. As the gap widens, the cycle of poverty will increase without appropriate social action.

WHAT CAN COUNSELORS DO?

What is the counselor's role in coping with the technogap between the rich and the poor? Is there anything that can be done other than form groups to "process the experience"? Should private practitioners move to Silicon Valley and cater to affluent clients? Should school counselors plan their career ladders around openings that develop within wealthier districts near the Research Triangle in

North Carolina? Should rehabilitation counselors focus their sights on clients with carpal tunnel syndrome in metropolitan Seattle?

No. The counselor's mandate is to become a social change agent wherever the technogap exists. Failure to become a proactive change agent, even among skilled Rogerians, is tantamount to negligence. Counselors must be catalysts for significant social, cultural, and economic changes through both individual and collective efforts to narrow the effects of the technogap.

Will Rogers once said, "Even if you're on the right track, you might get run over if you just sit there." Counselors who wait on the sidelines are developing a codependency with their technologically disadvantaged clients if they fail to develop the necessary knowledge and skills to cope with the world in the technological era.

IDEAS FOR COMMUNITY PROGRAMS

There are many social change agents who are attempting to improve the lives of people caught in the technogap. Some of them are counselors; most are not. The bulk of their efforts is focused on developing access to hardware, software, Internet connectivity, and training.

Reverend Cecil Williams of Glide Memorial Church (1997) in San Francisco's Tenderloin District has been a social change agent by sparking the creation of Computers and You, one of the most progressive learning centers ever designed to help underprivileged adults and children develop basic computer skills. Founded in 1989, Computers and You has successfully trained over 6,000 homeless and low-income adults and children in computer literacy. The computer learning center provides training in word processing, spreadsheets, graphics, desktop publishing, hardware, programming, and even MIDI. In addition, children are taught basic math, reading, composition, social studies, music, and art, all utilizing the computer. Although teaching computer literacy skills is one of the main goals of Computers and You, the program also addresses other student needs, such as resume writing and job interview skills, through classes, seminars, and individual counseling. The goals of the program are to facilitate students' learning and to increase their chances of breaking out of the cycle of poverty by providing valuable skills and training in a supportive atmosphere of ongoing discovery.

The philosophy of the center is expressed by David Bunnell, former publisher of *PC World* and *MacWorld* who helped found Computers and You: "Giving poor people access to personal computer technology can give them options: literacy, jobs skills, confidence and a bigger picture than they might have had."

The personal story of Ana Bolton typifies the successful outcomes possible for programs like Computers and You. Ana took IBM for Beginners, WordPerfect, Lotus 123, and Mac for Beginners courses at Computers and You and is now a full-time housing specialist/ community organizer with the San Francisco North Market Planning Coalition. "I was," she said, "indigent, ignorant, as well as intimidated by computers. Computers and You made learning affordable and created a safe atmosphere for me to face my fears and get the education, knowledge, and skills that gave me the extra edge to get the job done."

Street-Level Youth Media (1997), in Chicago, is another example of a social action program that addresses the problems of the techno-gap. This unique, nonprofit organization is designed to put the latest communication technology in the hands of urban kids. Through innovative courses in documentary production, computer art, and the Internet, Chicago's young people have the opportunity to address their issues and share their dreams with a global audience. Street-Level participants use the World-Wide Web, teleconferencing, and video technology as tools for education, self-expression, and social change.

The Street-Level Storefront, a program of Street-Level Youth Media located in the West Town community, is home base for administration, fundraising, and drop-in programming. Featuring staff work space, video production and editing facilities, and a dual platform computer lab with Internet access, the storefront is a place where youth create innovative media projects. The storefront drop-in program, Neutral Ground, is an afterschool program available to children 10 years old and up. Offered through the support of the City of Chicago Department of Human Services, Neutral Ground gives young people in West Town a safe place to hang out and explore their creativity. In the spring of 1996, students from Street-Level's classes premiered the first episode of their quarterly interactive television program *Live Wire*. The half-hour-long, youth-produced video magazine examined urban issues from the inside and gave youth a voice on the airwaves. In addition, each segment of the program was linked to the Street-Level web domain, allowing young people around Chicago and across the country participation in the production and critique of each episode.

Free expression by the participants on the Street-Level *Live Wire* web site has suggested how the program is working. One example was "Someone," a poem by Jamilah Covington:

Everyone needs a real true friend.
Someone in which they can depend.
Someone by your side because the world's a big place.
Someone to help you through the troubles you face.
Someone to change your frown into a smile.
Someone to help when you've been down for a while.
Some one who will be there till the end.
Someone you can call your very best friend.

From a younger but no less enthusiastic set of writers came this hopeful message full of self-esteem and career plans:

Hi, we are the Pottawattomie Park Cow Girls. We are from Field, Jordan, and Gale schools in Chicago, Illinois. We are 7 and 8 years old and are very pretty and cool. We love to pretend that we are cowgirls. We hate boys because they hit us sometimes. When we grow up we want to be doctors, lawyers, students, and singers . . . .
We wish peace to all the world.

And finally the boys, not to be outdone, answered with this retort, also embedded with self-esteem and career planning:

We are the Fresh Crew. We are boys and we don't like girls because they don't like us. We come from Jordan Community, Courtenay, and Armstrong Schools on the North Side of Chicago. We are fat and thin and cool and handsome and strong. When we grow up we want to basketball players, artists, astronauts, teachers, lawyers, and cops . . . .

In addition to Computers and You and Street-Level Youth Media, there is Plugged In (1997). This is a project in East Palo Alto,

California, that began in 1992 to provide afterschool, computer-based learning activities to youth. East Palo Alto has one of the highest homicide rates in the country, yet is situated only a few miles from Stanford University and the Silicon Valley. For the last 6 years, volunteers have staffed the center, worked with children in the community to use technology to improve their lives, and even raised money by designing and selling a special screen saver featuring the center's talents.

Two groups that do not work directly with clients but do work diligently to procure hardware for nonprofit use are the Detwiler Foundation and MindShare. The Detwiler Foundation provides matching grants to schools that obtain donated computer equipment from private industry. MindShare is a business that was developed in Brighton, Massachusetts, to address the technology needs of low-income families and the organizations that serve them. MindShare refurbishes and sells recent-model computers through a network of community-based, multilingual sales people. MindShare has also created a special donation program known as the MindShare Collaborative (1997), designed to help adult education programs and public-housing-based community programs acquire computers to be placed in the homes of their clients.

Technology accessibility in public and low-income housing is especially important if students are going to close the technogap in homework assignments. In Santa Rosa, California, the Burbank Housing Development Corporation spent $8,000 in 1997 to equip the community room of a subsidized housing development with computers. The choice of technology and software was made in consultation with residents and the local school district. The final purchase included an array of software in history, literature, geography, science, math, typing, Spanish, and French as well as an encyclopedia for school-aged students and both nonverbal and bilingual software for toddlers. If successful, the Burbank Corporation will expand the pilot project to its other 17 properties. The complex manager is Beth Kastrup, a counseling alumna of Sonoma State University (Mason, 1997).

IDEAS FOR SCHOOL PROGRAMS

The Burbank experiment is one of a growing number of projects that reflect counselor involvement in technology access and training.

Deena Davis (personal communication, 1994) reported that her school counseling effectiveness with Takini Elementary School on the Cheyenne Sioux Indian Reservation in Howes, South Dakota, was greatly enhanced through the use of technology.

> I have found that allowing them to draw pictures on HyperCard that reflect their feelings at the moment to be a good starting point for dialogue. Often they will come in and do a stack when they are free and leave it for me to view when I am free. Those that [sic] are shy about talking will leave messages regarding problems on the computer disk for me to respond to.

Another approach was reported by Sheila Kelley-Logan (1993), who organized the Panther Tech Computer Club at Surfside Elementary School in Satellite Beach, Florida, to work with at-risk students. These students used computer games to develop social skills under the counselor's guidance in addition to using a digital camera and editing software with word processing to do more creative work.

These counselors have discovered that computers offer greater opportunities for academic success among students who fail in traditional classroom modalities of group instruction (Casey, 1992). Indeed, the term *at-risk student* might more accurately be reframed *student in at-risk environment* when the learning environment emphasizes verbal and quantitative learning goals through auditory and visual channels alone. Gardner (1993) asserted through his theory of multiple intelligences that traditional instruction rewards verbal and quantitative intelligence at the expense of five other, equally important, intelligences: spatial, musical, bodily-kinesthetic, interpersonal, and intrapersonal. Computers, as an aid in instruction, offer learners who operate with strong alternative intelligences greater opportunities for learning and expression. Multicultural awareness can be also promoted through computer technology (D'Andrea, 1995).

Evidence that technology improves school success is limited but impressive. Researchers studying Apple Computers' Apple Classroom of Tomorrow (ACOT) at West High School in Columbus, Ohio, attributed reduced dropout rates, increased numbers of college-bound graduates, and increased awards of full scholarships to their technology-infused curriculum (Apple Computer, 1991). The randomly assigned seniors in the technology program outperformed their counterparts with fewer dropouts (0% vs. 30%), higher college matriculation (90% vs. 15%), and more full scholarships (33% vs. 6%). The ACOT program claimed to have achieved growth in eight competencies:

1. Explore and represent ideas
2. Experiment and problem solve with ease
3. Show high degree of social awareness and self-confidence
4. Communicate ideas effectively
5. Use computers productively
6. Learn independently
7. See themselves as collaborators and experts
8. Have positive orientation to the future.

There is still plenty of time to bridge the technogap. According to Larry Ellison of Oracle Corporation, 70% of homes in the United States had no computer access in 1997, as compared with 90% of homes in Japan and western Europe and 99% in the rest of the world. For change to occur, it will take counselors who will assume the role of social change agents and who will aggressively seek resources and training for both adults and students who are caught in the technogap.

BEYOND HARDWARE, SOFTWARE, AND TECHNICAL TRAINING: SOME SOCIAL IMPLICATIONS

In addition to hardware, software, and technical training, there is another critical area where counselors can play a leadership role: appropriate use of technology.

Inappropriate use of technology can sometimes be worse than no technology at all. Addiction to the Internet (Scherer & Bost, 1997) is one example where a disproprtionate amount of time spent using technology harms the individual. In a recent news story, a woman was arrested for locking her children in a small, feces-ridden room without ventilation or food so that she could spend hours on the Internet undisturbed. More commonly, technology may consume a disproportionate share of a person's daily routine, particularly when new "toys" are designed to appeal to the technophile and when industry profit is predicated on planned obsolescence. Mental and physical health can become casualties to overuse of technology as essential daily activities (healthy meals, exercise, friendships) are curtailed. Thus counselors can assist clients in drawing boundaries so that the client, not the industry, is in control of daily technology usage.

Appropriate use of technology should also include using technology with a social conscience. Allegations of dehumanization have surfaced as children and teens play aggressive warlike games (made by Sega, Nintendo, and other software designers), often with realistic images of blood and violence. In recent years, the U.S. Defense Department has scheduled annual meetings of game designers in New Mexico at which plans for military simulation software using the latest military hardware are discussed and developed concurrently for both military training and mass market consumption. Counselors have a social mandate to educate clients on the social implications of technology usage regarding human rights and compassion. Although the ratings system on commercial packages and censorship tools for Internet web site browsing are helpful, the ultimate determinant of judicious computer usage rests with the individual; counselors must be proactive in this educational process.

Traditional forms of community are changing dramatically during the technological era. Fraternal clubs and neighborhood watering holes are yielding to virtual communities. One interesting merger of the two eras is the Internet coffee house, where patrons can enjoy each other in person while also communicating worldwide via computers. Counselors can assist clients who experience loneliness, depression, or alienation by identifying their social needs for community and by clarifying appropriate uses of technology to help meet those needs.

One last, but certainly not least, example of approriate counselor use of technology may be to circumvent prejudicial barriers. The author was working with a university freshman on career planning recently when the client volunteered his desire to become a winemaker or, if successful, a vineyard owner. When an informational interview was suggested, the client quickly rejected the idea. He stated that he and his family had long been vineyard laborers and was sure that his Latino appearance would keep him from ever communicating with an owner. As an alternate plan, we decided that he should try sending E-mail messages through the links provided on some winery homepages located on the World-Wide Web. He planned to use his college E-mail address as a vehicle for return mail. Three weeks later, he enthusiastically brought in over a dozen electronic invitations for informational interviews with winery owners, including the vineyard where his family had previously worked. He discovered that he had an alternate path for communication that proved quite successful in overcoming potential prejudicial barrriers.

CONCLUSION

Workers with advanced technological skills are disproportionately favored in the United States today, and the gap between the technologically advantaged and disadvantaged continues to grow. As companies downsize, restructure, and reengineer, workers without technology skills are let go. The remaining front-line workers must, however, use their technology skills to work harder for less money, which means that corporate executives and stockholders reap windfall earnings because of increased productivity with decreased costs. A similar gap has also developed between wealthy K-12 school districts using state-of-the-art technology and poor districts struggling to meet basic needs.

Professional counselors have a mandate to be social change agents in combating these disturbing trends and developing a level playing field for all. Counselors must actively participate in procuring funds for hardware, software, and technical training. Moreover, counselors must be proactive in advocating for the appropriate use of technology, with emphasis on prudent time management, social conscience, community connectedness, and nonprejudicial communication. When counselors use their expertise to secure resources, create programs, and foster social activism in order to bridge the technogap, they fulfill their mandate and benefit all citizenry.

REFERENCES

Annie E. Casey Foundation. (1997). Kids count data book [On-line]. Available: http://www.aecf.org

Apple Computer (Producer). (1991). *Imagine: How computers are changing the way we learn* [Videotape]. Cupertino, CA: Apple Computer.

Casey, J. A. (1992). *Counseling using technology with at-risk youth.* Greensboro, NC: ERIC Clearinghouse on Counseling and Personnel Services. (ERIC Document Reproduction Service No. EDO CG 92 13)

Cohn, M. J., & Cohn, L. (1996). *Combating stress at work and home in the 90s and beyond.* Dubuque, IA: Kendall/Hunt.

D'Andrea, M. (1995). Using computer technology to promote multicultural awareness among elementary school-age students. *Elementary School Guidance and Counseling, 30,* 45-54.

Gardner, H. (1993). *Multiple intelligences.* New York: Basic Books.

Kelly-Logan, S. (1993). Getting started with technology in counseling. *Florida Technology in Education Quarterly, 6,* 65-70.

Kozol, J. (1991). *Savage inequalities.* New York: Crown.

Mason, C. (1997, February 16). Housing project gets computers for kids. *Santa Rosa Press Democrat,* p. B1.

Rich world, poor world. (1996, September 20). *USA Today,* p. 3B.

Scherer, K., & Bost, J. M. (1997). I can't—uh, won't—log off." *Treatment Today, 9,* 14-15.

Sklar, H. (1997, April 15). Chaos or community? Seeking solutions, not scapegoats for bad economics. *Santa Rosa Press Democrat,* p. B5.

PROGRAMS/WEB SITES

Glide Memorial Church. (1997). Computers and you [On-line]. Available: http://www.glide.org

MindShare Collaborative. (1997). [On-line]. Available: http:///www.citysource.com/mindshare

Plugged In. (1997). [On-line]. Available: http:///www.pluggedin.org

Street-Level Youth Media. (1997). The street-level storefront [On-line]. Available: http://www.iit.edu/~livewire

RESOURCES

Detwiler Foundation, 470 Nautilus Street, Suite 400, La Jolla, CA 92037
MindShare, P.O. Box 35389, Brighton, MA 02135

12

The Internet as a Potential Force for Social Change

JAMES P. SAMPSON, JR.

Futurists regularly predict profound changes in our society. In retrospect, some predictions have proven accurate and some have not, as could be expected. Computer technology has long been projected to reshape the nature of work, leisure, social interaction, and home life. Although the personal computer and computer networking has caused considerable change, the change has been most profound in organizations and in relatively affluent families with home computers. The evolution of the Internet into the information highway will accelerate societal change as the majority of our citizens gain direct access to computer technology.

Like other computer applications, the Internet is not inherently helpful or harmful. The Internet is simply a powerful tool. Successful use of this tool depends on selecting quality Internet resources that meet identified needs and then using these resources with a level of support that matches the readiness of the individual for learning. In particular, the Internet is a potential tool for counselors acting as agents of social change.

This chapter begins with a brief description of the Internet and the information highway and a discussion of Internet use. It then explores the potential benefits and problems in using the Internet as a social change resource. The chapter concludes with recommendations for action to maximize the benefits and minimize the problems associated with the use of the Internet.

THE NATURE OF THE INTERNET AND ITS USE

The Internet is an "interconnection of existing commercial (subscription) and noncommercial computer networks using standard conventions for exchanging information" (Sampson, Kolodinsky, & Greeno, 1997, p. 203). The World-Wide Web (WWW) is the portion of the Internet that "includes computer servers with graphic interfaces connected to the Internet which offer transmission of audio and video data in addition to text" (Sampson et al., 1997, p. 203). The graphic user interface, simple search features, and ability to easily link to other web sites make the WWW relatively easy to use and thus appropriate for a wide range of people in our society. As personal computers, cable TV networks, and telephone networks evolve into the information highway over the next 10 years, computing resources will be more available to the vast majority of our citizens (Gates, Myhrvold, & Rinearson, 1995).

The Internet provides individuals with access to an enormous quantity of data. The problem is that individuals can easily become overwhelmed by the amount and diversity of data available. Offer and Watts (1997, p. 3) noted that "the sheer quantity of unfiltered information can make it difficult for users to find and evaluate the information they need." What is required is a simple model that helps individuals select Internet functions that relate to their needs. Use of the Internet can be categorized into one of the following four functions:

1. *Identifying* problems and possibilities by using links to surf among Internet sites to discover the range of data that is available. This could also be termed *surfing serendipity*. For example, the mother of a young child is frustrated with the behavior of her 5-year-old son. She chooses to surf among Internet sites on childhood and children and notices several links to parenting sites. She links to three of these sites and learns that certain parenting styles can influence how children behave.

2. *Searching* for information to solve a problem or answer a question by using a search engine or an Internet site. For example, the mother uses an Internet search engine to locate sites that deal with parenting strategies for young children. By reading the brief descriptions of these Internet sites, the mother learns of the range of different parenting education resources available.

3. *Obtaining* information when users know what they want by accessing a specific Internet site or by using a search engine to

link to a specific Internet site address. For example, the mother links to a specific site to obtain information on specific parenting strategies for young children.

4. *Communicating* with others via E-mail, file transfer, chat mode, and videoconferencing. For example, the mother reads messages from and contributes messages to a mailing list related to the specific parenting strategies she has learned. Communicating with other parents who are applying the parenting principles with their own children allows the mother to explore issues with more experienced parents and to obtain support.

USING THE INTERNET AS A FORCE FOR SOCIAL CHANGE

POTENTIAL BENEFITS

Several potential benefits may result from using the Internet as a resource for social change. These include increased awareness of available counseling services, increased access to self-help psychoeducational resources, improved capacity to deal with multicultural issues, improved access to counseling, improved access to self-help groups, expanded opportunities for counselor supervision, and expanded opportunities for communication.

Increased Awareness of Available Counseling Services

The Internet is being commonly used to market counseling services (Offer & Watts, 1997; Sampson et al., 1997). Individuals who become aware of a problem can use the Internet to identify counseling services in their area that provide assistance related to their needs. Kurpius and Rozecki (1992, p. 177) noted that outreach involves "extending or making known available services to target populations." Outreach is an important element of social action, given that individuals in a specific target population may be unaware of information and services that are available. Effective social action requires that information and services actually reach the individuals who need assistance.

Increased Access to Self-Help Psychoeducational Resources

Self-help psychoeducational software can be used, without counselor support, by individuals for the prevention of problems or for self-diagnosed remediation of problems (assuming that the software was originally designed and validated for stand-alone use). Self-help psychoeducational software can also be used as a homework resource assigned by a counselor as part of the counseling process (Sampson, 1986; Sampson & Krumboltz, 1991). Specific self-help psychoeducational software can be developed for specific social action initiatives, such as parenting software for individuals who are at risk of committing child abuse. The self-help psychoeducational software should indicate the circumstances when counseling is needed (Allen, Sampson, & Herlihy, 1988). The Internet can provide links to counseling referrals as well as on-demand audio- and video-based help. Expert system elements of self-help software could identify problematic use of the resource by an individual so that a recommendation could be made to the individual to use the available audio- or video-based counselor support to address a specific problem (Sampson et al., 1997).

Improved Capacity to Deal With Multicultural Issues

It is possible to deliver multimedia-based assessment and information resources that match the ethnicity, age, and gender of the user (Sampson, 1990). Matching the demographic characteristics of multimedia presenters and clients can potentially contribute to the perceived credibility of the information and can reduce language and dialect barriers (Sampson & Krumboltz, 1991). For example, by indicating her ethnicity, age, and gender, a client could view an individual of the same demographic characteristics presenting assessment stimuli, delivering information, and modeling behavior.

Improved Access to Counseling

Videoconferencing via the Internet allows counseling to transcend geographic and physical barriers. Using this resource, the counselor and client can see and hear each other over great distances. Counseling services can be provided to clients in geographically remote areas where counseling services are limited or difficult to access. Clients who have transportation problems due to limited income or physical disability may especially benefit from Internet-based services. Being in different physical locations may make it safer for some clients to begin the counseling process (Offer & Watts, 1997; Sampson et al., 1997).

The delivery of counseling services via videoconferencing is an extension of telephone counseling services that have been offered for some time. Roach, Reardon, Alexander, and Cloudman (1983) observed that telephone counseling attracted previously underserved individuals, including home-based clients and persons with disabilities. Iscoe, Hill, Harmon, and Coffman (1979) noted that most clients served by telephone counseling had not sought previous counseling or information. Therefore, proactive outreach to typically underserved client populations as a social action initiative may be substantially enhanced by videoconferencing.

Improved Access to Self-Help Groups

The Internet can be used to enhance learning by promoting communication among individuals in different cultural settings and geographic locations (D'Andrea, 1995). Moderated mailing lists and moderated usenet news groups allow individuals with common interests to communicate with each other (Offer & Watts, 1997). Moderation by a counselor helps to ensure that individuals make appropriate use of the group and that counseling referrals are provided as needed. Self-help psychoeducational software can be used as a common resource for group members, providing a stimulus for group discussion. Moderated mailing lists and usenet news groups can also be used as an adjunct to counseling.

Expanded Opportunities for Counseling Supervision

Quality counseling supervision is a key element in the provision of effective counseling services. As counselors work toward being agents of social change, they will encounter client groups and circumstances that are new and challenging. Counseling supervision becomes especially important as counselors acquire new knowledge and develop new skills. The Internet can be a particularly useful resource that supplements traditional face-to-face supervision. Individual counseling supervision from specialists in remote locations can provide the unique support needed for a particular social action issue, such as a specific problem faced by a specific multicultural group. Group supervision can bring together counselors from various geographic locations who are dealing with common social change issues. E-mail, usenet news groups, bulletin board discussion groups, list servers, and mailing lists can provide counselors with supervisory support for dealing with clients (Casey, Bloom, & Moan, 1994; Marino, 1996; Myrick & Sabella, 1995).

Expanded Opportunities for Communication

As stated previously, one of the four main uses of the Internet is to enhance communication. Both counselors and clients can use the Internet as a communication tool to foster social change. Counselors can use E-mail, mailing lists, usenet news groups, and chat rooms to keep up to date with current social issues, public policy initiatives, legislation, and professional association initiatives. Clients interested in social action advocacy efforts can also use these Internet features to challenge issues of oppression, discrimination, stereotyping, and disenfranchisement. The sharing of information about issues and initiatives among counselors, clients, and policy makers can help all parties make more informed decisions about various social issues.

POTENTIAL PROBLEMS

Although Internet use may be beneficial, it is also possible that use of this technology will result in ineffective or harmful outcomes. Potential problems include overabundance of data, limited access to the Internet, lack of self-help psychoeducational resources on the Internet, inconsistent quality of self-help assessment resources, literacy barriers, confidentiality, credentialing, and misuse of group interactions.

Overabundance of Data

The amount of data available to assist individuals with problem solving and decision making has increased dramatically with the advent of the Internet. The problem is that access to an overabundance of data is as much of a problem as a scarcity of data. In both cases, the problem solving and decision-making capabilities of individuals are limited when they are unable to obtain and use the data that they need. Individuals who are overwhelmed with data sources can easily become discouraged when the data they locate does not apply to their specific problem or decision.

Limited Access to the Internet

Internet access is currently most available in organizations and relatively affluent families with home computers. Less affluent members of our society may find it difficult to access potentially valuable information and services (Noll & Graves, 1996; Offer & Watts, 1997; Sampson et al., 1997, Walz, 1996). The danger is that the economic gap between social classes will widen as affluent individuals and families gain access to information and services that are difficult to obtain without ready Internet access. As the future information highway integrates telephone, cable television, and Internet services (Gates et al., 1995), information access by low-income individuals and families is likely to improve. This evolution will take some time, however, to reach the majority of persons with limited incomes. The potential benefit of the Internet as a tool for social action will be substantially compromised if the target population can not access the resource.

Lack of Self-Help Psychoeducational Resources on the Internet

A great deal of self-help psychoeducational information is available in traditional print media. An increasing amount of information is available in audio and video formats. The problem is that very little print-, audio-, and video-based information has been adapted for computer delivery. Most of the current information available on the Internet simply presents existing print-based information via a new medium. The capacity of the Internet to deliver information that is motivational and promotes learning is lost when the capabilities of the medium are so poorly used. This is analogous to living in only one room of a three-bedroom house.

Taking full advantage of the capabilities of multimedia presentation of information is costly (Sampson, in press). Substantial design effort is needed to transform multimedia elements into an effective learning resource (Gerler, 1995). Although matching the demographic characteristics of clients with actors in a video helps to attend to multicultural issues in assessment and information delivery, the necessity of creating multiple versions of video content substantially increases production costs. Higher production costs may lead to higher purchase costs, which may in turn lead to reduced availability of the resource to individuals and organizations.

Inconsistent Quality of Self-Help Assessment Resources

Numerous self-help assessment resources are included in magazine articles and self-help literature to assist individuals in assessing various potential problems. It is rare for these self-assessments to include any evidence of the reliability or validity of the measure. As self-help resources become more common on the Internet, it is likely that self-assessments of questionable quality will be available. If invalid self-assessments are used by individuals to identify self-help psychoeducational resources relevant to their problem, individuals may not gain access to the information they actually need.

Inconsistent Quality of Available Data

An enormous quantity of data is currently available on the Internet. Some data are accurate and current, but other data are invalid or out of date. When poor quality data are delivered in self-help resources available on the Internet, or Internet-based resources are used as homework in counseling, individuals may subsequently make inappropriate decisions. This problem is exacerbated by the tendency of the public often to perceive computer-generated data as inherently accurate (Sampson et al., 1997).

Literacy Barriers

Although video- and audio-based information is increasingly available, the vast majority of information currently available on the Internet is text based. Very little of this text-based information is expressly written for individuals with limited reading proficiency. If the Internet is to succeed as a tool for social action, information resources that address a wide variety of self-help psychoeducational topics need to be developed for adolescents and adults with a range of literacy skills. Although the availability of multimedia-based assessment and information resources is helpful, care needs to be taken that the text that is typically presented along with audio and video is written at an appropriate reading level.

Confidentiality

The easy access to information provided by the Internet can result in damaging outcomes if the wrong individuals obtain sensitive data. Failure to maintain the security of text, audio, and video data transmitted over the Internet may result in a breach of confidentiality in counseling or supervision (Casey et al., 1994; Marino, 1996; Sampson et al., 1997).

Credentialing

Providers of Internet-based counseling services tend not to reveal adequate details about their credentials or do not have an appropriate credential for the type of service they are providing (Sampson et al., 1997). Counseling on the Internet can be delivered to unsuspecting clients by unqualified counselors. Individuals may also gain access to self-help psychoeducational resources developed by unqualified providers.

Misuse of Group Interactions

As stated previously, moderated mailing lists and moderated usenet news groups allow clients with common issues to communicate with each other. Internet use without moderation by a skilled facilitator may result in the provision of inaccurate or misleading information, domination of the group by a single individual or by a small group of individuals, or the manipulation of group members to purchase specific goods or services provided by a member of the group.

RECOMMENDATIONS

Given the potential benefits and problems that may result from using the Internet as a resource for social change, the following recommendations are offered:

- *Maximize Internet access for all individuals.* Counselors have an obligation to ensure that less affluent individuals have some readily accessible "public" location for connecting to the Internet.
- *Promote financial investment in Internet resource development.* Explore the feasibility of using public funding or public-private collaborations to develop software for relatively small special

populations where the likely limited return on investment will not encourage development by commercial businesses.

- *Emphasize the need for counselor initiative in developing Internet resources.* Counselors in training need to be made aware of indirect opportunities for helping clients by developing assessment and information resources for prevention and remediation (Sampson & Krumboltz, 1991). Conyne (1991) noted that although counselors are conceptually committed to prevention, their behavior clearly reflects a remedial orientation. Creating self-help psychoeducational resources that can be used both for prevention and remediation allows counselors with a developmental focus to support prevention efforts while working in settings that emphasize remedial services.

- *Identify relevant sites.* Counselors need to take an active role in identifying valid Internet sites that provide assessment and information resources related to specific problems and decisions. After reviewing various sites, counselors can then create (or make nominations for) gateway sites that recommend potentially helpful sites for specific client issues. Offer and Watts (1997) noted that the need to provide a filter that identifies quality Internet sites becomes increasingly important as the Internet becomes larger.

- *Develop valid and reliable self-assessment measures.* Assessments included in self-help psychoeducational software delivered over the Internet need to be designed and validated for this type of use (Allen et al., 1988).

- *Maximize data quality.* Counselors need to verify the quality of Internet-based data that they recommend to their clients. Whenever possible, counselors need to help their clients and the general public understand the importance of information quality and criteria for determining quality. Finally, counselors need to inform Internet-based providers of self-help psychoeducational resources of any inaccurate or out-of-date data.

- *Evaluate the efficacy of Internet-based information and service delivery.* To date, very little evaluation or research data are available on the efficacy of delivering counseling services or self-help psychoeducational resources via the Internet. Evaluation and research are obviously needed to help ensure that clients and the general public are well served by Internet-based information and services. Some evidence of ongoing Internet effectiveness will be required to stimulate capital investment in the high costs of multimedia software development.

- *Explore the similar, but not the same, impact of videoconferencing on counseling relationships.* It is unclear if counseling via videoconferencing on the Internet has any impact on the quality of the relationship between the counselor and the client (Sampson et al., 1997). Oravec (1996) noted that videoconferencing and face-to-face interaction were similar, but not identical, forms of communication. In comparison with face-to-face interactions, videoconferencing resulted in a more intense task focus and greater participant awareness of their physical appearance in the visual recording process. It is possible that these factors might influence or limit counseling relationships for some clients. Although it is likely that videoconferencing will be a powerful tool for facilitating learning and behavior change, videoconferencing is not the same as counseling face to face. We need to better understand the similarities and differences between these two modes of communication in order to make the best use of the full potential of counseling via videoconferencing and to avoid potential problems.
- *Maintain confidentiality of data.* Counselors and supervisors need to ensure that they are aware of potential limits to the confidentiality of data transmitted over the Internet and use the most up-to-date security procedures available.
- *Represent professional credentials accurately.* Internet-based self-help psychoeducational resources and Internet-based counseling services need to indicate clearly the credentials of the individual (or individuals) creating the resource or providing the service. Degrees need to include the title of the degree. Licenses and certifications need to include the complete name of the credential as well as the name and address of the credentialing organization.
- *Provide for counselor training.* Counselor preparation programs need to provide preservice training related to general skills associated with accessing and using the Internet, counseling strategies related to Internet-based service delivery, and ethical issues. Professional associations need to provide similar training for counselors who received their education prior to the emergence of the Internet.

- *Ensure professional standards.* Professional associations evolved at the turn of the century as a social action response to rapid social and economic changes in our society. The evolution from an industrial to an information-based economy is again creating a period of rapid social and economic change. Professional associations in counseling need to reevaluate their role and functioning in an information age in which psychoeducational assessment and information are readily available outside of the traditional counseling process. Professional associations in counseling and other helping fields need to collaborate in developing standards for the delivery of self-help assessment and information resources as well as counseling services over the Internet. Subsequent standards need to be widely disseminated and frequently updated if they are to have any positive impact on the quality of resources and services available to individuals around the world.

CONCLUSION

The Internet has emerged as a powerful tool for disseminating information and for communication. This tool can be used as a force for social change by counselors. To make effective use of this tool, counselors need to have appropriate Internet literacy as well as understand the potential benefits and problems associated with this tool. Counselors who are interested in helping clients in an indirect as well as a direct mode will need to take a leadership role in developing valid self-help psychoeducational assessment and information resources. Counselors need to experiment with various approaches to Internet-based counseling service delivery to document effective practice. Counselors, working through their professional associations, need to monitor the delivery of resources and services on the Internet and then attempt to shape Internet use in positive ways. Without the development of valid resources and effective counseling services, the Internet is unlikely to be a useful tool for social action.

REFERENCES

Allen, V. B., Sampson, J. P., Jr., & Herlihy, B. (1988). Details of the new 1988 AACD ethical standards. *Journal of Counseling and Development, 67,* 157-158.
Casey, J. A., Bloom, J. W., & Moan, E. R. (1994). Use of technology in counselor supervision. In L. D. Borders (Ed.), *Counseling supervision.* Greensboro, NC:

University of North Carolina at Greensboro, ERIC Clearinghouse on Counseling and Student Services. (ERIC Document Reproduction Service No. ED 372 357)

Conyne, R. K. (1991). Gains in primary prevention: Implications for the counseling profession. *Journal of Counseling and Development, 69,* 277-279.

D'Andrea, M. (1995). Using computer technology to promote multicultural awareness among elementary school-age students. *Elementary School Guidance and Counseling, 30,* 45-54.

Gates, B., Myhrvold, N., & Rinearson, P. (1995). *The road ahead.* New York: Viking.

Gerler, E. R., Jr. (1995). Advancing elementary and middle school counseling through computer technology. *Elementary School Guidance and Counseling, 30,* 8-15.

Iscoe, I., Hill, F. E., Harmon, M., & Coffman, D. (1979). Telephone counseling via cassette tapes. *Journal of Counseling Psychology, 26,* 166-168.

Kurpius, D. J., & Rozecki, T. (1992). Outreach, advocacy, and consultation: A framework for prevention and intervention. *Elementary School Guidance and Counseling, 26,* 176-189.

Marino, T. W. (1996, January). Counselors in cyberspace debate whether client discussions are ethical. *Counseling Today,* 8.

Myrick, R. D., & Sabella, R. A. (1995). Cyberspace: A new place for counselor supervision. *Elementary School Guidance and Counseling, 30,* 35-44.

Noll, C. L., & Graves, P. R. (1996). The impact of technology on career center practices. *Journal of Career Planning and Employment, 56*(3), 41-46.

Offer, M., & Watts, A. G. (1997). The Internet and careers work. *NICEC Briefing.* Cambridge, United Kingdom: National Institute for Careers Education and Counselling (Sheraton House, Castle Park, Cambridge CB3 OAX).

Oravec, J. A. (1996). *Virtual individuals, virtual groups: Human dimensions of groupware and computer networking.* Cambridge, United Kingdom: Cambridge University Press.

Roach, D., Reardon, R., Alexander, J., & Cloudman, D. (1983). Career counseling by telephone. *Journal of College Student Personnel, 24,* 71-76.

Sampson, J. P., Jr. (1986). The use of computer-assisted instruction in support of psychotherapeutic processes. *Computers in Human Behavior, 2,* 1-19.

Sampson, J. P., Jr. (1990). Computer-assisted testing and the goals of counseling psychology. *The Counseling Psychologist, 18,* 227-239.

Sampson, J. P., Jr. (in press). Computer applications. In C. E. Watkins, Jr., & V. L. Campbell (Eds.), *Using tests and assessment procedures in counseling* (2nd ed.). Hillsdale, NJ: Erlbaum.

Sampson, J. P., Jr., Kolodinsky, R. W., & Greeno, B. P. (1997). Counseling on the information highway: Future possibilities and potential problems. *Journal of Counseling and Development, 75,* 203-212.

Sampson, J. P., Jr., & Krumboltz, J. D. (1991). Computer-assisted instruction: A missing link in counseling. *Journal of Counseling and Development, 69,* 395-397.

Walz, G. R. (1996). Using the I-Way for career development. In R. Feller & G. Walz (Eds.), *Optimizing life transitions in turbulent times: Exploring work, learning, and careers* (pp. 415-427). Greensboro, NC: University of North Carolina at Greensboro, ERIC Clearinghouse on Counseling and Student Services.

13

Strategies for Social Change Research

WILLIAM E. SEDLACEK

Can research make a difference in bringing about social change? My answer is, it depends on how well it is done. This chapter offers suggestions as to what to do, and not do, to increase the chances of research making a difference, and provides examples of success or failure.

Doing good research has a particular meaning in this chapter. It is not necessarily the best design, most appropriate statistical analysis, or largest number of participants that is most important. Instead it is often the research strategies used that make the difference. This chapter first describes the basic research strategies of understanding your audience, defining research broadly, focusing your research question(s), and controlling the turf. The chapter then turns to the long-term view of research and explores the strategies of becoming a source, climbing the conceptual ladder, sticking to your principles, and being patient and persistent. The Banneker Scholarship Case at the University of Maryland helps to illustrate these long-term strategies and illuminate the power and potential of research.

BASIC STRATEGIES

UNDERSTAND YOUR AUDIENCE

The first question posed by the social action researcher should be Who do we wish to influence with our study? Is it university faculty, welfare recipients, state legislators, children? For each of these audiences we are likely to perform different kinds of studies and make different kinds of presentations.

If the topic is reducing prejudice, for example, in what ways has research influenced university faculty, welfare recipients, state legislators, and children? Note that as part of understanding an audience, the researcher should appeal to the audience's self-interests and choose data that will move the audience in what you regard as a positive direction.

University faculty generally regard themselves as scholars and are often uncomfortable with positions lacking an intellectual component. I have had success influencing faculty with scholarly, published research that demonstrates their racial attitudes in a way that meets rigorous challenges as to method and statistics (Sedlacek, 1995). Publishing and presenting at meetings as "one of them" increase the chances that most faculty will consider curricular change, better advising for students of color, or changes in campus activities.

Welfare recipients are not likely to be impressed with methodological issues, but they are likely to be influenced by examples and by case studies of people like them. Thus training counselors to provide individual or group counseling by using specific examples of other welfare recipients who followed certain paths can increase the chances that the clients will make the desired changes in their behavior. Changes such as following new welfare guidelines or securing employment are possible goals for the client. Such counseling could be seen as teaching welfare recipients to handle the prejudice that has been directed toward them by politicians, employers, and the general public. Learning to handle racism has been correlated with success for groups who experience prejudice (Sedlacek, 1996).

State legislators are commonly influenced by what voters in their districts feel about an issue. By detailing popular support on an issue and by illustrating those positions with examples drawn from their constituents, legislators can be influenced. If possible, arrange it so that politicians can take credit for being out in front on an issue and/or for initiating legislation. Recent concerns about affirmative action are an example. Surveying constituents about being fair to all citizens and helping those who deserve a chance, and providing examples of people who have benefited in a given district, can influence legislators. Direct contact with legislators and dramatic examples are likely to work best.

Children are often influenced by their peers and by what they see rather than by what others tell them. Therefore, to reach this audience, a community theater group and a research office in a school district combined to present an innovative program that made a difference. The research office checked the literature and did surveys in the elementary schools about the types of prejudice that were most likely to be seen and felt by the students. The theater group then developed skits and short plays around those themes. Students at various schools were recruited and included in the troupe. Students at each school where performances took place were also included. Surveys taken immediately afterward and some months later indicated that prejudice was reduced. Needs assessment and follow-up evaluation have been shown to be important parts of reducing prejudice in schools (Sedlacek & Brooks, 1976).

DEFINE RESEARCH BROADLY

Research can be defined as any systematic inquiry into a topic. The methods can be quantitative or qualitative, statistical or impressionistic, and involve paper-and-pencil techniques, computer technology, interviews, artistic perspectives, or naturalistic observations. Use what works best given your audience and available resources. If you have access to certain resources, such as a college research office, computers, and financial resources, by all means use them. If not, use what you have.

A technique I like to employ with research students is to ask them to pose a research question and then give them 1 week to make observations in the school, community, or campus they are studying and report back to the group on their conclusions. One such student wanted to study community violence and its causes. For a week he chose to observe the events taking place in a part of the community where people often congregated. He made observations about the events preceding hostilities between groups and developed some preliminary answers to his question, which he used to devise additional studies on the topic. His method limited him to certain kinds of data and certain answers to questions, but he was engaging in research.

Focus Your Research Question(s)

Although we want to think broadly about our definitions of research, we want to be very specific about the question(s) we wish to answer. Generally, it is better to have only one or a few questions to be answered. A clearer answer to one question is better than a vague answer to many. Other studies can be done to answer other questions. Concentrating on fewer questions helps sharpen goals and delineate what we want to learn.

Research questions can be categorized into one of three areas—information, attitudes, and behavior—and researchers should pick just one as a focus for their questions. Results in one area do not in general answer questions well in the other areas, and confusion on this point often works against the social action researcher.

Information is the first research area. Factual information, such as demographic data, frequency counts of events, or correct answers to test items fit here. The change agent often needs information to identify the issues or to know which way to go. At one time, learned people felt that earth, wind, fire, and water were the four elements in nature. Without research we would have no reason to think otherwise.

Sometimes information is compelling and results in immediate change. This is seldom true, however. The people and systems we are trying to change can often ignore or rationalize facts. Despite the evidence, they may continue to think, for example, that Blacks prefer to live in certain neighborhoods, women cannot handle management responsibilities, and welfare recipients are lazy. Sound familiar? Further, researchers have often assumed that the facts speak for themselves. Galileo, for example, assumed that once he presented his observations about the earth not being the center of the universe, the church would accept them. It did, but it was some 350 years later! Most of us prefer a quicker response.

Attitudes is the second area for research questions. Here any affective data concerning feelings, opinions, or perspectives are the focus of research and change. The link between attitudes and information is complex. Presenting information generally does not change feelings, but as part of a larger strategy the two may be linked. For example, in their stages of eliminating racism, Sedlacek and Brooks (1976) indicated that information on cultural and racial differences and racism, followed by attitude measurement, can lead to the desired reductions in racist behaviors. But changes in feelings should not be confused with information or behavior. In trying to change attitudes among groups, several conditions are required. One is that all groups should view the negotiating conditions as favorable. Others are that power among the groups to affect the outcome should be equal, and conditions for continued positive feelings should be developed (Dovidio & Gaertner, 1986). Assessments of feelings to determine the status of each of these conditions are important in any attitude-change process. The Situational Attitude Scale is a method of measuring prejudice that uses experimental and control forms of a questionnaire, can be applied to a variety of situations, and can be useful here (Sedlacek, 1996).

Behavior is the third area of focus for research. This is the area in which researchers often wish to concentrate, but in which it is difficult to foster change, and in which information and feelings commonly do not lead to behavior change. It is best to concentrate on reinforcing people to engage in the desired behavior without necessarily getting them to understand the information behind it or to feel good about it. If you get legislators to sponsor legislation that will help your cause, let the legislators do it for their reasons, not yours. If a university can increase its population of students of color by using different admissions procedures, do not worry about school officials not understanding the issues. Concentrate on research that will achieve the desired behavioral outcomes.

CONTROL THE TURF

An important part of social change is defining the issues to be argued. One valuable function research can serve in achieving social change is to control the area(s) of argument or debate. Counseling professionals too often react defensively to conditions set up by others. When we are told that the situation is a certain way, we often feel that we have to counter what those in control of the system have set forth. However, when we do research, we may put those in charge on the defensive and cause them to respond to our results. For instance, by providing information on how early detection of HIV/AIDS can save governments and insurance companies money, we can increase the chances of better treatment for the individuals involved.

THE LONG-TERM VIEW

Research can enable an examination of issues over time in a relatively constant manner, as in longitudinal studies that follow the same people or organizations over time to see how they change. This allows the change agent to avoid emotional context or a quick fix that may not solve the problem. Longitudinal studies of university students before and after matriculation, for example, have allowed me to observe the development of students of different races and groups and to provide others with some ideas on how developmental needs vary by race, culture, and gender. This has led to broader concepts and approaches to understanding student needs that are not apparent in an immediate crisis (Sedlacek, 1996). This approach to studying a university over time has also allowed me to see how the university has reacted to issues (Sedlacek, 1995). Without a historical and a projected futuristic context, it is easier to overreact to immediate concerns. If we do not understand the past we are condemned to repeat it.

Here is a place where quantitative and qualitative methods are useful. We can track numbers of students, their attitudes, and graduation rates, quantitatively, but we can also qualitatively explore the stories and issues behind the numbers. Public radio in the United States recently used a qualitative approach to help us understand the Civil Rights Movement. Instead of presenting the bigger stories and quantitative information already available, it presented smaller, more intimate stories of heretofore mostly unknown people who made contributions to civil rights in a program series called "Will the Circle Be Unbroken?" This deepened our understanding of the issues and helped those concerned with change in this area increase their chances of making deeper, more lasting changes in the future.

Conducting a series of cross-sectional studies to observe change over time, such as doing studies of people in a given community every 5 years, is also possible. The information community members have about, for example, recycling their used materials, their feelings about it, and their behavior are all data useful in research for social change. Note that many methods can be used to answer the same question.

BECOME THE SOURCE

By providing research results over a period of time, we can become reliable sources of data. Part of being a reliable source is providing data that are fair, honest, and not always slanted in a certain direction. As we watch the evening news, are we more apt to trust the results of a study done by a neutral party or by a representative of a political party? We should share results regardless of the outcome. By asking the right questions and putting them in a context useful for the change we wish to bring about, we can give the data the best chance to be used as we wish. However, research that is preconceived as to outcomes means suppressing undesirable outcomes, thus compromising our role as the source of reliable data.

The head of a state counseling association, for example, did a study showing that 25% of elementary school students were interested in some form of counseling. He was trying to influence counseling legislation in the state. He considered not using the data because 75% of the students were not interested. However, his advisers suggested he translate that 25% into actual numbers of students needing counseling, thus demonstrating to state legislators that the state counseling association could be trusted to give them the truth. The strategy worked, and the state passed some favorable legislation.

It is probably more important to be perceived as a reliable source, whether true or not, if the goal is social change. However, by providing topical data that have been useful to an audience over time, it is possible to have both perception and reality, as in research that I carried out at the University of Maryland for many years. When the University was faced with a lawsuit challenging its scholarship program for African American undergraduates (the Banneker Scholarship case), and the University administrators looked about for help in defending against the lawsuit, my colleagues and I were the only viable source of long-term information on the racial climate at the school. I became an expert witness.

The research provided four major types of evidence to document the University's racial climate. Most of the documentation was available through empirical articles in professional journals and internal campus research reports published before the lawsuit was initiated. The first type of research-generated evidence included numerous studies describing the needs, problems, and interests of African American students on the campus. Many of these studies had concluded that African Americans had unique problems and needs, such as the need for more African American faculty and staff and the need for help in dealing with a hostile campus climate. Many of the data were informational.

A second type of evidence came from research studies focusing on retention and identifying a series of variables that correlated with the success of African American students. The identified variables included having an ability to handle racism, developing a racial/cultural community on campus, and engaging in realistic self-appraisal despite the hostile environment. Many of the research articles were behavioral and suggested actions that the school could take to reduce racism on campus.

A third type of research-generated evidence came from studies examining the attitudes of Whites toward African Americans on campus over a period of 25 years. These studies generally showed that despite increasing numbers of African Americans and programs for them, Whites still had basically negative attitudes toward Blacks, and these attitudes were largely unchanged over the 25-year period.

The fourth type of research evidence was a historical analysis of the campus newspaper, again over a 25-year period. Examples of negative incidents involving African Americans were counted and cataloged. The result of this effort provided information as well as attitude and behavioral data, and showed that the examples depicting a negative racial climate for African American students and faculty/staff formed a continuous stream.

So what happened in the case? The University eventually lost after two rounds in the circuit and appellate courts. However, here is where an understanding of audience was useful. Although I would have liked to have seen the University win the case, I was also trying to change the University. Because the University used the research on racial climate and acknowledged the existence of the issues affecting African American students, I had achieved a goal that I had been working on for many years. As one top administrator put it after the University had won a round in court, "I was glad we won, but I wish we didn't have to admit we were racist to do it." Such thinking has led the University to assume more responsibility for programs in the scholarship and diversity areas that might not have been possible before the case.

CLIMB THE CONCEPTUAL LADDER

Research can help move conceptions of the problem to a higher level. For example, a town struggling with the quality of its water supply saw no improvement in pollution after several years of trying different treatments. Research made it clear that the pollution was being caused by factors outside the community, including industrial waste disposal upriver, runoff of chemicals from farms, and soil leeching from timber-cutting policies. Armed with data from their studies, the researchers were able to influence politicians from several states to adopt regional programs, and the community solved its pollution problem. The broader concepts provided by data made it possible to understand what needed to be done to provide clean water in the town.

In the Banneker Scholarship case, theories of racial identity (Helms, 1992) and eliminating racism (Sedlacek & Brooks, 1976) were used to organize the information and show how types of data influenced each another. The arguments in the case included presenting concepts that were more likely to result in change as opposed to presenting the issue as a molecular series of unrelated incidents. The scientific principle of induction suggests that we integrate the information we have into the broadest concepts possible so as to explain the results.

STICK TO YOUR PRINCIPLES

It is easy to lose track of goals when engaging in social change research. I have a colleague to whom more than one person has said that they were confused by her positions on certain issues. They thought she was "on their side." She usually explains that she tends to go where the data take her. Sometimes there is agreement with a position of a given person, sometimes not. If we start supporting people or organizations rather than issues, we are less likely to accomplish our social change goals.

In the Banneker Scholarship case, I worked out a set of principles to guide my activities and explained them to the lawyers and University officials involved. The first principle was to be helpful to the lawyers. Rather than to be self-righteous or guided solely by what any change agent with this unique opportunity might like to say, I attempted to put the research in a context that would be optimally useful to the lawyers and to concentrate work on the most salient issues for the case. As Sedlacek and Brooks (1976) noted, it is important for a social change agent to concentrate on what works, not on what he or she would like to see work. Although it was tempting to comment on many issues not directly raised by the research, an approach that focused on key research results seemed to have a better chance of being helpful to the lawyers and of making my contribution count.

For instance, there was evidence available indicating problems for students and faculty in racial/cultural groups other than African Americans or Hispanics (e.g., Arabs, international students, Jews, women, gays). Rather than try to tie together issues affecting these groups into broader issues, I focused on the more narrow issues in the case.

The second principle was to use the opportunity to reduce the racism against African Americans at the University. *Racism* was defined as policies or procedures (formal or informal) in an organization that result in negative outcomes for members of a certain group (e.g., African Americans) just because they are members of that group (Sedlacek & Brooks, 1976). Results, not intentions, are what count using this definition. The lawyers would have preferred a less forceful term to describe the problems faced by African Americans at the University, but adhering to this principle required defining racism and using the term in reports to the court.

Presenting the research in language the lawyers and a judge could interpret in legal terms while adhering to the second principal was a challenge, however. In reports to the court, I followed the second principle by concluding that there currently was racism against African Americans at the University and that there had been for some time. I also concluded that the scholarship program should be maintained exclusively for African Americans because it would take several, if not many, generations for African Americans to see the University as a comfortable place for themselves and their children to attend. Recruiting and retaining successful African American students was an important part of that process. The University needed to show its commitment to this goal by sticking with its programs, not by backing off under pressure.

The third principle was to reduce racism against Hispanics at the University. Many Hispanics resented what they perceived as more attention to the problems of African Americans than to those of Hispanics on campus. Hispanics also struggled with racism and prejudice from non-Hispanics (White & Sedlacek, 1987), and many Hispanics watched with suspicion as they waited to see how the University would respond to the case.

The third principle was implemented by calling for more University programs, including scholarships for Hispanics, in order to counter all forms of racism. Hispanics have unique needs and should not be lumped together with other groups or students in general. Research on campus had shown that a major difficulty for Hispanic students was deciding when to seek out programs for Hispanics and when to use general programs (Fuertes, Sedlacek, & Westbrook, 1989). Helping students in that process could be an important counseling/advocacy service to offer.

As often happens in a lawsuit, both sides decided to focus on a more limited legal point. Consequently, the Hispanic issue was dropped from the case. The lawsuit concentrated on whether to continue the scholarships for African Americans or to open them to all students. By indirectly avoiding the issue of Hispanics, this outcome could be interpreted as a racist position by the University. That is, the University could be seen as concerned with African American issues only, and as perceiving Hispanic issues as not important, which could have negative consequences for Hispanics seeking to reduce the racism engaged in by the University against them. Nevertheless, I did raise this issue in reports to the lawyers and the University, and the institution has initiated plans for several new programs for Hispanics.

The fourth and final guiding principle was to maintain personal integrity. The probability of encountering serious role conflicts was very high. It was important to make decisions based on the best course rather than on what was politically correct or expedient.

This fourth principle was implemented by avoiding opportunistic behavior and by concentrating on doing what seemed best overall. The University was going through a series of budget reductions at the time and was anxious to improve its relationship with the citizens in its state. Departments within the University were vying for favor with the administration by suggesting that they were the diversity "experts" or that they had something special to offer African Americans, Hispanics, the University in general, or the case in particular. By putting the goal of social change first, I hoped that I would have the best chance of contributing to the reduction of racism at the school in the long run.

Be Patient and Persistent

Any social change activity requires time and persistence. If one thing does not work, try another. The research component in social change also requires time and many attempts. In many of the examples given in this chapter, change took place slowly with help from many studies. Do not be discouraged by this. See each study as standing on its own and supporting key points you wish to make. Also see the research as fitting into a mosaic—as one more piece of a larger puzzle. Bigger gains can sometimes come from interconnected studies. More often, smaller gains lead to bigger ones. Do not go for it all too soon; be content with a smaller gain that moves your issue forward. Those who follow you can benefit from your work. Small victories attract allies and deter opponents (Weick, 1984).

In the Banneker Scholarship case, many students and colleagues over many years did the research that came together in that case. Many of those earlier studies resulted in changes in student services and academic programs, including admissions policies, counseling programs, cultural activities, and multicultural courses offered (Roper & Sedlacek, 1988; Sedlacek & Brooks, 1973). The culmination of the studies affected the University in a broader way and moved its leadership to see diversity as one of the school strengths, with resulting program funding.

CONCLUSION

Research can play a vital role in social change. Research alone can not bring about change, but dedicated professionals armed with good goals, good data, and guiding principles can make a difference. There are many references available in this publication and elsewhere on doing various types of research. I recommend the books by Isaac and Michael (1981) and by Webb, Campbell, Schwartz, Sechrest, and Grove (1981) (included in the reference list) for further reading.

We face many problems in our society, and there are many things that counseling professionals can do about them. Let us continue.

REFERENCES

Dovidio, J. F., & Gaertner, S. L. (1986). *Prejudice, discrimination, and racism.* Orlando FL: Academic Press.

Fuertes, J. N., Sedlacek, W. E., & Westbrook, F. D. (1989). A needs assessment of Hispanic students at a predominantly White university. *Counseling Center Research Report No. 21-89.* College Park, MD: University of Maryland.

Helms, J. E. (1992). *A race is a nice thing to have.* Topeka, KS: Content Communications.

Isaac, S., & Michael, W. B. (1981). *Handbook in research and evaluation.* San Diego, CA: EDITS.

Roper, L. D., & Sedlacek, W. E. (1988). Student affairs professional in academic roles: A course on racism. *National Association of Student Personnel Administrators Journal, 26*(1), 27-32.

Sedlacek, W. E. (1995). Using research to reduce racism at a university. *Journal of Humanistic Education and Development, 33,* 131-140.

Sedlacek, W. E. (1996). An empirical method of determining nontraditional group status. *Measurement and Evaluation in Counseling and Development, 28,* 200-210.

Sedlacek, W. E., & Brooks, C.C., Jr. (1973). Racism and research: Using data to initiate change. *Personnel and Guidance Journal, 52,* 184-188.

Sedlacek, W. E., & Brooks, C. C., Jr. (1976). *Racism in American education: A model for change.* Chicago: Nelson-Hall.

Webb, E. J., Campbell, D. T., Schwartz, R. D., Sechrest, L., & Grove, J. B. (1981). *Nonreactive measures in the social sciences.* Boston: Houghton Mifflin.

Weick, K. E. (1984). Small wins: Redefining the scale of social problems. *American Psychologist, 39,* 40-49.

White, T. J., & Sedlacek, W. E. (1987). White student attitudes toward Blacks and Hispanics: Programming implications. *Journal of Multicultural Counseling and Development, 15,* 171-182.

14

Using the Knowledge Base: Outcome Research and Accountable Social Action

THOMAS L. SEXTON AND SUSAN C. WHISTON

We are entering a new era of professional counseling—an era in which our role is broadening from being primarily focused on the individual to a consideration of family, society, and culture. It is an era in which we are moving away from being interested only in the development of our own professional knowledge and practice to an awareness of the impact that we have on our social context. This expanded role is based on the realization that any barrier between professional knowledge and society is only an artificial one. In fact, implicitly or explicitly, both as individual practitioners and an organized profession, we constantly mold the social environment. In a direct way, we play an important role as change agents for those experiencing personal and emotional problems. More indirectly, the theoretical constructs that make up professional counseling (e.g., self-esteem, self-actualization, self-awareness) become translated into the everyday language. As such, these constructs become part of the ways in which all of us understand and explain everyday experience. In this way, the belief systems constructed by professional counselors have a significant impact on what is considered good and bad in our culture.

The new era of professional counseling, heralded by this book, is one that acknowledges and embraces the role of social activist. The purpose of this chapter is to suggest that the professional knowledge base, as represented by the accumulated body of counseling outcome research, should be one of the primary foundations for our social activism. Outcome research can identify areas of cultural and social concern needing our professional attention. In addition, the use of outcome research helps legitimize and give credibility to our efforts to advocate for social change. To help make this case, the chapter first discusses the ways in which outcome research can and should serve as the foundation for our efforts in social action. The chapter then outlines social activist implications of outcome research, including the need to see counseling services as essential as well as the needs for counseling practice that is accountable, client service formulas that are flexible, treatments that are empirically validated and manual driven, and delivery systems that are diverse and responsive. The chapter next identifies future areas to which outcome research can turn in order to broaden its attention to areas of social concern. Finally, the chapter considers the need for a synergistic relationship among research, practice, professional training, and social action not only to provide a foundation for good service to clients but also to foster the development of credible and accountable social activism.

COUNSELING OUTCOME RESEARCH AS A FOUNDATION FOR SOCIAL ACTION

Outcome research has a long history in counseling. Over the last 60 years, thousands of studies have examined the variables that contribute to effective counseling. Over time, the questions that guide this research and the methods by which it is conducted have become increasingly sophisticated. Regardless of the method, the central question in any outcome research study is Does it work? For the most part, today's outcome research is characterized by high-quality studies, performed in multiple clinical settings, that have used validated treatments and reliable outcome measures. Even with these improvements, outcome research remains a complex undertaking, and the results of individual studies can be contradictory and confusing. However, the accumulated body of research yields substantiated trends that form a useful body of clinical knowledge.

What is most curious is the serious split between counseling research and counseling practice that exists, even though outcome research can provide a wealth of clinical guidance. This split between reliance on knowledge emanating from systematic empirical inquiry and reliance on knowledge resulting from clinical experience is one that many never expected. The split is often framed as one between those espousing the art of counseling (intuitive understanding based on clinical experience) and those proposing reliance on the science of counseling (based upon systematic study).

Although most of us probably think of counseling as both a science and an art, there is increasing evidence that the science portion of the equation is neglected. The extent of this neglect is illustrated by a number of recent surveys. Among the disturbing findings is evidence that practitioners do not read or engage in research and that counseling research currently has little or no impact on counseling practice. In addition, even with the increases in both the quantity and quality of counseling research, there appears to be little evidence that clinicians have adopted a more positive attitude concerning its relevance. Consequently, clinical outcome research is often neglected in favor of strategies based on clinical or personal experiences, clinical training, or therapeutic intuition (Kanfer, 1990). The gap between research and practice is a serious problem that is making it difficult for our profession to develop and to deliver the best possible services.

Many of the concerns about research are not without merit. Today's research is dominated by assumptions of logical positivism, based exclusively in quantitative top-down methods, and is theory-verifying rather than discovery-oriented. There is no question that we need an integrated approach based on a plurality of methods that involve cooperative partnerships between practitioners and researchers in real-life counseling settings (Sexton, Whiston, Bleuer, & Walz, 1997). Problems with outcome research do not, however, justify the abandonment of research for intuition. Instead they suggest that we need to expand the ways we conduct and use research. Although an expansion of clinical research methods will be beneficial, the current outcome research is substantial enough to be a valuable clinical aid to practicing counselors.

Regardless of unique specialty, professional counselors are linked by a common body of professional knowledge. Whether we are school counselors, marriage and family therapists, or mental health counselors, each of us uses this common knowledge. Outcome research can point a practitioner toward an intervention that has been shown to work with a particular type of client. Research can help us develop counseling programs in agencies and schools with a high probability of success. Furthermore, the profession of counseling is best served by integrating outcome research into all professional and clinical decisions.

In much the same way, research can and should be part of our emerging social action agenda. When informed by the systematic trends and scientific findings of research, our social agenda can be based on multiple perspectives, rooted in systemic inquiry, with conclusions that are ecologically valid. Research-based social positions will legitimize what we choose to support, will give us data from which to argue successfully, and will help develop the credibility of the profession as a field that can be trusted as a reliable social advocate. As a basis for social action, counseling outcome research can help make us both accountable and credible social activists.

SOCIAL ACTIVIST IMPLICATIONS OF OUTCOME RESEARCH

The accumulated body of outcome research has already pointed us toward a social activist agenda. Although a complete analysis of the outcome research and its impact on our social activism role is well beyond the scope of this chapter, looking at social activist implications of current outcome research will highlight ways in which research-based knowledge can be used to identify areas of social action and provide data-based findings that can be used to argue persuasively for social change. It is important to remember that research-based knowledge is substantial but not static; findings will evolve as we expand our research methods and gain new information. Consequently, our activist agendas will also change over time.

COUNSELING SERVICES ARE ESSENTIAL

Along with other health care providers, professional counselors are socially sanctioned to prevent and remediate developmental, emotional, and life problems. In fact, many of us went into the counseling profession to become "helpers." Once in the profession, we soon see that the varied social problems in our society are enormous and growing. For example, about one in five adults suffers from a diagnosable mental disorder, ranging from schizophrenia to depression to substance abuse. In addition, almost 12% of children under 18 experience serious emotional difficulties. Increasing numbers of people need counseling services. A survey of the adult population in the United States found that 59% of those surveyed reported that they could imagine circumstances under which they might benefit from discussing their psychological problems with someone (Kulka, Veroff, & Douvan, 1979). Of these, 26% had sought and received some type of psychological help. This rate represents a doubling of utilization from that reported a decade earlier. In a 1995 *Consumer Reports* survey, the utilization rate for mental health services increased to 31.36%. The cost of treating these problems is enormous—an estimated $273.3 billion in 1988 alone—and is increasing at an average rate of 13.9% annually. The prevalence of emotional problems has increased to the point where most people in our society now view them as a critical social issue.

Can counseling have an impact on these problems? Can professional counselors be successful change agents? The accumulated evidence leads to a relatively clear conclusion: counseling benefits most clients who become involved with skilled counselors. When compared to the impact in other fields, those produced by various methods of counseling and psychotherapy are typically as large or larger than those resulting from medical and educational interventions (Lambert & Bergin, 1994).

Based upon these findings, counselors should vigorously endorse an important social role for a wide range of counseling services offered by skilled professionals. As agents of social action, professional counselors can use these research findings to advocate credibly for counseling services with third-party payers, school administrators, local civic groups, both federal and state governments, and other potential clients. As social activists, professional counselors need to inform insurance organizations of the effectiveness of counseling. Furthermore, we need to educate the public about the substantial research base that supports counseling so that people will demand that these services be included in their benefit packages. Our activist message regarding the essential role of counseling services will have more influence in the political and business worlds when it is based on the empirical findings of counseling outcome research.

COUNSELING PRACTICE SHOULD BE ACCOUNTABLE

Attempts to manage both the volume and the cost of counseling services have ushered counseling into an era defined by accountability. Insurance review boards and managed care panels now control whether or not services are provided, the extent of those services, and the fees that fund the services. States are cutting mental health budgets and closely monitoring the services they provide. School districts want to know what services students are receiving and the efficiency of those activities. Counselors are, in this new environment, "under the gun" not only to provide good services but also to justify the need and efficacy of those services.

In order to attend responsibly to these social problems in an active and accountable manner, counselors need to provide the most effective services possible. To do so, we need to bring the best we have to bear in helping the clients. However, according to the current outcome research, not all counseling is equally effective. On the average, some 8 to 11% of clients get worse! Given this consistent research trend, the profession has a social responsibility to advocate for and promote those models of counseling that have demonstrable positive effects. A review of the outcome literature suggests that professional counselors should advocate, both inside and outside the profession, for models of counseling that are based on common therapeutic elements, with matched treatments, founded on a solid therapeutic alliance.

Numerous studies have examined the effectiveness of various theories. Surprisingly, with the exception of a small advantage found for some approaches (e.g., cognitive, cognitive-behavioral), the major theoretical approaches are relatively equal in their effectiveness. There do seem to be, however, a set of common factors that are a part of all effective counseling regardless of the counselor, theory, or technique. It is now safe to say that factors common across counseling approaches account for a substantial amount of client improvement. If the percentage of improvement in clients as a function of different factors were determined, 40% would be due to change factors outside of counseling, 15% would be due to expectancy or placebo effects, 15% would be attributed to specific psychological techniques, and 30% would be accounted for by common factors evident in all therapies regardless of the counselor's theoretical orientation (Lambert, 1991). If this analysis is correct, the impact of these common factors is twice that of specific psychological techniques.

Our best current understanding of common factors is that they are organized into three categories. The first is *support factors*, which include catharsis or positive relationship with the counselor, a therapeutic alliance, counselor warmth, respect, empathy, and trust. The second category is *learning factors*, which include advice, affective experiencing, corrective emotional experiencing, feedback, and assimilation of problematic experience. The third and final category is *action factors*, which include behavioral regulation, cognitive mastery, facing fears, mastery efforts, and successful experiences. These factors provide for a cooperative working alliance that leads to successful change (Lambert & Cattani-Thompson, 1996).

Even when these common factors are in place, however, a number of treatment protocols are particularly effective with certain client problems. For example, researchers can now say that depression, anxiety, panic disorders, and obsessive compulsive disorders are better treated by some techniques rather than others (for a complete analysis of which techniques are most effective with which specific client concern see Sexton et al., 1997). It is unfortunate that researchers have been unable to determine the most effective treatments for a wider array of client problems. However, as the sophistication of outcome research grows, identifying the most effective treatments for a broad spectrum of client concerns will become easier. Based on these outcome research findings, an effective model of counseling needs to incorporate the research-supported treatment protocols matched to the appropriate client problem.

Researchers have also learned that any formula of effective counseling must include a strong relational component. In fact, there is no other element of counseling more consistently related to successful outcome than the quality of the relationship between the client and counselor. What constitutes a therapeutic relationship has, however, been difficult to determine. Researchers now know that the counseling relationship is more than counselor-offered, facilitative-based conditions. Empathy, unconditional positive regard, genuineness, and respect alone do not account for a successful therapeutic relationship. Instead, there is substantial research support for counseling that occurs in the context of a therapeutic relationship in which the participants have mutual feelings of empathy and affiliation, and in which there are clear and agreed upon goals that are accomplished in collaborative ways. Positive outcomes are further enhanced when the counselor is viewed by the client as a credible helper (Sexton & Whiston, 1994).

There is no question that there is much more to learn about what constitutes *effective counseling*. Currently, the accumulated research directs us to teach and advocate for models of counseling that include the important common factors, are based on the successful matching of client problem with therapeutic approach, and contain a strong therapeutic alliance between the client and counselor (Orlinsky, Grawe, & Parks, 1994). Counseling based on these trends should reliably result in successful change that will further enhance the credibility of professional counselors. This is a model of effective counseling for which we can credibly and reasonably argue in the professional, political, and social arenas.

Formulas for Client Services Should Be Flexible

With the increases in the need and call for counseling, many changes are occurring regarding the type of counseling services being offered in our communities. Any practicing counselor knows the impact of managed care on health care delivery. A major concern for many counselors is that as managed health care systems become more powerful, a "single formula" for client services is emerging. Insurance companies are now determining the number of sessions and the type of treatment that should be given to those in our society who suffer from emotional and personal problems. Unfortunately, many of these decisions are made based on economic rather than efficacy reasons. As social activists, we, as professional counselors, should take the lead in defining what form counseling services should take. A review of the outcome literature suggests that the professional counselor should advocate for a flexible model of counseling based on client concern.

For example, in light of the economic pressures in the mental health marketplace, the optimal number of counseling sessions is of great interest. To be socially accountable, professional counselors need to deliver only that degree of help that is necessary. However, to be effective practitioners we need to give enough service such that clients change in lasting ways. A number of relatively consistent conclusions have emerged from the outcome research. In general, it seems that the road to recovery via counseling is a relatively short one. Regardless of the type of therapy, counselor, or client, there is evidence to support a curvilinear relationship between the number of sessions and improvement, with 50% of change occurring by the 8th session and 75% by the 26th session. However, the general trend is that the most effective therapy duration depends on the level of client disturbance, with different symptom clusters improving at different rates during different phases of treatment. Thus the effects of therapy may be relatively quick, but the nature of the client concern is an important mediating factor.

These findings coupled with the economic pressures of mental health services suggest that we advocate for short-term approaches to counseling. In addition, these data suggest that we argue for a model of counseling service that is flexible enough to determine the length of counseling based on the problem of the client. The combination of within-profession accountability for the length of counseling and system flexibility is the most defensible position given the current outcome research findings.

TREATMENTS SHOULD BE BOTH EMPIRICALLY VALIDATED AND MANUAL DRIVEN

The trend toward accountability has influenced two important trends within the professional organizations with enormous consequences for the social impact of counseling. The first is the establishment of clinical practice guidelines that outline which treatment best fits a client's concern. The second is a move toward treatment manuals intended to guide the clinician by standardizing psychotherapeutic interventions and by specifically outlining the steps in a particular type of intervention. The American Psychological Association has created multiple task forces to consider practice and training guidelines based on empirically validated treatments. Clinical practice guidelines are also currently being published by the American Psychiatric Association. Whether or not professional counselors support such efforts will have a major impact on the future role that counseling takes in our society. The outcome research does help outline a social position in regard to these initiatives.

Outcome research has established that there is a range of specific, well-documented treatments, with established efficacy, that can be used with various client problems. These treatments are not theory-based approaches but instead are specific interventions designed for specific client problems. Outcome research has suggested that technical proficiency increases with manualized treatment. The outcome literature has also suggested that even in the best of cases no single treatment, regardless of its skillful delivery, may fit all clients. Results of recent studies have suggested that certain clients respond better to the manual-guided treatment than other clients. It may be that counselors need to be skilled with multiple treatment protocols to work effectively with different clients. These findings have not suggested, however, that technical competence can overcome the need to be interpersonally skillful.

The current research has indicated that we need to advocate for a system that provides focused yet flexible services. It should be a system in which systematic counseling protocols are the guiding template for major client concerns—accompanied by flexibility and awareness of the relational component and the range of individual differences that are important if a treatment protocol is to be effective. It should not, however, be a system based on a simple match of broad problem labels with generic treatments.

DELIVERY SYSTEMS SHOULD BE DIVERSE AND RESPONSIVE

One of the more disturbing results of current outcome research has been the number of clients who either do not utilize or who do not continue counseling once they start. The majority of clients who enter counseling terminate by the eighth session, with the range only being from 3 to 13 sessions. The National Institute of Mental Health surveyed 350,000 children and youth involved in mental health services and found that 69% had 5 or fewer sessions, with only 12.5% continuing beyond 10 sessions. In a survey of private practice psychologists and psychiatrists, 44% of the clients made fewer than 4 visits while 16.2% of the sample made more than 24 visits. These clients, however, accounted for 57.4% of the expense of services. Almost 49% of clients referred for counseling never come to the first session (Garfield, 1994).

The outcome literature does contain studies that guide us in understanding these delivery problems. An early hypothesis was that the socioeconomic status of the client was related to dropping out. A number of studies did find that lower income clients are less likely to remain in counseling. Educational level seems to be related to length of time a client remains in counseling, with the higher the educational level, the longer the client is likely to remain in counseling. Occupational level was also significantly correlated with early drop out. It seemed that African American clients are more likely than White clients to terminate early from counseling. Asian Americans and Mexican Americans seemed underrepresented in the use of mental health services while African Americans overutilized services. Ethnic mismatch between client and counselor was related to premature termination for all groups but was not related to successful counseling. Hence, it may be that, in establishing a therapeutic alliance, it is not the ethnic, gender, or racial match of client and counselor that is most important, but rather the ability of the counselor to adopt the worldview of the client.

These findings tell us that the ways in which we deliver counseling services does not always correspond to the needs of those we could help. Regardless of the reasons, these findings should move us to advocate for the development of counseling services that are accessible and useful to people from varied ethnic backgrounds and economic levels. It seems that we need to understand the factors that engage clients in successful counseling so that they do not drop out. In addition, it seems clear that we need a delivery system that is accessible to the large group of potential clients who are currently not using these services.

We might need to consider novel ways in which we can deliver our effective services to those who are less likely to access them. For example, instead of expensive individual counseling we may need to consider accessible group and psychoeducational treatments. We might also consider home-based services in which counselors would go to clients' homes. Regardless of the specific method, the outcome literature points us toward advocating for a diverse range of services that fit the needs of a variety of social groups.

AN ACTIVIST RESEARCH AGENDA

To date, outcome research has focused almost exclusively on questions regarding whether counseling is effective and how we might improve its success. This information has proven helpful, but as social activists we need also to turn our attention toward broader social concerns. Outcome research can play a key role in our ability to enact social change. There are five current social issues in which outcome research could be used to clarify the direction of the activist activities and provide systematic data from which to argue credibly for social change. Although there are many social issues, these five are proposed as a stimulus for an expanded social action research agenda in professional counseling.

Issue: Crisis in Families

There is no question that many of the families in our society are struggling. Epidemiological studies have indicated that from 17% to 22% of youth under 18 years of age suffer developmental, behavioral, or emotional problems. The monetary costs for these troubled children and adolescents are staggering. For example, the Institute of Medicine (1989) estimated that in 1985 alone $1.5 billion was devoted to youths under the age of 14 with mental disorders. Divorce rates today typically average around 50%. It is now common for children to come from single-parent households, and it is not uncommon for children to live in multiple households. In many cities, juvenile crime and violence are now seen as major social problems and a public health hazard.

As social activists, professional counselors could take the lead in understanding and helping these families. Outcome research could help us address questions such as What are the factors that hinder family functioning? What are the most effective ways of helping these families? How can we tailor what we know about successful counseling to fit this population? What are the most efficacious delivery models for these families?

A number of encouraging initiatives illustrate ways research could be used to help these families. These efforts are, however, currently being conducted by groups outside the profession of counseling. For example, both the Centers for Disease Control (CDC) and the

U.S. Department of Justice have recently turned their attention toward the problems of family violence, substance abuse, and juvenile delinquency. The CDC set out to identify the most effective family treatment models based on the outcome literature in order to develop blueprints for a treatment model, which will then be disseminated to local communities. Once in place in local communities, evaluation research will help further define the most efficacious components of the models, further improving practice. Currently, Functional Family Therapy (Alexander & Parsons, 1982) has met the validity criteria and is moving toward field testing. With a broadened outcome research agenda, we could develop empirical information that might guide us in the development of additional treatments for troubled families.

ISSUE: CRISIS IN EDUCATION

Many local communities are becoming increasingly concerned about the academic achievement and educational preparation of school children. We have all heard about movements to return schools to a back-to-the-basics focus on academic achievement. Yet education takes places in an increasingly difficult social setting in which there are numerous roadblocks to learning. Students now come to school concerned about home life, struggling with peer relations, and challenged by the social climate of schools. We know that children are entering school climates that are increasingly more violent.

School counselors are positioned to have major impact on how to intervene successfully so that learning can occur. Unfortunately, research on which school counseling practices have a positive impact on academic and social development is lacking. According to a recent survey of counseling outcome research, school counseling has the least amount of empirical evidence available to practitioners (Sexton, 1996), and the range of methodological quality in the existing studies makes reliable conclusions difficult. Further, in the research conducted, the focus was often on outcomes that had little or no direct impact on education (e.g., self-esteem).

Understanding and intervening on the behavioral and social challenges that impede education could be an important social agenda for counselors. In order to play an activist role, we need to expand research into systematic analyses of the nature of these social problems and examine ways in which school counselors can have a positive impact with a wide range of students.

ISSUE: DIVERSITY AND PLURALISM

Gender, race, ethnicity, and culture are an important part of every layer of our social world. These issues increasingly occupy our professional dialogue and influence practice and theory. In many ways, the banners of diversity and pluralism have become synonymous with being socially active. In our search for understanding the importance of diversity, we have developed many beliefs about minority/majority cultures, clients, and counselors. Unfortunately, some of these beliefs are taken as "truth" without turning to the outcome research. Today we have little research support for our beliefs regarding gender, ethnicity, and race. Consequently, our efforts at social change are hindered.

In the pluralistic society in which we live, it is important for professional counseling to lead the charge in identifying counseling services that are effective for diverse clients. Unfortunately, the outcome literature has been of little help along this line. The studies provide equivocal conclusions regarding the impact of gender, ethnicity, and age on the outcomes of counseling. On the one hand, there is little research support for matching clients and counselors on any of these characteristics. On the other hand, it is clear that ethnic groups vary in the degree to which they utilize counseling. There are some data to suggest that certain characteristics of female counselors may contribute to successful counseling.

Outcome research is only beginning to sort out the complex interaction among these variables, and a broadened research effort is sorely needed. As a substantial body of research in this area grows, we will have a basis from which to determine how to argue responsibly for diversity and pluralism.

ISSUE: HEALTH-RELATED BEHAVIORS

As a society, we have become increasingly aware of the link between behavior and health. We know that smoking, exercise, and healthy diet have a direct impact both on length and quality of life. We know that sexual behavior can have a major social impact in regard to the transmission of the HIV virus. What we have yet to do is to determine what role professional counselors should play in this area. This is due, in part, to the fact that our outcome research has yet to turn its attention toward those counseling interventions that might successfully address health-related behaviors. A social activist agenda could include such a focus, and research could contribute to our understanding of the mechanisms that affect health behavior change. With a substantial body of research, professional counselors could make reasoned decisions when faced with questions such as Which health behaviors are related to common problems expressed in counseling? Which health behaviors contribute to the treatment of depression or anxiety? Which health behaviors contribute to a healthy lifestyle? With a research base, the profession would know how to make health a major point of social advocacy.

Issue: Impact of Professional Knowledge on Everyday Life

Some suggest that the knowledge base of professional counseling has, in addition to the noted direct influences, an equally important indirect impact on society. In the same way counseling theories are influenced by the norms of the culture, the culture is influenced by the beliefs, assumptions, and theories of the profession. Both explicitly and implicitly, the profession influences the values by which people, relationships, lifestyles, development, and communication are judged. As an example, just think of the number of ways in which the Freudian notion of the unconscious has become a common theme in literature, movies, and even everyday conversation. Sometimes the result of theoretical constructs, although professionally and theoretically useful, is inadvertently to limit those we may ultimately aim to help. As accountable social activists, we should also turn our attention toward investigating the long-term impact of our professional constructs on social values.

For example, diagnostic systems, such as the *DSM-IV*, may serve a useful function within the profession, but they may also have a potentially negative social impact. The original goal of a diagnostic system was to create a language to help us understand people better and to ensure reliable communication among professionals. However, since the introduction of the concept of neurosis (somewhere in the mid-18th century), the categories of mental disorder have grown geometrically. The *DSM-IV*, for example, contains over 200 categories of disorders. Once professionally established, these notions of disorder enter the cultural discourse and become "what everybody knows" about human behavior. As part of common language, these reified states then influence the way each of us constructs and makes sense out of everyday reality. As larger domains of behavior enter the ledger of problems subject to professional treatment, the construction of *infirmity* expands (Gergen, 1982). Thus, in an indirect way, we may have contributed to the proliferation of the very personal problems we have sought to remedy.

RESEARCH, PRACTICE, TRAINING, AND SOCIAL ACTION: A SYNERGISTIC ENTERPRISE

The key to developing a social action agenda based on our professional knowledge base lies with us. If we are ever to have outcome research inform activism, then we need to become more unified in our use and in our acceptance of the knowledge it provides. To do that, we have to overcome the research-practice gap. What gets lost in the struggle is the important fact that practice, research, training, and social action are not different; rather, they are mutually linked in two important ways. First, these activities share the same primary goal: effective and ethical services for clients and a positive impact on the larger culture. Second, although the specific duties of practice, research, and training differ, they are united by a mutual dependence on the same knowledge base.

A synergistic relationship among these activities needs to build on their common purposes, shared knowledge, and pragmatic approach. Each is practical in the sense that a common goal is the solution of conceptual, clinical, and social problems. As such, practice, research, training, and advocacy share the same motives— the best solutions to common problems. The best solutions are ones that work to further our knowledge and help clients change. When sharing a common purpose based on pragmatism, no one of these activities drives the others. Instead, each makes a different, yet equally important, contribution to effective counseling.

The roles of counseling practice and social action are in a synergistic relationship that goes beyond the traditional view in which we as clinicians merely draw upon science as the ultimate authority to solve problems. Instead, the counselor plays a crucial and unique role in the enhancement of the knowledge base in two important ways. First, practitioners are the ones in the trenches who apply the knowledge base in clinical settings. The identification of pertinent and relevant questions lies with them. Second, practitioners are local scientists who bring the skills of scientific inquiry to local phenomena, be they clinical or social. As such they also use the methods of inquiry to engage in an evaluation of their own effectiveness as action researchers, thus developing a local database that might be used to promote and guide their individual practice.

Research should also be viewed from a pragmatic standpoint and seen as a problem-solving activity. In the solution of problems, neither quantitative nor qualitative research is primary. Instead, methodological choice is based on pragmatic goals realized through pluralistic methods. Thus determining whether a quantitative or qualitative method is needed is based on the problem being investigated and the questions that need to be answered. Along this line, discovery-oriented questions are matched with opened qualitative investigations, whereas confirmation/verification questions use more traditional quantitative questions. The questions researchers study cannot be determined in isolation because questions need to emanate from the activities of practice and education.

If outcome research is to provide the direction and legitimacy to lead us toward an activist agenda, an expansion of acceptable clinical research methods is required. Research directed at the social problems will need to be pluralistic, multidimensional, and ecologically valid. Plurality will only occur when we take a pragmatic position and then use the best from among our systematic methods of outcome research. For example, traditional quantitative research is explanatory research with an "outside in" perspective from which we can identify broad trends that go beyond the individual. The qualitative process of phenomenological research and grounded theory analysis provides an "inside out" perspective, an approach in which the focus is on the contextually bound meaning of events for individual people. These approaches emphasize discovery-oriented

research focusing on, rather than controlling for, individual difference. A complete picture of the many complex social events requires
both perspectives.

The knowledge base that links these activities is an evolving one.
Information is continually infused as single research findings are
incorporated into the knowledge base. Common findings may take
the form of general principles by garnering significant support over
time and across varied situations. Rather than providing definitive
answers and ultimate truths, the knowledge base is constantly changing as new findings, interpretations, and questions are developed.
The conclusions of today are quite naturally replaced by the findings
of tomorrow. In our field the evolutionary nature of knowledge is
particularly evident. Some have suggested, for example, that the
half-life of psychological knowledge is somewhere around 10 years
(Kanfer, 1990). The implication is that the knowledge base must
be a consistent and integral part of all facets of counseling—be it
practice, research, training, or social action.

Practice, research, education, and social action each draw on
this knowledge base. In turn, each of these areas contributes to the
knowledge base by forming hypotheses, asking relevant questions,
and discovering new areas of interest. These questions become part
of the knowledge base to be acted upon by researchers. Critical in
these relationships is that the knowledge base is viewed as evolving
and is complete with strengths and limitations. For some questions,
research offers little guidance while in other areas there is a wealth
of relevant information. Even in those areas in which there are few
or mixed research findings, research could still be the foundation
of logical solutions to clinical problems. Thus the question is never
whether should research be integrated—but rather how. In the new
era of social action, counselors need to ask How is it that research
can form the basis of what we advocate? How can research help
us make persuasive arguments to carry out these advocacy agendas?

CONCLUSION

The expansion of our professional identity to include social activism is a necessary and important evolution for the profession of
counseling. Professional counseling plays an important role in the
social world. In the past, the profession has seemed somewhat

uncomfortable about adopting a socially active role, preferring to claim the neutrality and advocacy of the individual client. As we have come to see, the natural and synergistic relationship between professional knowledge and social values has caused these old barriers to fall away. As we embark on the new era advocated in this book, social action needs to be thoughtful, reflective, and based on the best of what we know about critical social problems. The profession is best served if we base our social action agenda on the over 60 years of accumulated and yet developing counseling outcome research that helps direct and give credibility to our efforts to advocate for social change.

REFERENCES

Alexander, J. F., & Parsons, B. V. (1982). *Functional family therapy*. Carmel CA: Brooks/Cole.

Garfield, S. L. (1994). Research on client variables in psychotherapy. In A. E. Bergin & S. L. Garfield (Eds.), *Handbook of psychotherapy and behavior change* (pp. 190-228). New York: Wiley.

Gergen, K. (1982). *Toward transformation in social knowledge*. New York: Springer-Verlag.

Institute of Medicine (IOM). (1989). *Research on children and adolescents with mental, behavioral, and developmental disorders*. Washington, DC: National Academy Press.

Kanfer, F. H. (1990). The scientist-practitioner connection: A bridge in need of constant attention. *Professional Psychology: Research and Practice, 21*, 264-270.

Kulka, R. A., Veroff, J., & Douvan, E. (1979). Social class and the use of professional help for personal problems: 1957-1976. *Journal of Health and Social Behavior, 20*, 2-17.

Lambert, M. J. (1991). Introduction to psychotherapy research. In L. E. Beutler & M. Crago (Eds.), *Psychotherapy research: An international review of programmatic studies* (pp. 1-23). Washington, DC: American Psychological Association.

Lambert, M. J., & Bergin, A. E. (1994). The effectiveness of psychotherapy. In A. E. Bergin & S. L. Garfield (Eds.), *Handbook of psychotherapy and behavior change* (pp. 143-189). New York: Wiley.

Lambert, M. J., & Cattani-Thompson, K. (1996). Current findings regarding the effectiveness of counseling: Implications for practice. *Journal of Counseling and Development, 74*, 601-608.

Mental health: Does therapy help? (1995, November). *Consumer Reports*, 734-739.

Orlinsky, D. E., Grawe, D., & Parks, B. K. (1994). Process and outcome in psychotherapy—NOCH EINMAL. In A. E. Bergin & S. L. Garfield (Eds.), *Handbook of psychotherapy and behavior change* (pp. 270-368). New York: Wiley.

Sexton, T. L. (1996). The relevance of counseling outcome research: Current trends and practical implications. *Journal of Counseling and Development, 74*, 590-600.

Sexton, T. L., & Whiston, S. C. (1994). The status of the counseling relationship: An empirical review, theoretical implications, and research directions. *The Counseling Psychologist, 22*(1), 6-78.

Sexton, T. L., Whiston, S. C., Bleuer, J. C., & Walz, G. R. (1997). *Integrating outcome research into counseling practice and training.* Alexandria, VA: American Counseling Association.

PART THREE

Social Action: A Focus on Professional Issues

15

Preparing Counselors
for Social Action

BROOKE B. COLLISON, JUDITH L. OSBORNE, LIZBETH A. GRAY,
REESE M. HOUSE, JAMES FIRTH, AND MARY LOU

Conscious strategies to teach social action must be a central part of the counselor education curriculum if we expect counselors to become effective social activists. It is possible that some counselors might become social activists through a natural developmental process, or social activists might become counselors; but, our contention is that counselor education programs should include intentional philosophy, curriculum, and processes that prepare graduates to work as social activists in their professional settings. Just as we include preparation program components to assure that graduates possess counseling skills, we should also include preparation components that prepare counselors to become effective change agents who can work to improve the lives of their clients in a variety of ways.

Socially active counselors are those who intervene in the lives of their clients and in the world around them (Courtland C. Lee & Garry R. Walz, personal correspondence, February 14, 1997). Further, counseling should be directed toward the "significant social, cultural, and economic issues that often impact negatively upon the lives of clients in contemporary American society" (p. 1). Eldridge (1983) has presented similar ideas. To become socially active and make those interventions, counselors must see themselves as social change agents, and we, as counselor educators, must model those same skills and attitudes in our preparation programs. This chapter briefly looks at counselor advocacy and action in the past and then outlines a frame of reference for social action that includes the law, professional ethics, moral codes, social condition and data-based frameworks, research, and personal belief systems. The chapter next explores a personal frame of reference for social action decision making that considers the system, the client group, style issues, self-view, information, and consequence. The chapter concludes with a discussion of counselor education and social action that stresses the importance of counselor educators modeling a social conscience for their students.

ADVOCACY AND ACTION IN THE PAST

Change agentry is not a new concept for counselors or counselor educators. Several authors have presented ideas about this process that can be classified as promoting assertive change. Lofaro (1982) described how counselor education needed to change to prepare counselors for assertive work on the behalf of clients with disabling conditions. Brigman (1994) described how counselors need to respond actively to challenges from religious or political groups that seek to eliminate use of various school counseling materials. Kurpius and Rozecki (1992) used the word *advocacy* as one of the role descriptions for school counselors and have described characteristics of that role for counselors; however, they were silent on how counselor education should prepare counselors to be advocates.

In her presidential address to the Association for Counselor Education and Supervision (ACES), Griffin (1993) challenged counselor educators to use a constructivist philosophy in order to build a framework for preparation of counselors who would do more than just work with clients one at a time. Her emphasis on a social constructivist philosophy "forces the consideration of the social, cultural, psychological, economic, and political circumstances on which our professional behaviors are based" (p. 4).

In a reflection on the history of ACES and the profession in the 25th anniversary edition of the journal *Counselor Education and Supervision*, Engels and Muro (1986) stated that counselor educators and supervisors need to provide leadership in "services, teaching, research, credentialing, policy, and law" (p. 289). Their position was that counselors have professional expertise and commitment to issues of civil rights such as freedom from discrimination because of "race, religion, sex, sexual orientation, and related characteristics"

(p. 296). Engels and Muro explained that the world needs leaders who understand positive change and who believe that "constructive, informed change is possible for others" (p. 297). They cited Herr (1985), who stated that early versions of the constitutions of the American Association for Counseling and Development (AACD) and ACES have been forces for change in that they included language that encouraged individual members and organizational units to remove barriers to individual development.

The current mission statement of the American Counseling Association does not include direction for the members or the association to take an advocacy stance on behalf of clients or other groups. The Code of Ethics (ACA, 1995) does include words in the Preamble that "members are dedicated to the enhancement of human development throughout the life span" (p. 1). A reading of the Code of Ethics, however, does not encompass a call to action for counselors to act assertively beyond the required reporting and duty-to-warn situations that are discussed in every beginning counselor education class. In short, although ACA has developed convention themes, programs, and workshops that speak to social injustice, there is no strong organizational statement that counselors should take on an advocacy role in their professional lives. However, enhancing human development demands an assertive response from counselors and their association—an advocacy position. Counselor education programs, and ACA programs, should also include these components.

Organizations, like people, are dynamic, changing, and developmental in nature. If a system does not change over time, it is in some kind of death process. As counselor education moves toward a perspective that adequately responds to society's multifaceted needs, the changes that take place will include a posture of activism and advocacy. The markers for those changes may occur so slowly that counseling professionals who are in the center of the change may not notice them; however, there are ways to assess the philosophical shifts. For example, Thompson and Walker (1995) examined the family studies literature in the mid 1980s and again a decade later to determine the degree to which feminism was reflected in the research publications of that discipline. Thompson and Walker's conclusions were extensive and, in general, support the premise that feminist scholarship is increasingly reflected in recent literature in family studies and subsequently has influenced policy in that same area. Their excellent summary could be a model for counselor educators to use in assessing the degree to which the counseling literature has shifted with the times or is fixed in a former era.

Policy considerations are another domain for counselor educators to examine. Pratt (1995) explained how professionals can be involved in policy creation when she spoke to family and human development issues. She used work by Miringhoff to explain the difference between values, politics, and capability. Values reflect what people believe should be; politics reflects what can be supported; and capability reflects service technology or what is actually possible when addressing a problem. She recommended that academicians be actively involved in all three domains, with special emphasis on use of their research knowledge to support and define values and politics and to develop capabilities.

The future of counselor education was described in Orwellian terms by Stripling (1984). He was able to use his long history with the profession to reflect on an interesting transition from the early days of the profession to the height of the Rogerian orientation that shifted from seeing the client as dependent patient to responsible client. Additional emphases have included systems theory, brief therapy, and feminist therapy—all calling for different active behaviors from the counselor. The next orientation, a social activist stance, may enable counselors to see their own roles as being that of power brokers to enhance the lives of clients, in part by directly addressing the issues that create problems for their client groups.

A FRAME OF REFERENCE FOR SOCIAL ACTION

Counselor educators can expand on the Lee and Walz definition (cited at the beginning of this chapter) as well as on the Lee and Sirch (1994) position and say that social action is an individual or collective action taken to right some injustice or to improve some condition for the benefit of an individual or group. In order to describe a condition or situation as *unjust*, there must be a standard, a set of criteria, or a frame of reference for determining that an injustice exists or that a condition is unfair. That frame of reference can be described in terms of the law, professional ethics, moral codes, social condition frameworks, data-based frameworks, research, or personal belief systems.

The Law

Counselors work with numerous legal criteria that can be used to say that a person or a group is experiencing injustice. For example, federal legislation entitles children to an education in the least restrictive environment (Education for All Handicapped Children Act of 1975), mandates that there should be fairness in men's and women's athletic activities (Title IX of the Education Amendments of 1972), and stipulates that the content of school records must be open to the persons affected by those records (Family Educational Rights and Privacy Act of 1974). Persons with disabling conditions must have accommodations made that enable them to access public services (Americans With Disabilities Act of 1990). Decisions about individuals in any public agency must be made with reasonable attention to due process as a basic constitutional right. Civil rights legislation has made it illegal to discriminate on the basis of race or ethnicity. If the counselor observes that one of these legal rights is being abused, then there is a frame of reference for defining action to be taken.

Professional Ethics

Counselors show their professionalism by adopting a code of ethics. Codes of ethics are typically linked to a professional organization or licensing body and describe not only practices and behaviors that counselors should follow in their practice but also behaviors that clients can expect. The limits of confidentiality, how research subjects are to be treated, when counselors must refer, with whom a counselor can consult and why, and what constitutes an inappropriate relationship are all described in counseling codes of ethics (ACA, 1995). When counselors see questionable practices, they may use the codes of ethics to respond in ways that will protect the rights of clients. If that action means that they address the behavior of other counselors, then the professional counselor must respond.

Moral Codes

Numerous moral codes exist within any social order. Moral codes can be shaped by religious institutions, expressed as common practice among a group of people, or defined by community standards. A moral code might indicate that all people are to be treated fairly, that abusive behavior is wrong, that elderly persons are to be respected, or that standards of dress or appearance have limits. Moral codes are among the most controversial frameworks to apply to human behavior because they include descriptions of behaviors that may be viewed as unacceptable by one group of persons but acceptable by another. When counselors observe that persons are treated unfairly according to a moral code, then the counselor must respond.

Social Condition Frameworks

Descriptions of social conditions can be used as a framework for a definition of injustice. If an individual or a group has inadequate food or poor housing, it points to an injustice. If health care is not available to a group of individuals, then an injustice exists. Counselors who examine community health data will probably learn that young unmarried women who are sexually active and become pregnant often have low-birth-weight babies. Those babies are likely to experience persistent learning problems as they move through their school years; thus the social conditions associated with early unprotected sexual activity may have long-term effects in many other arenas. These examples of social conditions reflect complex injustices that counselors must be able to address.

Data-Based Frameworks

Counselors need to have as complete a picture of their client group as they can develop in order to develop assertive responses where needed. Thus counselors should be able to use a variety of data sources to develop a framework for describing what exists. For example, census data can provide an expanded picture of the area in which clients live. Population growth rates have implications for future school enrollments, immigration rates point out needs for second language instruction, employment rates have implications for social support systems, and rates of births to different age groups tell of contemporary issues for adolescents and future issues for schools.

RESEARCH

Research provides counselors with the knowledge that enables advocacy decisions based on an understanding of effective practice. For example, current research on at-risk adolescents has strongly suggested that more resilient youth have a higher degree of self-efficacy, have a more internalized locus of control, are involved in their own decision making, and live in a home or school environment that is not highly authoritarian (Hawkins, Catalano, & Miller, 1992). Counselors who observe that educational practice is such that it removes decision making from students in favor of external control and discipline may use the research base to work assertively to revise educational philosophy or practice. Their alternative is to continue to work with students who have varying degrees of symptoms associated with the system in which they live and work.

PERSONAL BELIEF SYSTEMS

Each counselor and counselor educator operates from a personal belief system that adds to the larger framework for identifying conditions that are unfair, unjust, or not equitable. Those personal belief systems incorporate a set of other beliefs—laws, professional training, ethics, moral values, research knowledge, and cultural tradition. How counselors utilize their personal belief systems to determine that a situation is wrong and then address it is part of the personal decision–making process described in the following section.

A PERSONAL FRAME OF REFERENCE FOR SOCIAL ACTION DECISION MAKING

All persons must first examine their own framework for deciding if they are to take an advocacy position on an issue, how active they are to be, what style they will use in developing an advocacy response, and what they are willing to risk. These decisions are made within the larger framework of law, professional ethics, moral codes, social condition frameworks, data-based frameworks, and research already described. Counselor education programs should provide students with opportunities to examine themselves along each of six personal activism dimensions that are included in making decisions about what to do (see Figure 15-1). These six personal dimensions, which serve not as a model of personal social activism but more as a guide to the complex factors of personal decision making, are as follows: (a) being inside or outside the affected system (the system), (b) being in or out of the affected group (the client group), (c) style of intervention (style issues), (d) perceived self-efficacy (self-view), (e) amount and accuracy of information (information), and (f) personal and organizational consequence of the action (consequence). Other dimensions may be equally important to examine, but these six cover much of the decision process individuals experience prior to implementing a social activist strategy. These six dimensions, when combined with any (or all) of the external frameworks previously described, present a picture of how a person determines whether or not an injustice exists and if he or she will respond.

The System

The activist might be either a member of or external to the system he or she is trying to impact. A faculty member in a counselor education program who is trying to get the counselor education program to revise grading policies is clearly inside the system. A member of the community who is lobbying for changes in grading practices is outside the system. In attempts to change policies, the two persons operate from different assumptions, use different tactics, and experience different consequences. Depending on the issue and on the system, being either inside or outside the system may or may not add strength to a position.

The Client Group

It is ironic that advocacy by persons outside the client group may have more impact on decision makers than advocacy by members of the client group. For example, males who speak up for women's rights may be heard more seriously than females speaking to the same issue; heterosexuals speaking up for gay rights may have more potent voices than homosexuals saying the same thing; and members of numerical majorities can speak more strongly for rights of numerical minority groups than members of those groups themselves.

Figure 15-1
Dimensions of Personal Decision Making

In   Out

System

Central   *Peripheral*

Client Group

Indirect   **Confront/Direct**

Style

Personally Effective   Personally Ineffective

Self-View

Little   Much

Information

Major   Minor

Consequence

However, the person who can speak with the most authenticity about conditions is the member of the client group that is the focus of an action, even though his or her voice may be more difficult to hear. Counselors will find themselves, at times, either in or out of the client groups for which they are taking an advocacy position.

STYLE ISSUES

Social activism usually involves some form of conflict—conflict of information, methods, goals, or values. Persons vary in styles of dealing with conflict, ranging from very direct confrontational styles dealing with conflict, ranging from very direct confrontational styles to behind-the-scenes indirect methods. In order to be an effective social advocate, persons must understand their own styles of action in situations where there is injustice or inequity. Their style of action may be different for small groups than for large groups, and it may differ depending on whether they are in or out of the system. Similarly, style may vary if they are members of the client group affected. Style of activism is an additional dimension of counselor self-knowledge that is important in making a personal decision to become involved in an issue.

SELF-VIEW

All persons have a self-view of their degree of effectiveness in various situations. This dimension of self-efficacy can be described as the ability to accomplish goals or be successful in usual efforts. This self-view has an impact on whether persons take on a social activist strategy. It also has an impact on the style of intervention that they choose and the risks that they are willing to take. Counselors need to acknowledge their own self-efficacy in the arena of advocacy efforts and take steps either to get training or help to become stronger in their view of self. Counselor education programs can encourage collaboration during preparation and continued consultation follow-ing graduation in order to assist in developing positive self-views.

INFORMATION

An informed individual is better able to develop strategic interven-tions than an uninformed person. In matters that call for social action or advocacy, information plays an important part. Some persons can act based merely on their personal convictions; however, institutions often respond more to information than personal conviction. Effec-tive social activist strategies make good use of information. There is a place in counselor education programs for students to learn both how to access sources that describe social conditions and how to acquire information on successful strategies for remediation.

CONSEQUENCE

The consequence of implementing a social activist strategy in some situations can be anticipated in advance, but seldom measured with accuracy. History and fiction are filled with stories of persons who took social activist positions of various kinds; readers of history often know the consequence to them as individuals and to the organizations they represented. Martin Luther King, Jr. was killed for his efforts; Karen Silkwood was harassed and perhaps murdered for speaking out about conditions in the plant where she worked; Maggie Kuhn gained fame as an effective Grey Panther spokesperson for issues related to the elderly; and Marion Wright Edelman has had awards heaped on her as a strong voice for children. There are undoubtedly stories within each counselor's organization or community about persons who were punished for their protest actions or about efforts that failed or backfired in the organizations where the change was attempted. Consequences must be discussed in making decisions to become an activist.

COUNSELOR EDUCATION AND SOCIAL ACTION

Counselor education programs should include social action as a core component in their graduate education programs. It is not enough just to praise the individual student who takes on a cause or who speaks out for underrepresented groups. It is more appropriate for counselor education programs to have social action components within the regular preparation program. It is more likely that counselors in preparation will develop a professional stance of social activism if (a) social action is included in the counselor education program philosophy statement; (b) course syllabi include readings and assignments that address advocacy issues; (c) internship sites reflect a broad range of socially appropriate practice before being endorsed; (d) class projects give priority to social activism; (e) required and supplementary reading lists include advocacy materials; (f) terminal projects for graduate degrees or programs include dimensions of social activism as valued skills that students must acquire; (g) follow-up studies of graduates include discussion of the way that they work as social advocates; and (h) faculty model social activism in a way that personal behavior and program philosophy are shown to be consistent.

PHILOSOPHY STATEMENTS

Social responsibility is included as part of the authors' institutional and program philosophy and mission statements. Inclusion of these statements has been valuable in recruiting new faculty, and student applicants have raised questions with us as to whether or not we as counselor educators really believe and practice what we say we do. We have found that the students who are attracted to our program because of our mission statement or who have questioned us have been among our better students and that they seem to be making career choices because of passion rather than convenience.

COURSE WORK

Within the CACREP standards is language that reflects "social and cultural" dimensions of counseling practice. This language can be interpreted to be supportive of a social advocacy posture. Course assignments can easily include discussion of advocacy, readings about advocacy, or demonstrations of activism. In the first program orientation session, students are informed that the standard of usage will be nonsexist language in both written and verbal expression. The standard is justified as a requirement of the publication manual that is used in graduate study (APA, 1994), but more importantly, it is explained in terms of what the research says about the differential effect on males and females of noninclusive pronoun use.

INTERNSHIPS

The quality of the counseling internship and the supervision that interns receive is extremely important in any graduate program. It is equally important that the overall actions of the internship site reflect a philosophy, as well as behaviors, that are consistent with the comprehensive practice of counseling; therefore, placing an intern in a site that does not support socially responsible counselors should be avoided as much as possible. In addition, interns who encounter inappropriate behaviors should be encouraged to work to address those actions in ways that are consistent with their intern role and to debrief their intervention processes during their internship seminars.

PROJECTS

Any number of advocacy projects can be conducted by students as part of their graduate programs. Students have developed projects that address differential treatment of students in schools based on their economic level, sexism in the public schools, or justification for special programs for students where census data can be used to draw inferences about need. Students have implemented strategies for increasing the support for counselor education programs, for increasing the availability of Spanish interpreters in a hospital setting, and for creating an adventure-based course for troubled adolescents. When professors place a priority on projects that reflect a social advocacy position, students follow.

READING ASSIGNMENTS AND EVALUATION PROCESSES

Counseling courses are replete with readings about individual change; they also need to include readings about societal and organizational change. Perhaps in addition to the chapters on client-centered counselors, students should read descriptions of curbstone counselors like Saul Alinsky (1971), a community organizer with a fabled reputation. Inquiry about how students will practice their social activism or where they will direct their energies to battle injustice can be included in the dialogues that make up their degree exit process. As part of the final portfolio evaluation, the authors routinely ask students in their final 2-hour committee meeting, "What will you do in your professional life to address injustice?"

FOLLOW-UP AND CONTINUED PROFESSIONAL DEVELOPMENT

CACREP programs must conduct periodic follow-up studies of graduates. It is appropriate to determine how students are putting their advocacy philosophy to work in their jobs and communities. This means that the standard follow-up question of "How well were you prepared to do your job?" might be supplemented by "What is something that you have done in the past year to address an injustice?" Based on the kind of answers received, it is incumbent on counselor education programs to modify curriculum or to develop workshops and seminars for graduates and others in the field that would assist them to become more effective in their jobs and communities.

MODELING

For a counselor education program to ask students to become more socially active without the faculty modeling that same activist behavior is to be hypocritical in all respects. Years of teaching at various levels in the educational system have led the authors to believe that students quickly lose respect when faculty don't practice what they preach. Faculty in a program that prepares students for social activism must be activists themselves. Students must see their mentors stepping out, speaking out, and being out with their own activism. Faculty need to be ready for students to challenge them just as they expect students to challenge community inequities. Perhaps one of the most powerful lessons for students in a counselor education program to learn is that they can venture out to challenge inequities or injustice in their own graduate program and then watch faculty respond in such a way that the program improves. In the end, counselor educators must do the right thing for the right reason.

CONCLUSION

Adopting a socially activist orientation to counselor education is not without its incumbent challenges. If such a philosophy challenges students to question the status quo, they may do that—and challenge the preparation program in the process. As faculty and students become more active in their challenges, they may run the risk of offending the funders. If socially active admissions procedures result in a more diverse student population, preparation programs may need to change so as to build on the different languages or different experiences of students. In short, faculty must be ready to receive as well as give. Counselor education can do no less.

This book represents a call to action for counselors to address the social injustice that exists in their world. Counselors will be best prepared to answer that call when the counselor education programs that they attend place a high priority on social activism within all aspects of the counselor's preparation. More than that, however, counselor educators must model what they ask their students to do. The personal examination for effective personal decision making suggested for students can begin with counselor education faculty. In time, that philosophy and practice can permeate the profession, the professional associations, and professional preparation. Our clients will thank us.

REFERENCES

Alinsky, S. (1971). *Rules for radicals.* New York: Vantage Books.

American Counseling Association. (1995). *Code of ethics and standards of practice.* Alexandria, VA: Author.

American Psychological Association. (1994). *Publication manual of the American Psychological Association* (4th ed.). Washington, DC: Author.

Americans With Disabilities Act of 1990, Pub. L. No. 101-336, § 2, 104 Stat. 328 (1991).

Brigman, G. A. (1994). Coping with challenges to school counseling materials. *Elementary School Guidance and Counseling, 29,* 47-59.

Education for All Handicapped Children Act of 1975, Pub. L. No. 94-142.

Eldridge, W. D. (1983). Affirmative social action and the use of power in clinical counseling. *Counseling and Values, 27,* 66-75.

Engels, D. W., & Muro, J. J. (1986). Silver to gold: The alchemy, potential, and maturing of ACES and CES. *Counselor Education and Supervision, 25,* 289-305.

Family Educational Rights and Privacy Act of 1974, Pub. L. 93-380.

Griffin, B. (1993). ACES: Promoting professionalism, collaboration, and advocacy. *Counselor Education and Supervision, 33,* 2-9.

Hawkins, J. D., Catalano, R. F., & Miller, J. F. (1992). Risk and protective factors for alcohol and other drug problems in adolescence and early childhood: Implications for substance abuse prevention. *Psychological Bulletin, 112,* 64-105.

Herr, E. L. (1985). AACD: An association committed to unity through diversity. *Journal of Counseling and Development, 63,* 395-404.

Kurpius, D. J., & Rozecki, T. (1992). Outreach, advocacy, and consultation: A framework for prevention and intervention. *Elementary School Guidance and Counseling, 26,* 176-189.

Lee, C. C., & Sirch, M. L. (1994). Counseling in an enlightened society: Values for a new millennium. *Counseling and Values, 38,* 90-97.

Lofaro, G. A. (1982). Disability and counselor education. *Counselor Education and Supervision, 21,* 200-207.

Pratt, C. C. (1995). Family professionals and family policy: Strategies for influence. *Family Relations, 44,* 56-62.

Stripling, R. O. (1984). Orwell: 1984 and counselor educators. *Counselor Education and Supervision, 23,* 260-267.

Thompson, L., & Walker, A. J. (1995). The place of feminism in family studies. *Journal of Marriage and the Family, 57,* 847-865.

Title IX of the Education Amendments of 1972, Prohibition of Sex Discrimination, Pub. L. 92-318.

16

Interdisciplinary Collaboration for Social Change: Redefining the Counseling Profession

FRED BEMAK

As the counseling profession enters the 21st century, it is an opportune time to raise questions regarding the scope and mission of the counseling field. This is especially true as we examine the role of counseling as an agent of social and political change in contemporary society. This will require a revaluation of the fundamental philosophical principles underlying counseling; a reconceptualization about the meaning and strategies to engage individuals, groups, communities, and societies in healing and change; a critical look at reconstructing counselor education; and a rethinking of the role and direction of research in the 21st century.

Contemporary counseling is markedly deficient in linking the field to the larger society and world as a social change agent and/or advocate to address the social, political, cultural, and economic problems faced by hundreds of millions of people. Gladding (1996) summarized the common factors in counseling as identified by the American Counseling Association and the Counseling Psychology Division (17) of the American Psychological Association. They agreed that counseling is a recognized profession; counselors deal with personal, social, vocational, and educational issues; counseling fosters empowerment in clients; it is theory driven; it is a process that helps clients identify new ways of thinking, behaving, and feeling, and subsequently, of making decisions; and counseling includes various subspecialties. The absence of social activism is striking, especially because there has been a call for counselors to promote social and political change for the past three decades (e.g., Banks & Martens, 1973; Bemak & Hanna, in press; Dworkin &

Dworkin, 1971; Maslow, 1977; Sherman, 1976; Smith, 1971; Wrenn, 1983). Multiculturalism has forced counseling away from an individualistic ethnocentric worldview (Sue & Sue, 1990); and Howard (1993), Wolleat (1993), and White (1993) have written about the need to address the social and political context of clients. Even so, the counseling field remains focused on maintaining the status quo rather than on helping to facilitate deep-rooted change to address the effects of exploitation and oppression by dominant systems and cultures on individuals, groups, or families.

The predominant emphasis of counseling on individuals has, in effect, neutralized social and political concerns, and resulted in maintaining traditional Eurocentric values, such as individualism, independence, self-development, competition, autonomy, and self-reliance. The consequence of this professional stance has been to preserve tradition, that is, a position of neutrality and dominant paradigms. The paradox is that there is a discrepancy between the professional expectation that counselors should reflect and critique their own process and efficacy, and the profession itself that ignores crucial contemporary issues and maintains the status quo.

To address our lack of rigorous self-evaluation as a profession, it is essential, as we move into the next century, that there be a critical examination of the strengths and deficiencies of our current model. How can we as a profession grow and change? What directions must we take as a professional discipline to define the most efficient paradigm as we face the changing nature of personal and social challenges of modern and future times? This is especially vital because there are marked changes in socioeconomic, cultural, and political structures that impact on the disintegration of traditional family structure, substance abuse, racism and discrimination, economics and poverty, physical and sexual abuse, growing violence, and changing demographics regarding age, race, and ethnicity (e.g., Bemak & Hanna, in press). It is apparent that to keep up with the complexity and depth of these changes new roles and competencies will be required of counselors.

One important area of agreement affecting the changing role of counselors is the relationship among social, cultural, psychological, educational, political, health, and economic problems. Bronfenbrenner (1986) wrote about the association among social, psychological, and educational needs and mental health derived from work in schools. In addition, Heath and McLaughlin (1987) argued that the scope of problems in distressed schools and families are so complex that to solve them we must collaborate with community resources. It has been pointed out that the development of new models to address multifarious problems requires multidimensional, multifaceted, and interdisciplinary partners to achieve positive results and change (Boyer, 1990). In fact, major foundations such as the Ford Foundation, Annie E. Casey Foundation, and W.K. Kellogg Foundation have been funding projects aimed at interagency and interdisciplinary cooperation. These projects lead toward new collaborative directions for the counseling profession and necessitate a careful examination regarding reforms that incorporate interdisciplinary interventions and research.

This chapter first emphasizes the need to incorporate interdisciplinary collaboration into mainstream counseling as a means toward social change by discussing redefinition of the profession through realigning power, fostering hope, considering the social context, and keeping pace with relevant developments. Because counseling has a history of advocacy, the redefinition will be an extension of contemporary counseling as well as compatible with the values, professional mission, and contemporary issues of the profession. The chapter then explores actions and strategies for interdisciplinary collaboration by presenting 17 guiding principles for promoting interdisciplinary collaboration as an essential component of social change.

REDEFINING THE PROFESSION

To question modern day thought or to introduce interdisciplinary collaboration as a means for social change, and thereby confront and challenge acceptable standardized counseling practices and roles, is a major undertaking. In order to evolve from a profession that values theories based on Euro-American thought with an implicit emphasis on individuals and families independent from the sociopolitical context, current paradigms must be deconstructed and the counseling profession redefined. An example of the difficulty achieving this may be evident with the strongly accepted movement to standardize graduate training programs. Programs are regulated by established certification and licensure standards for the counseling profession. It is questionable whether there is room for innovative interdisciplinary programs or developing curricula that train counseling professionals in areas such as teamwork, leadership, social action, poverty, public health, sociology, anthropology, or advocacy. Critics of current licensure and certification standards have labeled them as rigid and insular while disempowering faculty from planning new coursework and programs of study (Aubrey, 1983; Thomas, 1991; Weinrach, 1991). This inhibits introducing new coursework, training, and skills into the profession. Thus there are structural barriers implicit in the culture that prohibit initiating new concepts to keep pace with changing needs, roles, and functions.

Fundamental to this change is the need for counselors to become social change agents or advocates. This parallels a highly flawed assumption that counseling as a profession can effectively stand alone. Rarely in training programs, practice, supervision, or consultation is there mention of interdisciplinary collaboration. Rather, we revert back to our counseling theories and strategies within the isolated framework of the profession, exploring solutions without acknowledging the value of perspectives from other professional disciplines. This is particularly striking given the complexity of commonly shared problems that many of our clients, families, schools, institutions, and communities face and the multitude of human services agencies that can simultaneously become involved with one individual, family, school, or community. Yet counselors are not introduced to a value system that encourages and supports an interdisciplinary effort nor provided with skills to work in collaborative teams comprised of varying professions. In fact, the American Counseling Association previously issued a call for greater interprofessional collaboration between human services and primary care professionals.

REALIGN POWER

Although all societies are constantly undergoing change, the counseling profession should assume an active role with the focus on planned change. This requires systematic interventions that can influence basic structures in society and impact on individual and social values, attitudes, behaviors, and policy. It is a particularly sensitive matter because social change involves a realignment of power. More specifically, if one group, agency, or profession attains more power in reaching its goals and objectives, another group will experience less power. This, in effect, changes the accepted status quo and establishes new paradigms by challenging existing political and social structures. When models are shifted to incorporate interdisciplinary collaboration, it means that some participants who have been accustomed to being in positions of power must share in decision making and authority.

To illustrate, examine the introduction of interdisciplinary teams in school systems. As community agencies, businesses, and parents enter into alliances with schools to address school-based problems, there are shifts in the balance of power and authority. This is contrary to tradition whereby school administrators exhibited full command in the school environment. Effective collaboration with community agencies, parents, and businesses so as to address human and social service concerns necessitates that school executives and supervisors share both authority *and* decision making about issues that effect the entire community inclusive of the school.

FOSTER HOPE: A KEY INGREDIENT

One important aspect of redefining the profession and creating change is to foster hope and project vision about the change. Hope has been identified as a precondition for enduring action. Without aspirations, hope, and vision, the foresight is lost and the momentum for change diminishes. Thus to design a drug prevention program in an inner-city low-income area requires not only patience, skills, and endurance but also a belief and vision about the possibilities of change. Penn and Kiesel (1994) described the role of the African American psychologist as one of defining hope and the ability to discern a future vision that enkindles the commitment for unity and solidarity. I propose that this definition be broadened beyond African American psychologists to embrace all counselors becoming social change agents.

CONSIDER THE SOCIAL CONTEXT

As a result of the multitude of problems facing our society, counselors are presented with individuals and groups whose potential for fulfilling lives is thwarted and inhibited by oppressive forces within society. As counselors we are challenged to address these issues with clients in a broader sense than just individual counseling and regard the magnitude of the problem in its fullest sense. The reconceptualizing of the problem necessitates a redefinition of the traditional counselor role to include directly assailing systems and structures that adhere to socially normative behavior, and demanding and challenging oppression in whatever form it manifests. This will result in counselors becoming social change agents.

Making the transition or adaptating to incorporate advocacy or social activism into our work as counselors may be especially difficult. Because the essence of counseling has primarily been defined as facilitating change for clients on an individual, group, or family basis, more substantive changes that address the environment and systems that may have created, or significantly contributed to, the problems have been limited. Thus the paradox is that the profession of counseling promotes transformation in individuals but has been slow and inept in addressing larger social issues. Boyer (1990) coined the term *scholarship of application* when he described the need for researchers to investigate the application of knowledge through problem definition and solutions that are beneficial to both individuals and institutions. He described how at the beginning of this century the ultimate goal was not only to contribute to but also to reshape society. This is particularly striking given the context of the shifting problems that accompany national and global trends.

Keep Pace

In one sense counseling may be regarded as one of the major professions designed to promote change; yet, as a profession, it is not keeping pace with the relevant shifts in social, economic, cultural, political, and technological developments that critically impact society. It is not surprising, for example, that there is a danger of school counselors becoming obsolete or of mental health counselors lacking training to handle some of the presenting problems of clients. Thus to keep pace with the times the profession must reexamine the basic foundations of counseling. This self-scrutiny will serve to determine how the field needs to change in order to address the problems of contemporary culture. Such a shift will lead us to incorporate interdisciplinary collaboration as a powerful vehicle for contributing to social and political change.

ACTIONS AND STRATEGIES FOR INTERDISCIPLINARY COLLABORATION

Restructuring new models to introduce interdisciplinary collaboration effectively as a means to social change requires major shifts in conceptualization and practice. There are well-established areas of territoriality that are clearly associated with funding, traditional sectors of responsibility, and compartmentalized professionally prescribed areas of expertise. Breaking down the boundaries and barriers is a monumental task. Yet it can be done. Use the following 17 guiding principles to promote interdisciplinary collaboration as an essential component for social change.

1. *Identify with counseling as a profession.* One of the criticisms of the counseling field regards the search for an identity (Hanna & Bemak, 1997). Before counselors can effectively work with other professional disciplines, there must be a clearer definition of the similarities and differences with other professions such as psychology, social work, marriage and family therapy, and psychiatry.

2. *Overcome interprofessional hostility and phobia.* Ambiguously delineated territoriality has been a basis for conflict and disagreement among various professional groups and agencies. This is true even when multiple agencies and professionals are serving the same individuals or families for separate but interrelated problems. This has generated interprofessional hostility and phobia. To work with the complexity of modern day problems and to address causal factors rather than symptoms, interagency and interprofessional mutual trust and respect must be established and maintained.

3. *Remember counseling solutions are not always the answer.* Working from a multidisciplinary perspective, it is important to acknowledge that each discipline has values, perceptions, and philosophical bases from which to view and address problems. Mutual respect means that counselors approach interdisciplinary collaboration with authentic openness, that is, they

acknowledge that other professions have important contributions that are not counseling based. Adler (1986) argued that the melding of different professional cultures to problem solve is more effective, and Bergan (1995) and Caplan, Caplan, and Erchul (1995) asserted that this held true for school problems. Within this framework, it is crucial that counselors acknowledge that the best solution may not always come from a counseling perspective.

4. *Establish mutually defined projects and goals.* A critical aspect of multidisciplinary cooperation to promote social change is jointly agreeing upon outcomes and objectives. Shared responsibility and equal participation in establishing goals results in mutuality in ownership. For counselors or other disciplines to impose their authority by virtue of their profession will not create a cohesive team and will cause ongoing problems with the development of projects and goals.

5. *Design mutual projects to meet those goals.* To establish cooperative projects and goals as described in the preceding principle creates unified outcomes. Of equal importance is facilitating and succeeding at the process to reach that outcome. Therefore, the interdisciplinary teams must work cooperatively to meet their objectives. How an interdisciplinary team achieves its objectives, works together to problem solve, and savors shared accomplishments is critical to cultivating a hardy and vigorous work environment.

6. *Redefine professional roles.* The history of counseling and current belief systems have prescribed beliefs, values, philosophy, and definitions about the counselor's role. This is similar across professional disciplines. In order to work effectively across professional boundaries, counselors must deconstruct assumptions about their function and role, and recreate a new definition within the framework of interdisciplinary teams. This requires breaking traditional boundaries and charting unfamiliar territory that will, by nature of the task at hand, precipitate discomfort and anxiety. Thus the ability to work with the challenge of uncertainty will be a key factor in collaboratively reconstructing the counselor and other professional roles.

7. *Share power and decision making.* Friend and Cook (1996) identified parity and shared decision making as distinguishing features of collaborative teams. Traditionally there has been a hierarchy established within the helping professions with psychiatry assuming the role as the authority. Power differentials are evident within other professional disciplines, as well, and have the potential to impact the efficacy of the multidisciplinary team negatively. The experience of the author has been that teams with a designated facilitator, rather than with a leader by virtue of his or her profession, have proven to be the most formidable structures for fostering cooperation and best utilizing the knowledge and expertise of all team members.

8. *Set up interprofessional exchanges.* Public and private agencies, organizations, departments, institutions, and schools should introduce specific programs for interprofessional exchanges. This can be done across disciplines. For example, the author designed in Nicaragua a year-long pilot staff exchange program between the ministries of social services and education in order to address more efficiently the problems of troubled youths who were orphans of the war. The same type of exchange was duplicated between a Maryland social service agency and an urban school-to-work program helping with aggressive, troubled youth. A condensed version of this might be an Interprofessional Exchange Day whereby agencies and schools designate days as informal open houses for other professionals or even conduct 1-day professional exchanges.

9. *Reconstruct incentives.* As a rule, scholarly, professional, or merit rewards are based on accomplishments within one discipline. This system should be revamped to incorporate an incentive system that supports interdisciplinary collaboration aimed at social change. There may be professional association awards that honor the best social change project utilizing an interdisciplinary approach (possibly cosponsored by dual organizations), best innovative projects, papers, or presentations to create societal change, similar university awards and grants, and even agency- or school-based awards that promote social change via multidisciplinary work.

10. *Restructure offices.* Offices could be restructured to reflect a team approach to problems rather than a single-discipline-centered approach. If there is a fundamental value shift to support interdisciplinary teams in mutually addressing problems, it follows that there will be a basic shift in the base of operations to champion the team approach. This has been done in some of the projects in which the author has worked by, for example, housing more human services agencies within schools, creating family space within schools, or reserving office space for school personnel and other team members within community-based agencies.

11. *Redesign funding schemata.* Interdisciplinary teams must have individuals whose funds and/or time to participate in a collaborative project comes from their respective work sites. Developing new paradigms requires major shifts in resources. An example is a project designed by the author in an urban region where the school district committed a substantial start-up budget for a school-community-family-developed team project. This underscored the commitment to the team concept and prompted an allocation of resources, staff, funding, and the pursuit of a team-based grant by regional human services and educational facilities.

12. *Conduct whole team training.* As just noted, if there is dedication to the new model, then activities for interdisciplinary efforts will be designed around the team rather than in traditional disciplinary formulations. This also holds true for training. An example is a 3-day training start-up for new teams, implemented by the author, in which role, task, function, and relationships were redefined. The training utilized the essential elements described by Johnson and Johnson (1997) for effective teams, including collaborative skills, group processing, positive interdependence, personal accountability, and direct communication. Barriers to collaboration were addressed as well as strategies for establishing common language and vision. Team goals were developed during the training based on Villa and Thousand's (1988) premise that common, agreed-upon goals result in positive collaboration.

13. *Establish graduate interdisciplinary training.* It is essential that universities investigate multidisciplinary training models that establish prototypes for graduates from the programs. Currently, graduate level training is encapsulated in discipline-specific training. Interdisciplinary graduate training, coursework, and applied practicums have been identified as having long-range implications for facilitating cooperation (Golightly, 1987; Humes & Hohenshil, 1987). An excellent example of cross-departmental training, developed at the graduate school at the University of Utah, included prospective teachers, special educators, counselors, administrators, and school psychologists (Welch et al., 1992).

14. *Understand change theory.* In order for counselors to assume a role as social change agents, they must understand organizational and social change. To undertake this endeavor without the tools will only produce failure and frustration. Therefore, counselors must have exposure to works such as Alinsky (1971) and Hanna and Robinson (1994) in order to better understand how to operationalize new roles within reconstructed paradigms.

15. *Encourage interdisciplinary publications.* Even in cross-disciplinary projects there is generally little cross-fertilization of scholarly publications. Individuals should publish across professions, however. School counselors, for example, could write in education administration journals about research and recommendations for change in school counseling positions rather than publish only in counseling professional journals.

16. *Make collaborative cross-discipline presentations.* The author received a grant for a project to decrease school violence and aggression in a major urban school system by developing a comprehensive school-community-family partnership program. The project involved school counselors, mental-health-agency-based counselors and social workers, school principals, central and regional office school administrators, teachers, various community agencies representatives, social workers, psychologists, nurses, parents, and business people. Rather than present the successes of this project independently at the American Counseling Association annual meeting, representative professionals

and individuals involved with the project were invited to participate. The result of not only working together daily but also
actually collaborating and presenting this work at a major
national forum was highly beneficial and consistent with the
design of the project.

17. *Cooperate in documentation and research.* To demonstrate the
efficacy of interdisciplinary projects there must be applied
research. This requires cooperation between universities, agencies, and institutions that are initiating multidisciplinary programs aimed at social change. The evaluation and measurement
of success for change, as well as the benefits of the interdisciplinary process itself, are crucial to sustaining long-term change.

CONCLUSION

The 21st century requires a critical reconception of the role
of counselors that incorporates interdisciplinary collaboration and
social change. The passage to a new century provides the counseling
profession with a unique opportunity to reexamine itself as a professional discipline. Historically, there was a call for social action as
a core professional responsibility. Modern times have significantly
changed the cultural and sociopolitical context within which counselors work. It is only logical that the role, structure, and function
of the counseling profession transform to address the complexities
of the 21st century. Joining with other professions and collaborating
with other departments, agencies, and institutions that go beyond
the profound but limited scope of counseling will be crucial if the
counseling profession is to make a significant contribution to social
change and a better world.

REFERENCES

Adler, N. J. (1986). *International dimensions of organizational behavior.* Boston: Kent.

Alinsky, S. D. (1971). *Rules for radicals.* New York: Random House.

Aubrey, R. (1983). The odyssey of counseling and images of the future. *Personnel and Guidance Journal, 62,* 78-82.

Banks, W., & Martens, K. (1973). Counseling: The reactionary profession. *Personnel and Guidance Journal, 51,* 457-462.

Bemak, F., & Hanna, F. (in press). The 21st century counselor: An emerging role in changing times. *International Journal for the Advancement of Counselling.*

Bergan, J. R. (1995). Evolution of a problem-solving model of consultation. *Journal of Educational and Psychological Consultation, 6,* 111-123.

Boyer, E. (1990). *Scholarship reconsidered: Priorities of the professorate.* Princeton, NJ: Carnegie Foundation for the Advancement of Teaching.

Bronfenbrenner, U. (1986). Ecology of the family is a context for human development: Research perspectives. *Developmental Psychology, 26*(6), 723-742.

Caplan, G., Caplan, R. B., & Erchul, W. P. (1995). A contemporary view of mental health consultation: Comments on "Types of Mental Health Consultation" by Gerald Caplan (1963). *Journal of Educational and Psychological Consultation, 6,* 23-30.

Dworkin, E. P., & Dworkin, A. L. (1971). The activist counselor. *Personnel and Guidance Journal, 49,* 748-753.

Friend, M., & Cook, L. (1996). *Interactions: Collaboration skills for school counselors* (2nd ed.). White Plains, NY: Longman.

Gladding, S. T. (1996). *Counseling: A comprehensive profession.* Englewood Cliffs, NJ: Merrill/Prentice Hall.

Golightly, C. J. (1987). Transdisciplinary training: A step forward in special education teacher preparation. *Teacher Education and Special Education, 10,* 126-130.

Hanna, F. J., & Bemak, F. (1997). The quest for identity in the counseling profession. *Counselor Education and Supervision, 36*(3), 194-206.

Hanna, M. G., & Robinson, B. (1994). *Strategies for community empowerment: Direct action and transformative approaches to social change practice.* Lewiston, NY: Mellen.

Heath, S. B., & McLaughlin, M. W. (1987, April). A child resource policy: Moving beyond dependence on school and family. *Phi Delta Kappan,* 576-580.

Howard, G. (1993). Thoughts on saving our planet: Political, economic, cultural, and bureaucratic impediments to ecological activism. *The Counseling Psychologist, 21,* 597-617.

Humes, C. W., & Hohenshil, T. H. (1987). Elementary counselors, school psychologists, school social workers: Who does what? *Elementary School Guidance and Counseling, 1,* 37-45.

Johnson, D. W., & Johnson, F. P. (1997). *Joining together: Group theory and skills* (6th ed.). Englewood Cliffs, NJ: Prentice-Hall.

Maslow, A. (1977). Politics. *Journal of Humanistic Psychology, 17*(4), 5-20.

Penn, M. L., & Kiesel, L. (1994). Toward a global world community: The role of Black psychologists. *Journal of Black Psychology, 20*(4), 398-417.

Sherman, P. (1976). The counselor as change agent: A revolution? Not likely. *The Counseling Psychologist, 12*(2), 111-116.

Smith, P. M. (1971). Black activists for liberation, not guidance. *Personnel and Guidance Journal, 49,* 721-726.

Sue D. W., & Sue, D. (1990). *Counseling the culturally different: Theory and practice.* New York: Wiley.

Thomas, K. R. (1991). Oedipal issues in counseling psychology. *Journal of Counseling and Development, 69,* 203-205.

Villa, R., & Thousand, J. (1988). Enhancing success in heterogeneous classroom and schools: The power of partnerships. *Teacher Education and Special Education,* 144-154.

Weinrach, S. (1991). CACREP: The need for a midcourse correction. *Journal of Counseling and Development, 69,* 491-495.

Welch, M., Sheridan, S. M., Fuhriman, A., Hart, A. W., Connell, M. L., & Stoddart, T. (1992). Preparing professionals for educational partnerships: An interdisciplinary approach. *Journal of Educational and Psychological Consultation,* 3(1), 1-23.

White, M. (1993). The histories of the present. In S. Gilligan (Ed.), *Therapeutic conversations.* New York: Norton.

Wolleat, P. (1993). Environmental counseling: Postmodern counseling psychology? *The Counseling Psychologist, 21,* 628-634.

Wrenn, G. (1983). The fighting, risk-taking counselor. *Personnel and Guidance Journal, 61,* 323-326.

17

Professional Counseling in a Global Context: Collaboration for International Social Action

Courtland C. Lee

As the world prepares to enter the 21st century, there is growing awareness of a new global interconnectedness. While old ideological barriers fall and new alliances replace long-standing animosities, there is great anticipation about a new era of mutual respect and cooperation among nations. This has been heightened by universal improvements in communication and travel that have made the world, in many respects, a *global village*.

As the concept of global interconnectedness continues to grow, it has prompted efforts in many parts of the world to reconfigure social and economic institutions to make them more responsive to interactions across national boundaries. As part of this, many professions are exploring ways to adopt a global perspective in order to address more effectively challenges that increasingly transcend political borders. In recent years, for example, the counseling profession has taken a series of significant steps to internationalize the scope of mental health and educational intervention. This has resulted in an emerging process to develop an international helping paradigm that will encompass a universal consensus for social action to promote human development.

The purpose of this chapter is to present ideas for facilitating international collaboration among professional counselors so as to address contemporary global cultural, economic, and social challenges. It begins with a personal reflection on the misery that the world's children and women face on a daily basis and that impels counselors to try and relieve conditions of suffering. The chapter then describes ways in which to do this through international professionalization and collaboration in counseling and through a global social action agenda that includes assisting in nation building, challenging intolerance, and promoting the integrity of the family. The final section discusses some of the many challenges to global cooperation that counselors will encounter as they strive for change.

INTERNATIONAL SOCIAL ACTION: A PERSONAL REFLECTION

Several years ago I had the opportunity to visit South Africa. My trip took place in the waning days of the apartheid regime. During my stay I visited a squatter camp outside of Johannesburg with a worker from a South African social welfare agency. The camp was set up behind a school and provided temporary housing for thousands of people from throughout South Africa who had been displaced by the violence that led up to that country's historic 1994 election. The camp had one source of fresh water, an open spigot in the middle of the camp, and the only toilet facilities were several open pits.

Many of the families in the camp were living in crowded temporary classroom buildings. In one such building that my companion and I visited, there were at least 15 large families living together in hot, cramped, and extremely unsanitary conditions. The male members of these families were off either looking for or doing low-paying odd jobs in Johannesburg. It was lunchtime when we arrived, and the women were tending to the children who were eating a meager meal of rice, beans, and cabbage out of small plastic bowls. Most of the children looked severely malnourished, and many had open sores on their faces.

The image that is most vivid in my memory is of one small girl who, while running with her bowl, tripped and fell. As she did, the contents of her bowl spilled onto the ground. At that moment at least five other children rushed up with their spoons trying to scrape up spilled rice. The social service worker remarked to me that this accident was very costly because food was scarce, and this would, no doubt, be the only meal that the children would eat that day.

This image and the worker's statement struck me hard. Soon I would be returning to my comfortable accommodations in Johannesburg, looking forward to a nice dinner. I would also be leaving South Africa in a few days to celebrate a joyous Christmas with my family in the United States. However, these children would still be in the squatter camp. Christmas Day would be just another day of hunger and misery for them.

This dichotomy between my reality and that of those children made me feel both guilty and angry. Guilty that I should have so much and they so little, and angry that political and social circumstances should impact upon the lives of children in such a cruel fashion. Driving away from the squatter camp that afternoon, I vowed that, as a professional counselor and a human being, I would take some type of action.

When I returned to the United States I made the following proposal to my colleagues in the counselor education program: rather than hold a faculty holiday dinner at an expensive restaurant, which had become our custom, we should make a donation to the relief agency that was working in South African squatter camps. My colleagues eagerly agreed to this, and we sent a sizable contribution to the relief agency.

Although this example of social action is small, it does demonstrate, to some degree, professional counselors taking initiative as social advocates. Our contribution made a statement about our belief as professionals that children starving anywhere in the world is a socially and morally unacceptable situation. We hope, in some small way, that our contribution empowered social welfare officials to battle more effectively the hunger and despair of the children in that squatter camp.

COUNSELING: INTERNATIONAL PROFESSIONALIZATION AND COLLABORATION

In the last two decades, major initiatives have been undertaken by counselors to establish international professional links. These links have been forged through international forums for the exchange of ideas and research on counseling and human development. An implicit goal of such forums is the establishment of an international perspective on the role of counseling in promoting human development and in addressing social challenges.

One such forum that has been in the forefront of establishing a global perspective on counseling is the International Round Table for the Advancement of Counselling (IRTAC). Since its founding in 1966 by Hans Z. Hoxter, IRTAC has been an international association with scientific and educational aims concerned with the interdisciplinary study of counseling. Through its sponsorship of seminars and conferences that have been held in Europe, Canada, and New Zealand, IRTAC has played a major role in the development of counseling services in many parts of the world. It has offered advice and information to governmental and nongovernmental organizations in both industrialized and developing countries. Most importantly, however, IRTAC has provided a professional forum for counselors and those in related educational and psychological fields, from throughout the world, to gather together and examine differences and commonalities in counseling practices.

As IRTAC has continued to develop global linkages among mental health professionals, established counseling associations in a number of countries have also attempted to expand their missions to include international collaboration. As an example, the American Counseling Association has held several successful bilateral professional conferences with counseling associations in England, Mexico, and Scotland. These conferences have proven to be fertile ground for exploring differences and commonalities in the issues that confront professional counseling organizations as they address both the professional development of their members and the mental health issues of citizens in their respective countries.

Through the efforts of the International/Interprofessional Collaboration Committee of ACA, a number of collaborative relationships have been formed between ACA and international counseling associations. Most recently, such relationships have been developed with the British Association for Counselling (BAC) and the Indian Academy of Counselling. For nearly a decade, an informal relationship between ACA and BAC has provided the opportunity for leaders of both organizations to exchange visits to national conferences in the United States and the United Kingdom. This has provided for a cross-fertilization of diverse ideas on counseling issues and practices.

The emergence of an international perspective on counseling and human development portends a new era of global interconnectedness among professional counselors. In many parts of the world, counselors and counseling organizations are moving beyond provincial conceptions of theory, research, and practice to join in collaborative efforts to foster notions of mental health and human development that stretch across geopolitical boundaries.

A GLOBAL SOCIAL ACTION AGENDA FOR COUNSELING PROFESSIONALS

As this international professional collaboration among counselors increases, so too does the need for a strategic view of counseling and human development in a global context. This view should be translated into an international action plan with a unified mission and a set of goals and objectives to guide counseling activities. Such a plan should have broad applicability across borders and cultures. This is particularly important given the significant transformations that have occurred throughout the world in recent years (Lee, 1997). These transformations can be found in such areas as the nature of employment, cultural diversity, migration and refugees, the roles of men and women, increasing rates of innovation and expanding technology, and major changes in patterns of local, regional, and national identity. The scope of these transformations has often negatively affected the function of those institutions that promote human development in many parts of the world, including the family, school, workplace, social welfare agencies, government agencies, and religious institutions. As the impact of these institutions has been weakened, the potential of counseling and related services has increased.

This potential can be realized through a strategic plan that stresses global social action on the part of counseling professionals. Through international collaborative efforts, counselors can work to help people lessen the impact of social transformations on their lives and well-being. Additionally, through social action, counselors can be a part of a process that promotes global interconnectedness. Given this, the global mission of the counseling profession should be to promote human development within the unique context of national, cultural, and individual realities.

The goals and objectives that can be derived from this mission form the basis of a global social action agenda for counselors. Important aspects of such an agenda might include assisting in nation building, challenging intolerance, and promoting the integrity of the family. Although these agenda items are not exhaustive, they represent ones that are of current interest to a number of national professional counseling organizations.

ASSISTING IN NATION BUILDING

There is a great need for wide-ranging technical expertise in many areas of the world where old regimes have disintegrated and countries struggle to construct new social orders. Experts are needed to help build institutions or restructure old ones for the social and economic empowerment of people in newly emerging nations. Professional counselors have an important opportunity to lend their expertise to these nation-building efforts. For example, by working collaboratively, counselors from a number of countries can address the mental health and educational challenges in the nations of the former Soviet Union as they attempt to restructure their social order based on the principles of free enterprise and individual freedom.

Likewise, there is much potential for counseling in the new Republic of South Africa as it strives to establish an inclusive society after years of excluding the majority of its population under apartheid. Counselors can help remediate the psychological ravages of that brutal system and promote new models for advancing psychosocial development. For example, counselors could help organize a school counseling system that will facilitate academic, career, and personal-social empowerment among young people who have historically been denied educational access. For another example of professional collaboration in this part of the world, counseling for Post-Traumatic Stress Disorder could be provided to the victims and the perpetrators of apartheid violence.

CHALLENGING INTOLERANCE

While political barriers are falling throughout the world, levels of intolerance and violence appear to be rising. In many countries, groups of people, often acting on age-old prejudices, have become increasingly unwilling to share social or political privilege with, and are oppressive toward, other groups who differ in terms of race, ethnicity, religion, or sexual orientation. Wherever they occur, acts of violence associated with intolerant attitudes hinder efforts to form working alliances for progress. More importantly, they impact negatively on the psychological and social development of people across the life span.

Whether it is Bosnia, Rwanda, Cambodia, Northern Ireland, the Middle East , or the United States, racism, sexism, ethnic hostility, religious intolerance, and homophobia poison the quality of life for both the victim and perpetrator of intolerant acts. Counselors, therefore, should use their facilitation skills to promote dialogues for understanding across the lines that divide groups of people. Significantly, models for such group facilitation at the international level have been offered in recent years (Rogers, 1987; Rogers & Ryback, 1984). The collaborative efforts of counselors should focus on helping people challenge intolerant attitudes and move beyond mere tolerance to a position of mutual respect and understanding.

PROMOTING THE INTEGRITY OF THE FAMILY

The family, in all its varied forms, is at the center of human experience. Therefore, it is crucial that counselors collaborate internationally to help empower families. New interventions are needed for people around the world who confront dysfunction that interferes with the quality of life, both inside and outside of the family structure.

International professional counseling efforts should be undertaken to assist parents in promoting self-esteem, pride, self-discipline, healthy physical habits, spirituality, and academic skills in their children. If families are to be empowered, counselors should find ways for the generations that comprise them to work together. When considering family empowerment, it is important to be aware of cultural differences in the perception of family life. Although certain aspects of family interaction are universal, it must always be remembered that spousal relationships and the dynamics of child-rearing often have a specific cultural context.

Many complex issues affect family life throughout the world. For example, child labor is a serious global problem. It is the single most important source of child exploitation and child abuse in the world today (International Labour Organization, 1996a). According to revised estimates by the International Labour Organization's Bureau of Statistics, the number of working children between the ages of 5 and 14 is at least 120 million (International Labour

Organization, 1996a). The overwhelming majority of these children are in developing countries in Africa, Asia, and Latin America. Numerous children work in occupations and industries that are plainly dangerous and hazardous—from factory work to prostitution (International Labour Organization, 1996b).

A child working is a future denied. This is because working children miss out on education. Today, lack of education is especially damaging because both individual and societal well-being increasingly depend on literacy and numerical competence. Working children are disadvantaged in other ways as well. According to Forastieri (in press), the early involvement of children in work can have serious health and developmental consequences.

Counselors working in proactive international partnerships with governmental agencies and nongovernmental organizations can effectively challenge the issue of child labor. The manifesto for any social action on behalf of the world's children should be *The Convention of the Rights of the Child* that was adopted by the United Nations General Assembly in 1989 (UNICEF, 1990). It is the first legally binding international document to incorporate the full range of human rights, including children's civil and political rights as well as their economic, social, and cultural rights.

Within the context of *The Convention of the Rights of the Child* the first priority for social action might include focusing resources on eliminating the most intolerable forms of child labor, particularly that involving girls and the very young, such as slavery, debt bondage, child prostitution, and work in hazardous occupations and industries. The second priority should be to address the problem of the invisibility of working children in many parts of the world. Any effort to protect children from workplace hazards, therefore, must begin by making the global public aware of working children and the dangers they face.

Advocating for the rights of women is another example of global social action for counselors that relates to the integrity of the family. It is important that counselors understand how the status of women, in playing their ascribed roles in society, is affected by cultural, economic, and social issues. Progress toward gender equality is unsatisfactory in a number of countries. In many parts of the world there are still major gaps in educational attainment and employment opportunities for men and women. Economic development and growth appear to be intricately related to the advancement of women. Where women have advanced, economic growth has usually been steady; where women have not been allowed to be full participants, there has been stagnation. Strategic objectives and actions are needed, therefore, to promote the quality of life for women in a variety of areas, including equal access to education and employment, quality health care, violence prevention, and greater roles in political decision making.

As with universal children's rights, the United Nations has taken action to advance the status of women. In 1946, the U.N. established the Commission on the Status of Women to monitor the situation of women and promote their rights in all societies around the world. This commission is the global advocate for equality between women and men. Building on this, the U.N. General Assembly adopted the *Convention on the Elimination of All Forms of Discrimination Against Women* in 1979. The Convention defines what constitutes discrimination against women and sets up an agenda for national action to end such discrimination. Finally, in 1993 the U.N. adopted the *Declaration on the Elimination of Violence Against Women* (U.N., 1993), which defined what constitutes violence against women and which outlined actions governments and communities should take to prevent such acts.

The United Nations observed 1975 as International Women's Year and held the first world conference on women in Mexico City. Subsequently, three other U.N. conferences on women have been held: Copenhagen in 1980, Nairobi in 1985, and Beijing in 1995. At the 1985 Nairobi conference, *The Forward-Looking Strategies for the Advancement of Women to the Year 2000* (U.N., 1985) was adopted. This was a blueprint for women's advancement, dealing with the entire spectrum of women's role in society. This blueprint was followed by a *Platform for Action* (U.N., 1995), adopted at the 1995 Beijing conference. This document addressed 21st century challenges and demands for women.

These United Nations conferences, conventions, and declarations provide the framework for collaborative social action on the part of the world's counseling professionals. Through their efforts, both individually and at the association level, counselors should advocate for or reinforce national efforts to promote laws and programs that increase the access of women to productive resources and equal opportunity.

CHALLENGES TO GLOBAL COLLABORATION

Several important challenges to international collaboration among professional counselors must be considered. The most obvious are differences in language and culture. As professional counselors begin to collaborate across geopolitical boundaries, they must be sensitive to language differences and be aware of unique cultural realities and differences in worldviews. A crucial aspect of international collaboration must be the development of multicultural awareness and competencies (Sue, Arredondo, & McDavis, 1992). Counselors must have an understanding of, and appreciation for, cultural diversity. These must be at the center of counselors' global professional consciousness.

An even greater challenge to international collaboration, however, is the fact that counseling, as it has been conceptualized and practiced in North America for most of the 20th century, does not exist as a profession in many other parts of the world. Counselors must consider that social action efforts may be hampered in many parts of the world due to the lack of a traditional North-American-like counseling infrastructure. It might be necessary, therefore, to form working alliances with professionals from related mental health disciplines, such as psychology or psychiatry. Likewise, collaboration in many countries may need to take place with professionals from allied health fields. Counselors may also need to form social action alliances with indigenous helpers/healers. In many cultures that predate those of the countries in North America, people have for centuries found guidance to resolve personal problems and make decisions from individuals who are acknowledged within their communities as possessing special insight and helping skills. These individuals have been commonly recognized as healers and are believed to possess awareness, knowledge, and skills that grow out of a timeless wisdom. These healers are the keepers of this wisdom, and they enlist it to help people solve problems and make decisions (Lee & Armstrong, 1995). Social action initiatives in many countries may need to be predicated on forming collaborative relationships with such healers (Lee & Armstrong, 1995; Lee, Oh, & Mountcastle, 1992; Vontress, 1991).

CONCLUSION

As the world enters a new century, professional counselors have the opportunity to assess the philosophy and scope of mental health intervention. The philosophy of counseling in the 21st century must encompass a commitment to social change that focuses on helping to empower individuals to meet the challenges of global transformation. The scope of this commitment must entail a worldwide collaboration among counseling and related mental health professionals who have the awareness, knowledge, and skills to promote human development locally, nationally, and internationally.

REFERENCES

Forastieri, V. (in press). *Danger: Children at work.* Geneva, Switzerland: International Labour Office.

International Labour Organization. (1996a). *Child labour surveys: Results of methodological experiments in four countries, 1992-93.* Geneva, Switzerland: International Labour Office.

International Labour Organization, (1996b). *Child labour: Targeting the intolerable.* Geneva, Switzerland: International Labour Office.

Lee, C. C. (1997). The global future of professional counseling: Collaboration for international social change. *International Journal of Intercultural Relations, 21,* 279-285.

Lee, C. C., & Armstrong, K. L. (1995). Indigenous models of mental health intervention: Lessons from traditional healers. In J. Ponterotto, J. M. Casas, L. A. Suzuki, & C. M. Alexander (Eds.), *Handbook of multicultural counseling* (pp. 441-456). Thousand Oaks, CA: Sage.

Lee, C. C., Oh, M. Y., & Mountcastle, A. R. (1992). Indigenous models of helping in nonwestern countries: Implications for multicultural counseling. *Journal of Multicultural Counseling and Development, 20,* 3-10.

Rogers, C. R. (1987). Steps toward world peace, 1948-1986: Tension reduction in theory and practice. *Counseling and Values, 32,* 12-16.

Rogers, C. R., & Ryback, D. (1984). One alternative to nuclear planetary suicide. *The Counseling Psychologist, 12,* 3-12.

Sue, D. W., Arredondo, P., & McDavis, R. J. (1992). Multicultural competencies and standards: A call to the profession. *Journal of Counseling and Development, 70,* 477-486.

United Nations. (1979). *Convention on the elimination of all forms of discrimination against women.* New York: Author.

United Nations. (1985). *The forward-looking strategies for the advancement of women to the year 2000.* New York: Author.

United Nations. (1993). *Declaration on the elimination of violence against women.* New York: Author.

United Nations. (1995). *Platform for action.* New York: Author.

UNICEF. (1990). *The convention of the rights of the child.* New York: Author.

Vontress, C. E. (1991). Traditional healing in Africa: Implications for cross-cultural counseling. *Journal of Counseling and Development, 70,* 242-249.

CONCLUSION

Conclusion

18

A Summing Up and Call
to Action

COURTLAND C. LEE AND GARRY R. WALZ

Washing one's hands of the conflict between the pow-
erful and the powerless means to side with the power-
ful, not to be neutral.—Paulo Freire

This statement by the famous Brazilian educator, philosopher,
and social activist provides a challenge to any profession. It
suggests that anyone in a position to make a difference who is not
a part of the solution to the issues that confront society is, by
default, a part of the problem. As professional counselors we need
to consider Freire's statement as we assess our roles as helpers.
This book advances the concept of intervention not only into client's
lives to help with problem resolution or decision making but also
into the world that affects those lives. All the authors contributing
to this book emphatically stress that social action is often pivotal
to promoting psychosocial development.

Recently the Governing Council of the American Counseling
Association adopted a definition of professional counseling that
underscores the principle of social change:

> The practice of Professional Counseling is the application of
> mental health, psychological, or human development principles,
> through cognitive, affective, behavioral, or systemic intervention
> strategies, that address wellness, personal growth, or career devel-
> opment as well as pathology.

This definition includes systemic intervention as a primary aspect
of counseling practice and provides the basis for social action on
the part of professional counselors.

Social action in counseling requires a paradigm shift. Counselors need to consider roles and functions that, heretofore, have not necessarily been associated with their profession. A goal of this book is to provide a context for social intervention and action on the part of professional counselors.

A close reading of this book suggests that part of the paradigm shift required for counselors to become agents of social change involves new ways of conceptualizing the theory and practice of professional counseling. These new ways of viewing counseling are predicated on the notion that counselors and their clients live in an environment of constant social, cultural, and economic change. Counseling theory and practice, therefore, must continue to be dynamic and responsive to the realities of rapid and consistent social change.

This final chapter discusses eight action steps that incorporate and synthesize the ideas presented in the preceding chapters. These steps provide a context to the concept of social action as it has been defined and discussed in this book. They also serve as points to consider in future theory-building related to the practice of professional counseling.

ACTION STEPS

1. Commit to Acquiring Greater Competence in the Use of the New Information Technologies as a Means to Further Professional Renewal

The availability of new information tools, such as the Internet, websites, listservs, national databases (ERIC online and CD ROM) and virtual libraries, has immeasurably increased access to greatly expanded sources of counseling-relevant information. Availability is a twin-edged sword, however. The tools provide more information from more sources, but the information is frequently unauthoritative and contradictory, and may even be misinformation. If counselors are to devise and/or use knowledge-driven rather than speculative social change interventions, they need to expand their knowledge and use of the new information technologies continually so they can both use the new knowledge to enhance their own professional competence and share it with their clients. Traditional sources of information, such as print media in the form of books and journals, are still important for counselors, but hardly sufficient. Much of the vital, fast-breaking, and broad-based information is available primarily to counselors who have the technological savvy to use the new information technologies to separate out relevant and worthy information from junk information.

2. *Focus on Acquiring and Using Multiple Assessment Procedures That Are Designed to Reflect Adequately the Characteristics of Persons From an Increasingly Diverse and Pluralistic Society*

Assessment is an important and vital aspect of the counseling process. Appropriate and valid assessment of both groups and individuals, however, cannot be achieved through the use of a few favorite tests. Counselors constantly need to update their knowledge of, and competence in the use of, the new and socially responsive assessment procedures so that they facilitate the psychosocial development of persons rather than hinder, stigmatize, or falsely categorize them.

3. *Assign a Higher Priority in Counselor Education Programs to the Preparation of Counselors as Agents of Social Change*

This book's authors consistently speak to the need for greater attention in courses, the practical, and field experiences to exploring why and how counselors can become agents of social change. Much more than book knowledge needs to be emphasized. Counselors must begin with an analysis of their own values regarding social change and form their own personal philosophies and action strategies as regards their role as agents of social change. Counselor attitude toward the role of social change agent is crucial, and each counselor should develop a personal perspective formed by active involvement rather than by passive adoption of the views of others.

4. *Commit to the Personal Utilization of Counseling Outcomes Research to Promote Greater Public Support of Counseling and Counselors by Documenting the Efficacy of Various Counseling Processes*

Counselors traditionally look to many sources in deciding how to intervene in a particular counseling context. The more counselors are able to make choices from an array of interventions of known effectiveness, the broader their public creditably and support is likely to be. At a time of increased competition for health care resources, it is probable that those providers who can make the best case for what they do will win the lion's share of public dollars. Counselors fortunately are able to document the worth of much of what they do if only they will choose to do so. Most importantly, counselors must use outcome data to make their decisions about what to do rather than rely on speculation and levels of personal comfort with different interventions.

5. *Intervene Into the Environments of Clients to Eliminate or to Promote Change in Those Aspects of the Environment That Stifle Psychosocial Development and at the Same Time Enhance the Resilience and Invulnerability of Persons to Those Same Debilitating Aspects*

In the best of worlds, counselors would be able through enlightened social action to bring about systemic changes in the environments of their clients, which are the real problems. But in this imperfect world, injustice and discrimination will continue despite the best efforts of many. Given this condition, it behooves counselors to teach clients the strategies successfully used by some young people and adults to cope successfully, even sometimes gain strength and power, by overcoming the land mines of environmental deprivation through which they must negotiate their way. When and if it can be successfully implemented, the quintessential strategy is bipartite; that is, it both removes major obstacles to client psychosocial development by concerted caregiver social action and also empowers individual clients to deal with the obstacles they face through the strength of their own resilience.

6. *Help to Create Alternatives and Opportunities for People*

People, particularly those who have been marginalized or rendered powerless, need more life choices. This may mean addressing the root causes of poverty, racism, sexism, homophobia, and other forms of social or economic discrimination. Counselors may need to help clients cope with such issues in the short term while helping to empower them ultimately to take control of their long-term responses to these forces. This needs to be done in a socially active way in order to improve the quality of life for all people and to address social challenges within an environment of change.

7. Work to Improve Institutional Policies With Respect to Human Welfare and Development

Counselors should examine the internal policies of agencies, schools, and other social institutions with regard to the needs of people. Institutional policies need to be based on a better understanding of cognitive, affective, and behavioral functioning. Counselors can help to ensure that institutional policies do not stifle individual development or empowerment.

8. Advocate at All Levels of Government

In order to help empower people to take effective action to improve the quality of their lives, a supportive policy framework is needed at all levels of government. Legislation and government policies must be sensitive to human psychological and social development. Legislation and policies should also promote initiatives that empower people and address their concerns. Counselors should have the skills to advocate at all levels of government to raise awareness and increase legislative involvement in creating alternatives and opportunities that result in educational, career, and personal empowerment.

A FINAL NOTE

The action steps model a process that we, as this book's editors, believe that those motivated to make a larger commitment to counseling and social action should go through. This book contains an enormous collection of inspiring ideas, presents much viable information, and suggests potentially rewarding interventions, all within an overarching social action framework. Just reading it is a heady experience. But to benefit significantly from the book's contents, readers must sort out and put into some kind of organized framework those ideas and actions that they resonate with and want to act on.

The eight synthesized action steps presented in this chapter are illustrations of what has meaning at this point in time to us. But even as we write this, our ideas are changing and expanding. It is an exciting process to be going through, and we hope readers will be able to share what has particular meaning and significance with others, the authors of the different chapters, and us. Whether by letter, FAX, E-mail, or phone, we want to hear from readers. And hopefully, at conferences, such as the ACA Convention, we will have the opportunity to communicate with readers directly.

Read, ponder, highlight, but most of all take action—now!

Courtland C. Lee
Curry School of Education • Department of Human Services
University of Virginia • 405 Emmet Street
Charlottesville, VA 22903-2495
804/924/3119 • FAX: 804/924/0747
E-mail: cl8r@virginia.edu

Garry R. Walz
ERIC Counseling and Student Services Clearinghouse
201 Ferguson Building • University of North Carolina at Greensboro
P.O. Box 26171 • Greensboro, NC 27402-6171
800/414/9769 • 336/334/4114 • FAX: 336/334/4116
E-mail: ericcass@uncg.edu

Appendix

ABOUT ERIC AND ERIC/CASS

ERIC/CASS (originally ERIC/CAPS) was one of the founding clearinghouses that started the system in 1966 and that has since grown to be the world's largest educational database with nearly 1 million entries.

The ERIC system has as its mission to improve American education by *increasing* and facilitating the use of educational research and information on practice in the activities of learning, teaching, educational decision making, and research, wherever and whenever these activities take place.

ERIC/CASS has as its major foci serving the needs and interests of care givers and helping specialists such as counselors, therapists, and career specialists at all ages and educational levels and in all settings—school, college, government, business, and private practice.

ERIC/CASS's basic goal has been to improve decision making through increased access to information. More importantly, ERIC/CASS wants, through the many resources and services it offers, to empower users to realize more fully their goals—and their dreams.

ERIC/CASS WEBSITE, 201 Park Building,
UNCG • P.O. Box 26171, Greensboro, NC, 27402-6171;
http://www.uncg.edu/~ericcas2

One of the best sources of educational information is ERIC—
the Educational Resources Information Center. An appropriate first
step in gaining access to ERIC is to locate the ERIC/CASS Website
and through it identify a multitude of educational resources. Numerous "hotlinks" to other databases and websites can also be reached
through the ERIC/CASS Website.

Through ERIC/CASS, the U.S. Department of Education's extensive educational resources can be assessed as well as special services
of the ERIC system (AskERIC, Access ERIC, and other ERIC
Clearinghouses). Among the specific resources available on the
ERIC/CASS Website are

- capability to search the ERIC database and the U.S. Department
  of Education resources
- information on forthcoming ERIC/CASS Listservs
- full text of ERIC/CASS Digests
- information on forthcoming conferences and workshops
- shopping mall of publications and resources.

For more information on ERIC/CASS, call (336) 334-4114, FAX
(336) 334-4116, E-mail: ericcas@hamlet.uncg.edu, or access the
ERIC/CASS Homepage at http://www.uncg.edu/~ericcas2.

Index

317